THE ALIEN ART

Also by Michael Collie

George Gissing: A Bibliography
George Gissing: A Biography
George Meredith: A Bibliography

MICHAEL COLLIE

THE ALIEN ART
A Critical Study of George Gissing's Novels

DAWSON · ARCHON BOOKS

Framingham State College
Framingham, Massachusetts

First published in 1979

© Michael Collie 1978

All rights reserved. No part of this publication may be reproduced, stored in a retrieval system, or transmitted, in any form or by any means, electronic, mechanical, photocopying, recording or otherwise without the permission of the publishers:

Wm Dawson & Sons Ltd, Cannon House
Folkestone, Kent, England

Archon Books, The Shoe String Press, Inc
995 Sherman Avenue, Hamden, Connecticut 06514 USA

British Library Cataloguing in Publication Data

Collie, Michael
The alien art.
1. Gissing, George – Criticism and interpretation.
I. Title
823'.8   PR 4717   78-40730
ISBN 0-7129-0874-9

Archon ISBN 0-208-01731-3

Film set in 10/12 point Baskerville
Printed and Bound in Great Britain
by W & J Mackay Limited, Chatham

Contents

Preface	vii
Acknowledgements	ix
1 The Struggle for Acceptance	1
2 'Tableaux Vivants': the Composition and Revision of *Workers in the Dawn*	20
3 1880–5: 'By Indirection Find Direction Out': Gissing's Apprenticeship	42
4 Experiments in Naturalism	68
5 *The Emancipated* and *New Grub Street*	103
6 *Born in Exile*	127
7 The Art of Social Alienation	146
8 Conclusion	164
Notes	173
Appendix A Chronological Listing of Gissing's Works	189
Select Bibliography	190
Index	195

Preface

THIS book consists of a set of closely related essays on various aspects of George Gissing's fiction. Taken together, they are intended to demonstrate that Gissing's sense of the potential of the novel form developed steadily throughout his career. That this development was in some respects un-English and more in tune with Continental European fiction than with what Leavis called the Great Tradition is suggested as one of the reasons for the relative neglect of his novels during the first fifty years of the century. Whereas it was once fashionable to think about the English novel in chiefly insular terms, it is now realized (or at least is here argued) that critical and historical distortions result from a neglect of the European context. Novelists like Gissing and Meredith were European writers who happened to be English, just as Ibsen was a European writer who happened to be Norwegian. Consequently it may prove useful to discuss the features of Gissing's work that made him seem an alien in his own country.

Taken singly, it is hoped that the essays will, in different ways, demonstrate the traditional usefulness of critical attention to the novels themselves, in the right edition, as opposed to types of discussion where it is assumed from the outset that all of Gissing's work was in one way or another autobiographical. Because there is a received and fairly widely accepted view of Gissing as a writer who was preoccupied with his own experiences and yet failed to transpose them into art, the first chapter includes a brief mention of some of the matters that appear to have influenced people's response to Gissing's work. Received opinion is often a barrier that holds a new reader away from first-hand encounters with an author's work. The first chapter is not intended to fan the flames of controversy among those whose opinions of Gissing are already set, but rather to prepare the way for a straightforward discussion of what Gissing wrote and how he wrote it. Given the rigidity of the historical mould within which late nineteenth-century novelists are often seen, this seems a necessary first step.

Much of the work for this book was completed while I was preparing a Bibliography a few years ago and, for the help and advice I received then, it is a pleasure to have this chance to thank once more the staffs of research libraries in which the Gissing papers are preserved, and in particular the Berg Collection of the New York Library, the Carl H. and Lily Pforzheimer Library, the Miriam Lutcher Stark Library and the Library of the Academic Center at the University of Texas, Austin, the Huntington Library and the Beinecke Manuscript Library and Rare Bookroom at Yale. Access to these collections made the book possible, while the generosity and counsel of librarians made the work itself extremely enjoyable.

Sections of the introductory chapter, 'Gissing's Fights with Publishers', have been used in a paper entitled 'The Struggle for Acceptance', published in *English Studies in Canada*, vol. 1, no. 4 (Winter 1975), pp. 434–49. An earlier version of chapter 2 appeared as 'The Lost Realist' in *English Studies Today*, fifth series (1973), pp. 359–85 (and earlier still, as a paper given at the IAUPE Istanbul conference in 1971), and the *New Grub Street* part of chapter 5 was published as 'George Gissing's Revision of *New Grub Street*', in *The Year Book of English Studies*, vol. 4 (1974), pp. 212–24.

Acknowledgements

IT is a pleasure to thank the following libraries for permission to quote from the unpublished autographed letters of Gissing in their collections: Yale University Library for the letters in the Beinecke Rare Book Room and Manuscript Library; the Carl and Lily Pforzheimer Foundation Inc., for the letters in the Pforzheimer Library; the Henry W. and Albert A. Berg Collection in the New York Public Library, and the Astor Lenox and Tilden Foundations, for the letters and diaries in the Berg Collection.

The book derives in large measure from a study of George Gissing's manuscripts in American libraries undertaken some years ago and supported then by the Canada Council. It is pleasant to have this further opportunity to record my appreciation of the Council's most generous support. Once again I am indebted to Margaret Bowman for her expert help with the typescript.

1
The Struggle for Acceptance

In the Château de Fourchambault is still preserved the black leather swivel chair and writing desk which George Gissing took with him from England to Paris when he went to live with Gabrielle Fleury towards the end of his life. Mme Le Mallier, the present owner and Gabrielle Fleury's cousin, has preserved the rooms at the top of the house which Gissing and Gabrielle Fleury used when they were there, including several shelves of Gissing's books. These rooms, and particularly this quiet corner with chair, table, and books which Gissing had used for his writing, recall the way he had organized his existence throughout the twenty-five years of his career as a novelist, for his determination to be a novelist had never slackened and there were only brief periods between 1878 and 1903 when he did not sit at such a desk or table for several hours a day.

That Gissing did not need much more of a material kind from life than he had as a guest at Fourchambault has to be imagined as an essential part of an intellectual and literary career that was almost exclusively devoted to the writing of a modern novel. The books, the desk, the hiding place were his essentials. Whether rich or poor, happy or unhappy, married or living by himself, he worked steadily at the task, in novel after novel, of discovering by experience and sustained hard work a kind of fiction that was both within his own powers and at the same time appropriate to the age in which he lived. His stone-flagged cellar off the Tottenham Court Road at the beginning of his career and all his later studies, garrets, attics, rented sitting-rooms and hotel bedrooms served the same purpose. The life of the imagination, his real life, occurred when he was sitting at a desk with pen in hand, so it is as a practising writer, a tireless experimenter, an artist ever willing to learn from his own mistakes that he can best be understood. In this solitary way, such is the enigma of his writing life, Gissing tried to come to terms with what he took to be the social and psychological realities of his age, his own uprootedness making him sympathetic, as artist if not as human being, to the dislocations and fractures of contemporary existence. Preoccupied with place as the environment that determined the shape of other people's lives, he himself resisted environment by leading a migrant existence in places which had no deep associations for him, thus chronicling other people's miseries in the act of observing theirs while concealing his own. Modern critical discussion seems to confirm that, at least in the best of his novels, he succeeded in creating distinctive fictions, whose strengths (and perhaps weaknesses) derived from this dispassionate, distant scrutiny of the contemporary scene.

Behind Gissing's determination to devote his life to literature was a *fin-de-siècle* imagination for which a fragmented vision of reality was more credible than a coherent one. Gissing reacted violently against what he thought of as the Romance fantasies, conventions, and idealizations of previous generations, such as the idea that a person's life might make sense as a whole, or that love might be the basis of a good marriage, or that there was a meaningful relationship between the individual and the society in which he lived. Like many other decadent or nihilist writers of the end of the nineteenth century, he believed a person's life was so subjected to exterior pressure, was so much a response to factors outside its control, was so unresponsive to will-power and initiative, that it made sense only for brief periods if at all, romantic love constituting a delusion which distracted sensible people from the need to accommodate themselves to the grim conditions of existence. The negative of what other people cherished and believed had a fascination for him. Sometimes with subtlety, sometimes without, he satirized bourgeois or middle-class aspirations and habits, whenever they seemed to him more based upon fantasy than fact. This was most of the time. He had no personal reason for believing in the moral stabilities represented by authors of the previous generation like George Eliot, indeed was deeply convinced for both emotional and philosophical reasons that they were chimerical, and he observed for himself, especially in London, that large numbers of his fellow human beings had to manage as best they could in life without the assistance of stable institutions. What he observed, he accepted and worked with as fact: he was not a reformer.

As will be seen, his satire, his disbelief, his negative reaction to experience were part of Gissing's literary universe, quite distinct from the world of social action inhabited by some of his friends. It will be seen, too, that his vision of reality was associated with an extremely fragile, private, agnostic ethic of great importance to Gissing and people like him, though of little relevance to the world at large. Gissing's position, throughout his writing life, was a special one, in that he successfully devised for himself a type of fiction in which his essentially negative or nihilistic response to experience became the means by which this private, alienating world view could be expressed. He rarely attempted to write the kind of novel that other English novelists had written;[1] on the contrary, he tried – as a consciously un-English novelist – to solve new sets of problems which were peculiar both to him and to the period in which he wrote. These problems stemmed from the fact that, while he believed in literature, the importance of writing novels, and (in a special sense) the social role of the novelist, he did not believe in what most of his compatriots took for granted, tending always, therefore, to create characters who were nihilists and situations that they felt were not susceptible to resolution, or else characters to whom the novelist attributed his own nihilism and for whom he devised situations beyond their power to resolve.

This nihilism and lack of resolution, both European and not merely British states of mind, were consistent with a world view in which social incoherence was of necessity accepted. Mid-Victorian values, virtues, ideas, and institutions had been found wanting. So Gissing believed. Furthermore, Gissing fully understood, from 1880 onwards, that his nihilistic world view, together with the social critique it involved, were shared by important European writers like Ibsen and Turgenev. In England, he knew he was one of a minority; in the larger European community he could in all justice associate himself with the most powerful living authors. This he felt strongly. But was it actually possible in England in the 1880s, to write a modern, *avant-garde*, cosmopolitan novel and have it accepted by English publishers who had every reason to be cautious and conservative? Was it possible from a commercial point of view? And was it possible from a technical point of view? Technically, Gissing had to struggle hard to discover a formula that would satisfy the reading public and yet allow him to be true to his own vision. Like many of his contemporaries, certainly like Ibsen whose initial impact on the British imagination occurred at the same time, he had to offer a social critique that was devasting in its implications in a form which would nonetheless ensure that he was read. Commercially, he had to struggle to get published at all, and even then frequently suffered editorial interference and mutilation.

Looking back over the years, we can see that Gissing's determination to find for himself a type of novel appropriate to his overall view of things was justified in that he succeeded in portraying nineteenth-century life imaginatively in one of its most important aspects, specifically that aspect characterized by eroded belief, uncertainty of action, personal alienation and social frustration. And quite apart from that portrait of an age, which is interesting both as literature and as social history, is the fact that he in the end wrote a number of books as good as any produced by any of his contemporaries. For this reason, it seems worth attempting to study his novels on their own terms, which means, in the first place, establishing what those terms might be. It will be suggested in this book that if one looks at the various things Gissing wanted or needed to do in a novel, judging this on the basis of the novels themselves, it is in practice useful to acknowledge that his attitude to the art of the novel was at first alien to the English imagination and that, in bringing together both an all-pervasive nihilism and the appearance of a social conscience, he created an obstacle to easy popular acceptance which in turn affected the type of novel he was able to write. The chapters which follow constitute a close examination of this idea.

To approach Gissing's fiction in this way is to make allowance for several aspects of his career that are at least interesting enough to think about: for example, his 'outsider's' vision of English urban life; his admiration for foreign writers, like Schopenhauer and Turgenev; the influence of his important visits to France, Italy and Greece; his difficulties with publishers, particularly the difficulties that resulted from differences of moral attitude or belief; and most of all, perhaps, the time it took him to learn how to write his own type of novel. These matters clearly have a bearing on the process by which Gissing matured and developed as a novelist. They do not need to be a matter of dispute, for they are well known and well documented.[2] The weight that any particular reader will attach to any one of these aspects will obviously not represent a critical constant; nor is it for a moment being argued that there is only one correct critical approach to this intriguing nineteenth-century novelist who has been attracting increasing attention during the 1960s and 1970s. Not to attach any importance to the factors which made Gissing's art seem foreign and unusual when his books were first published would, however, be a mistake – except, that is, for someone willing to sweep away so much of interest and importance with a simple prejudicial assertion that Gissing was different from his contemporaries simply by being second rate.[3] Such foolishness apart, the extent to which Gissing deviated from the main tradition of English fiction deserves attention.

Gissing's normal work habits entailed their own difficulties. He did not hit on a formula for writing a slightly unusual type of novel and then apply it, but rather worked towards a type of novel that would constitute the best artistic resolution of the apparently discordant elements he seemed to want in the one book. This learning as he worked makes his career as a whole difficult to analyse, because he sometimes gets into technical difficulties in the handling of the very stuff of his fiction, sometimes because of his essentially experimental approach. This means that a few words have to be said at the outset about how he worked, so that there can be some appreciation of the complexity of his self-appointed task. His usual practice was to end a long, often painful, essentially private, even secretive period of gestation with an intense, equally private period of work during which he wrote steadily all day and every day until the novel in question was finished. There is little evidence to suggest that he discussed his work with anyone while it was in progress, and for that matter, for much of his life, there was no one with whom he could have discussed it, except in the most general terms.[4] He then took or sent it to a publisher almost immediately, often on the very day he wrote the last word. This meant that, once the intense creative energies of producing a final draft had abated (for the creative process may be as intense for the realist as for the Romantic novelist), he left himself little time for reconsideration. From the substantial and significant changes he made when he had occasion to revise a book for a new edition, one can see the shape that a novel might have had originally had he given himself time to think it over. Wishing to sell each book as quickly as possible he rarely gave himself that time. At the beginning of his career, he found it easier, when he was working hard, to write a new book rather than revise an old one. There are a number of clear instances of a Gissing novel implicitly constituting a commentary – a commentary concerning art and technique – on the one which preceded it, as *Thyrza* is a commentary on *Demos*, for example, and *The Odd Women* on *Born in Exile*. As Gissing once said himself, he was one of those people who never imagined the cancellation of possibility, least of all the cancellation imposed by the brute reality of life coming to an end. Always there would be a next time. He could always think, and he always did, that in the next novel he would have a chance to resolve the technical and artistic problems he encountered while writing the last. This meant that his attitude to the art of fiction was pragmatic: his sense of art was satisfied when he hit upon a structure of credible disturbances, failures and alienations, but he had a tendency at first to be too easily satisfied, so it seems, by a novel that derived its form merely from the negatives of fractured human relationships and broken hopes. His career as a whole makes a kind of sense not equally revealed by individual novels.

This meant in turn that he had a somewhat cavalier and, from a business point of view, unassertive attitude both to the sale of his work and to the way in which it was received. If he could sell a book outright or obtain an advance, he would be able – whether the financial arrangements were satisfactory or not – to continue to live and write and, in writing, experiment. This attitude was reinforced by his experience of Victorian taste as expressed by publishers and publishers' readers, who rarely accepted a novel exactly in the form Gissing had submitted it. There was a close relation, of course, between Gissing's battle with publishers about the alleged immorality of his work and the difficulty he had commercially with those same publishers. Whether he succumbed too easily to demands that his novels be rendered inoffensive before they could be accepted for publication, or whether publishers took advantage of him, is sometimes difficult to determine. Some of the responsibility clearly lay with Gissing himself. Nevertheless, it was this problem of how he could get the Victorian publisher to accept the kind of work he wanted to do that determined the shape of Gissing's career, as a brief review will here suggest and the later chapters demonstrate.[5]

Gissing accepted the fact, however much he grumbled about it, that if he wished to write an alien or unfamiliar type of novel which stemmed as much from the Continental European as from the English tradition, he might well encounter opposition from those whose ideas about the novel were quite different from his own. He broached the matter directly in a letter to his friend the radical, positivist man-of-letters, Frederic Harrison:

> It would be much better for me if I could write so as not to offend people, and yet I cannot do it. I have no circle to encourage me in the course I have chosen, and no one to follow; it is simply that I feel the irresistible impulse to strive after my ideal of artistic excellence. It is true, as you said, that I have a quarrel with society, and that, I suppose, explains the instinct. But the quarrel is life-long; ever since I can remember I have known this passionate tendency of revolt.[6]

We must note that Gissing doggedly held to the word 'art' when he was speaking about his own work, particularly in the early years and particularly when defending himself against antagonistic readers, who included members of his family in Wakefield. This may seem surprising to anyone familiar with the unevenness of some of the early work: on the other hand, surprising or not, his retention of the word provides a clue to Gissing's attitude to novel writing which should not be overlooked. When he used the word 'art', he did not mean anything of a qualitative kind, as though to imply that his work was better than that of his contemporaries: he used it because of the way he worked, because of the way his imagination coped with experience, because he saw himself as a person who had an insight into the phenomena of contemporary life that only by a certain type of creative process could be converted into viable fictions. At all events, he started courageously by publishing *Workers in the Dawn* in 1880 at his own expense (actually with the legacy on which his first marriage depended). Then success. His next novel 'Mrs Grundy's Enemies', was accepted by Richard Bentley, who paid him an advance of £50, while Chapman & Hall published *The Unclassed* in 1884 and *Isabel Clarendon* in 1886. This was success in the sense that when Gissing began to write *Demos* in 1885 he was still only twenty-seven years old, had published two novels and had two others accepted for publication. What more could a young author have wanted? Later in his life he became embittered when acknowledged literary success did not bring him an adequate income, but in 1885 this was not the way he thought.

Behind the scenes, some of the difficulties that were to beset him throughout his life had already emerged. *Workers in the Dawn* had failed to make an impact on the reading public: too few copies had been sold. This was because he had been too ambitious, had attempted much too much – too much, that is, given his limited technical experience in 1879. In the next chapter, detailed discussion of the manuscript of *Workers in the Dawn* (which is now in the library of the Academic Center at the University of Texas, Austin), will show that even though Gissing paid for the publication of the novel himself, he had to delete a large number of supposedly offensive passages, as well as weakly written and repetitive ones, in order to get it published. Here one sees straightaway that questions of taste (the supposed limits of what a reader would accept) and questions of art (how to write a novel that would satisfy both novelist and reader, and work for both) were inextricably bound up, so that the process by which Gissing learnt the art of the novel necessarily involved, as a major component, stratagems for gaining acceptance for foreign, unusual, dangerous or alien material. The extent to which Gissing himself thought along these lines shows up in his later (second) version of *Workers in the Dawn*, as will be seen.

As for Gissing's next novel, R. A. Gettman, in his excellent book on the Bentley papers, has shown that Bentley, perhaps having accepted 'Mrs Grundy's Enemies' without appreciating the full extent of its satire, attempted to have the manuscript bowdlerized by an Oxford don before deciding against publication after allowing several years to slip by. Again, the gap between novelist and publisher was one of technique, of art. The substance of the novel was seen to be important: could it be turned into a book which would be accepted and sell? Before this question was settled, Bentley turned down *The Unclassed* on the grounds that to portray the redemption of a prostitute glossed over a social evil; Chapman & Hall accepted it but, on the advice of George Meredith, required that it be rewritten. Gissing's initiation was obviously a stern and testing one: he scarcely managed at all financially but as a practising writer he learnt a lot.

Isabel Clarendon, also published by Chapman & Hall, represented the youthful Gissing's attempt to write a 'polite' novel with inoffensive, middle-class characters, a desperate reaction, obviously, to his recent ordeals. Meredith, still in his capacity as reader for Chapman & Hall, advised him not to repeat this experiment but to return to his own more serious subjects, which he did. In the course of a few years, Gissing had experienced in the most direct way possible the type of collision with well-established Victorian publishers with which other writers were already very familiar. No wonder Gissing later complained to Hardy that it was impossible for an English writer to put in 'honest work'.[7] His apprenticeship was in a sense over when he published *Isabel Clarendon* but, for all that, he continued to experiment with different novelistic strategies for writing a book which would both address itself to what he thought were the serious issues of the day and at the same time satisfy, or at least not offend, the moral sensibilities of his publishers.

Perhaps because of his bizarre private life, it was easier for him to read than to meet his contemporaries. Not until later, in the mid-1890s, when he returned to London from Exeter when his second marriage began to disintegrate, did he have much chance to discuss the predicament of the novelist with writers whom he respected. In retrospect, it is reasonably simple for us to see, for example, that there is the strongest possible connection between the treatment of the 'pure woman' in *Tess of the D'Urbervilles* and *The Unclassed* (Gissing sent Hardy a copy of the second edition), and between Meredith's *One of Our Conquerors* and Gissing's *The Whirlpool* and *In the Year of Jubilee.* The three writers took each other seriously, read each other's books, responded positively to each other's innovations. But in the mid-1880s Gissing's struggle was a solitary one. He seems to have read Hardy's novels as they appeared and, impressed by *Diana of the Crossways,* re-read Meredith in the important first collected edition which began to appear in the same year, that is in 1885. Hardy's and

Meredith's later novels had also been shaped by their keen appreciation of the extent to which the art of the novel was a function of a complex relationship with both publisher and reader. They had transcended that relationship, however, as in the end did Gissing. He had studied how they contrived to do this long before he had the opportunity to meet them. He read widely, omniverously, but with keen determination. The result of this reading was a tough-minded appraisal of his contemporaries and a knowing assessment of their strengths by comparison with the strengths of their predecessors. He did not, in short, neglect his English fellow novelists, yet – that said – it remains true that they learnt as much from him as he did from them, while he himself cast further afield in his reading of French, Russian, German, and Italian works.

In the late 1880s Gissing immersed himself in contemporary European fiction, as he had during previous periods of his life. Gissing's wide reading has been often noted but rarely assessed. Salient in any study of it would be his reading of Goethe and Heine in 1876 (and throughout his life), Eugène Sue and Henri Murger (in 1878 *Scènes de la Vie de Bohème* was deeply influential), Comte (notably *Cours de Philosophie Positive* in 1878), Turgenev (in 1884 – but also constantly, for by the end of the decade he had read *Fathers and Sons* five times), Molière, Georges Sand, Balzac, de Musset (whom he called 'indispensable' in 1885), Ibsen (in German, in the late 1880s), Zola, Dostoevski, the Goncourts (at least by the early 1890s). Gissing read with equal ease in French, German, Greek and Latin, and these from an early age. Later he added Italian and late in life some Spanish. The scope of his reading thus confirmed his cosmopolitan attitudes and he tended to have read at first hand what most of his contemporaries had merely heard about.[8] He soon noticed that the kind of thing he (and evidently Meredith and Hardy) wanted to do in fiction was already being done in other countries and that there was something peculiar to the English reader, in his resistance of the contemporary, which presented a special challenge to the English novelist, or else constituted an additional, probably unnecessary burden.

It must be emphasized that one is not here talking about influence, as though Gissing's novels would have been altogether different had he never read, say, Murger, Turgenev and Ibsen. It would be a naïve notion of literary influence indeed that assumed a direct cause and effect relationship between a writer of powerful intellect and a book he had read. One is rather talking about the way in which the sensibility of a period is fashioned or fashions itself by a thousand accords and compatibilities, as by a thousand rejections and avoidances, in an imaginative process in which the artist gathers up what he can use, what he feels happy with, what seems true. For Gissing, Murger's Bohemia was more true than the microcosm of Middlemarch: the deeply felt disbelief of characters in *Fathers and Sons* was more true than the assurances of Silas Marner: the sharp insight into sexual politics in *Hedda Gabler* was more true than the tonal or verbal felicities of *The Mill on the Floss*; not philosophically true in any absolute sense, of course, but true because felt to be consistent with his experience of life, an experience which had convinced him of the futility of conventional morality and the inadequacy of social institutions. A frank acceptance of the fragility of relationships, of human fallibility, of confusion of motive, of the mundane, the sordid, the ordinary, was – in these and other authors – congenial to him, the more so because of what he took to be the evasions of earlier Victorian writers. He wanted to be a *modern* novelist. He believed in the novel as the *modern* form *par excellence*. He was therefore interested in things as they were, not as they were supposed to be, and for this reason could more easily associate, through his reading, with foreign writers whose sense of human consciousness was amoral, detached, even cynical and negative. He did not directly imitate the foreign writers whom he admired, however; rather he experimented with the novel form until he hit upon a type of fiction which expressed his nihilistic world view. He repeatedly said that he was not a documentary writer, but an artist, and he repeatedly said he had more in common with European than with English writers. It is part of the purpose of this book to enquire, in detail, into what he meant.

Gissing developed as an artist in stages that can readily be identified, in that his major novels fall naturally into groups. The first group consists of *Workers in the Dawn* (1880), *The Unclassed* (1884), *Demos* (1886), *Thyrza* (1887) and *The Nether World* (1889). As mentioned already, these novels demonstrate a close affinity with the naturalistic novel of the Continent and it is partly in this context that they are discussed in the first few chapters. It will be shown, particularly in chapter 4, that there was a logic to Gissing's naturalistic experiments up to the writing of *The Nether World* or, if 'experiment' is too grand a word, that by trial and error he worked out for himself how far he could go in combining a brutal and uncompromising type of social realism with a Schopenhaurian view of character. This logical development represented the early stages of the artist's development, but they were identifiable stages nonetheless. A second natural grouping is *The Emancipated* (1890), *New Grub*

Street (1891), *Born in Exile* (1892), *Denzil Quarrier* (1892), and *The Odd Women* (1893), all extremely interesting novels which mark Gissing's swing away from working-class, social realism towards a greatly increased interest in the psychological relationships of thinking but socially dislocated characters. Broadly speaking, these novels were divided from the first group by his travels in the late 1880s and by an intensive spell of reading in French and German. Except for *The Emancipated*, which is the first novel to show his move away from naturalism, they were written during the excitement of his second marriage. In terms of technique, Gissing discovered that a less rigid type of narration, involving a multiple or relativist point of view, was needed for novels whose overall design had to do with meetings and avoidances, confrontation and alienation, partial misunderstandings and total misunderstandings – in other words, for confused, tense, even tragic types of human relationships, especially when more than two characters were involved. Certainly there are thematic similarities between the novels of the first and the second group, but what Gissing was trying to do with the novel had now altered in significant and interesting ways. A third group has at its centre Gissing's most important late novels, *In the Year of Jubilee* (1894), *The Whirlpool* (1897) and *The Crown of Life* (1899), which are discussed together in chapter 7. In the 1890s, Gissing became preoccupied with the types of alienation that characterized urban capitalist societies and, as was his habit, made several attempts at depicting the forces of alienation at work. That these novels are much better than people realized during the period when Gissing was neglected seems certain: they have their own integrity, they are without the blemishes that marred Gissing's earliest work, and they represent – so much has Gissing's understanding of a certain type of character been combined, artistically, with his understanding of capitalism – a powerful treatment of the complex web of existence that made up late nineteenth-century English life. Again there are thematic similarities between this last group and Gissing's earlier books, but the differences are interesting and worth discussion.

The broad outline of Gissing's development as a novelist is not mentioned here for the sake of argument (for, of course, detailed discussion of the matters raised in the previous paragraph will be found in the chapters which follow), but merely for convenience. While readers who know Gissing may well argue about whether a particular novel belongs in a particular group, it will be useful for the reader less familiar with Gissing to see that the present study has its own strategy based on the idea that Gissing thought of the novel in artistic not in documentary terms, that some of his difficulties derived from the fact that the type of art he wanted was unfamiliar in England and that, notwithstanding the difficulties, he did succeed in making an important contribution to the art of fiction, despite a pervasive nihilism with which fiction was at first sight incompatible. Gissing was not alone in this, for as the gap between novelist and reader widened, or as the novelist made it widen in order to obtain new imaginative effects – not effects based upon shared assumptions, but ones brought about by the author's real or pretended detachment from what the reader believed – so novelists like James, Conrad and Meredith found themselves devising much more complex novelistic strategies, more complex fictional ironies, than had been needed or desired by their predecessors. Each of these novelists played upon the difference between what the reader was supposed to expect and what the novelist's characters discovered to be, for them, true. This implied a development, for better or worse, in the art of fiction – a development to which it will be seen Gissing made a distinctive contribution.

The emphasis in this book on the development of Gissing's art will inevitably draw attention away from Gissing's less successful fiction, as well as from his short stories and his non-fiction prose work, though these are by no means to be dismissed out of hand. In the first category are the short, commissioned novels Gissing wrote in the 1890s, when the tide of public opinion had so changed and the reading market so increased, that publishers and editors sought out work from established writers like Gissing, often for popular series of the kind that Gissing disliked. When he needed the additional income to pay for his growing family, and also to allow him to return to London, Gissing wrote *Eve's Ransom* (Lawrence & Bullen, 1895), *The Paying Guest* (Cassell, 1895), and *Sleeping Fires* (T. Fisher Unwin, 1895).[9] It is generally agreed that these are lightweight works, even pot-boilers, written well within Gissing's powers and not indicating any new direction or strength. In other words, they do not greatly affect the discussion of Gissing's development or his literary skill at any particular point in his career.

Much the same is the case with the short stories. By no stretch of the imagination could one agree with Pierre Coustillas' claim, in his introduction to *George Gissing Essays and Fiction*, that the short stories he included are 'delicacies to the connoisseur'[10] which will stimulate new readers to try the major novels. Those stories are not delicacies at all, but unpublished early attempts which have little to do with either Gissing's development as a novelist during the 1880s or his return to the short story form in the mid-1890s. No useful purpose is served by such extravagent claims for what Coustillas acknowledges to be ephemera. More judicious is Jacob Korg's curt dismissal in his *George Gissing: a Critical Biography*, where he called the stories 'interesting' despite their lack of 'social idealism' and 'earnestness' and then qualified the interest in the following terms: 'Some of them deal with the manners of lower-class people like those in *The Nether World*. Others exploit the quaintness of character exhibited by helpless bibliophiles, underdogs, and social outcasts, often displaying sympathy but ending with a cruelly ironic twist.'[11] Korg's dismissal is not absolute, of course, as can be seen from his discussion of individual stories, but on the other hand, when he came to mention *Human Odds and Ends* (1898), the only volume of stories to be published during Gissing's lifetime, he correctly refrained from suggesting that the collection in any way affected Gissing's status as a writer. Published after Gissing's death were four other volumes of stories: *The House of Cobwebs and Other Stories* (1906), *Sins of the Fathers and Other Tales* (1924), *A Victim of Circumstances* (1924) and *Brownie* (1931). In Thomas Seccombe's extremely useful 'introductory survey' to *The House of Cobwebs*, he said that the stories derived their interest from the thematic relationship with the novels but that they constituted, at least the best of them, 'perfectly characteristic and quite admirable specimens of Gissing's own genre, and later, unstudied, but always finished prose style.'[12] In other words these stories reflect but do not contribute to Gissing's development as a writer of fiction. Most of the stories are vignettes written in a dispassionate, low-key, ironic fashion, the irony obviating the need for a full working out of character and motive. As a short-story writer, Gissing was in no sense an innovator: in fact he failed to generate the tensions, energies, movements that the form needs. He simply used the form when he had to, that is, when a magazine editor needed the story and he, Gissing, needed the money.[13]

Finally, three important books appeared late in Gissing's life: a commissioned critical book, *Charles Dickens* (Blackie, 1898);[14] an idiosyncratic travel book, *By the Ionian Sea* (Chapman & Hall, 1901);[15] and that immensely intriguing belle-lettristic indulgence – and minor classic – *The Private Papers of Henry Ryecroft* (Constable, 1903).[16] Apart from the fact that these books appeared late in Gissing's life and so could hardly be expected to reflect much of the creative stress of the early formative periods, they in any case have little bearing upon the main argument of the present book – which is not to dismiss them out of hand, of course, but merely to put them, for the moment, to one side. The Dickens book will be mentioned again in a later chapter, but it is worth noting straightaway that Gissing very well understood the ways in which he was different from Dickens. For example he once said: 'I am constantly astonished to think of the small use Dickens made of his vast opportunities; in the matter of observation among the lower classes. The explanation of course is, that he did not conceive of a work of fiction as anything but a *romance*. The details which would to me be most precious, he left aside as unsuitable, because unattractive to the multitude of novel-readers.'[17] This puts the matter clearly enough. In *Charles Dickens* his stance is equally clear. On the first page, he explained that 'the time which knew him as one of its foremost figures . . . is already made remote by a social revolution of which he watched the mere beginning',[18] while in an important later chapter called 'Comparisons', having dismissed a possible comparison of Dickens with Thackeray as an absurdity only discussed 'in country towns or London suburbs',[19] he compares Dickens, not with any English authors at all, but with Balzac, Hugo, Dostoevski and Alphonse Daudet. Evidently this was the context in which for Gissing Dickens had to be appraised. In other words, Gissing's book on Dickens – genuinely an act of appreciation and homage – is at the same time a testimony to Gissing's own cosmopolitan interests and his broad familiarity with European literature.

This study, then, will be based chiefly upon Gissing's principal novels, in the three groupings that have already been mentioned. But there is a further complication. Gissing revised his early work when the occasion arose, and one would expect the revisions to provide additional information on the way he worked. If it is true that in the early days he tended to complete a draft of a novel in a single, sustained period of work, what happened when he was presented with a chance to reconsider it? Whenever the revision was extensive enough to be taken seriously, as is often the case, it ought to have a bearing on whether or not Gissing was becoming more skilful as a literary craftsman. In such a case, does a study of the process of revision support the idea of marked developments in the art of fiction? Although Gissing sometimes revised a book merely to make it shorter (often a matter of removing the extraneous incidents and dialogue that had filled out the original three volumes), there are a number of situations which in later chapters will be looked at closely. The first concerns the original manuscript taken by itself; it will be seen that the manuscript frequently reveals the pressures under which Gissing worked. The second concerns revision for a second edition: it will be seen that, when Gissing shortened a novel for publication in one volume, he sometimes also restructured it, altered the balance, altered the relationship between characters, altered, then, its overall effect. The third concerns the two, corrected manuscript and later revision, taken together: here it is sometimes possible to reconstruct the process by which the novel achieved its final form, as is the case with *Workers in the Dawn* and *Born in Exile*. It will be suggested that as the years passed, Gissing developed a firmer touch, a better sense of structure and a more sophisticated feel for characters and the interplay of characters, so that the revisions do in fact demonstrate an advance in art.

Initially, therefore, the present book has a double thrust. Of the dozen or so manuscripts that have survived, which, if any, throw light on the way Gissing worked and on his development as an artist? Secondly, of the revisions of his early work for publication by Lawrence & Bullen in single volumes in the 1890s, which are important? The chapters which follow constitute an answer to these two questions seen within the larger context of Gissing's struggle, as an artist, simultaneously to discover or create his own novel and to accommodate his basically European approach to novel writing to conditions that prevailed in the English publishing world. In the process, it will be possible to clarify questions of copy-text. Gissing's work, when available, has often been available only in the wrong – that is to say, unrevised – text. Critical opinion has often been based on the early versions of the early novels, the critics simply not bothering to take Gissing's revision of his own work into account. Because of this, it seems important to reconsider the overall shape of Gissing's writing and publishing life, for only in this way can one do justice to him as a serious writer who successfully worked out for himself fictional formulations by which his nihilist vision of the world could be expressed. In this consideration, the revisions for Lawrence & Bullen turn out to be particularly important.

While still in Exeter, Gissing in fact revised more of his early work than Lawrence & Bullen eventually published. He began, and perhaps finished, both the extremely important revision of *Workers in the Dawn* which is discussed in detail in chapter 2 (the revisions were indicated in but not incorporated into Robert Shafer's two-volume edition for Doubleday in 1935), and the revision of *Isabel Clarendon* (the corrections to a copy of the first edition now in the Alexander Turnbull Library are listed in the Introduction to the Harvester Press photographic reprint of the first edition). Whereas the corrections to *Isabel Clarendon*, not yet incorporated editorially into any edition, were of no greater significance than those minor corrections Gissing made for the second editions of *The Nether World* (Smith, Elder, 1891) and *The Emancipated* (Lawrence & Bullen, 1893), the revision of *Workers in the Dawn* was substantial and in fact amounted to a complete restructuring of the book, which has unfortunately never been published in its revised form. The restructured, more tightly organized, shorter *Workers in the Dawn* is a much more readable novel than the first edition version. Even where no strong case can be made (on the grounds of literary significance) for the twentieth-century republication or publication of the revised text, it still seems unreasonable that critical opinion should be based upon the wrong text. In point of fact, so much Gissing material is unknown and inaccessible to the general reader that scholarly editions of both *Workers in the Dawn* and *Thyrza* (at the very least) are badly needed. With this sort of thing in mind, a somewhat technical account of *Workers in the Dawn* is given in chapter 2 – an account whose technicality is justified, it is felt, by the importance of that material in later novels, while *Thyrza*, one of the more important early novels, is discussed in chapter 4. A case can also be made, and is made here in chapter 5, for taking seriously Gissing's revision of *New Grub Street* for Gabrielle Fleury's translation into French. Because Smith, Elder refused to release the copyright, Gissing had no occasion to revise the novel for Lawrence & Bullen, but the revision for the French translation, a revision which makes *New Grub Street* a vastly better book, shows what he could have done had the opportunity presented itself.

It goes without saying that a novelist's artistic skill can be discussed without any consideration at all of the way he worked, the extent to which he revised his work, the relation of one edition to another, the novelist's dealings with his publishers, or the thousand and one other matters that come into the mind of someone interested in the process of publication. How else could one manage in cases where information on these matters were unavailable? More significantly, the essential act of criticism occurs when a reader attends to the book in front of him, for the while excluding all else. *The Alien Art* is not, then, intended as a salvo in the running fight between pure critic and literary historian. Nothing of a doctrinaire kind is intended here at all. On the other hand, it has to be accepted, first, that Gissing, on the whole, has not been properly considered as a serious artist, partly because people more interested in his life than in his books have misrepresented him,[20] and secondly, because his novels have either not been available at all or have been available in the wrong texts.[21] In situations of this kind it is quite normal to make some attempt to establish the text, which is an important aspect of much of the discussion which follows. Even then, however, the purpose is not to prove that a certain text or a certain attitude to a text is absolutely to be preferred, but rather to let certain questions see the light of day, with whatever evidence seems necessary, so that the reading and re-reading of the works of this important novelist may proceed in the normal manner.

It is hoped that the present study, with its textual emphasis, will build upon and complement the relatively recent work that has brought about a renaissance in Gissing studies. Anyone who thinks about the subject at all must be deeply indebted to the work of Gettman, Young, Korg and Coustillas. R. A. Gettman's *A Victorian Publisher. A Study of the Bentley Papers* (1960) was quickly followed by his *George Gissing and H. G. Wells. A Record of their Friendship and Correspondence* (1961). In the same year A. C. Young published *The Letters of George Gissing to Eduard Bertz.* Critical momentum was maintained through the 1960s by Jacob Korg's *George Gissing. A Critical Biography* (1963),[22] which was in turn followed by the editorial work of Pierre Coustillas, notably in *The Letters of George Gissing to Gabrielle Fleury* (1964) and *George Gissing: Essays and Fiction* (1970). When one adds to this list Pierre Coustillas' subsequent work,[23] it is easy to see why a critic writing about Gissing must in 1978 feel more confident than he would have felt in, say, 1958. Recent contributions to this now more informed discussion are Gillian Tindall's *The Born Exile* and Adrian Poole's *Gissing in Context.*[24]

Despite all this valuable spade work, however, it is still necessary to proceed cautiously in any reassessment of Gissing's work. Looking at what Gissing actually wrote seems safe enough (and that is the main intention here) and yet – as suggested elsewhere[25] – there remain in circulation so many preconceptions about Gissing, especially preconceptions (mostly of a naïve kind) about his having been an autobiographical novelist,[26] that it seems best in an introduction of this kind to review the main evidence on which a view of Gissing has had to be built. Until Gissing is accorded the same kind of straightforward critical attention as, say Mrs Gaskell[27] or Thomas Hardy,[28] there will remain the possibility that Gissing, the writer, is relatively unknown because his books are hard to come by and because he does not fit into existing academic packaging arrangements,[29] while Gissing, the man, is thought to be known, and is in any case fascinating, because of the half-truths about him that were for so many years hawked about. Opinions on this matter will vary. Suffice it to say, for the moment, that there are strong grounds for being cautious in the use of what seem primary sources of information, so much so that a brief summary will be given here.

In the case of published material, editorial disturbance and interference had been considerable. *The Letters of George Gissing to Members of His Family* (1927) on which the general reader and most students have been obliged to depend, was disasterously but quite understandably bowdlerized when Algernon and Ellen Gissing prepared the correspondence for publication.[30] Unpublished autograph letters from Gissing to members of his family survive in large numbers;[31] many of them, however, were omitted from *The Letters of George Gissing to Members of His Family*, while many others, perhaps a much larger number, were suppressed. Understandably enough Algernon and Ellen tried to render their brother respectable by making his life consist of what he had suffered, not what he had done. This inadequacy in a crucial volume has long been recognized. Similarly, Gissing's letters to Bertz, as edited by A. C. Young, had been previously selected by Bertz himself who destroyed many of the letters dating from before Gissing's second marriage because he feared they might be used unscrupulously.[32] The letters to Gabrielle Fleury had likewise been edited, and 'censored', by Gabrielle Fleury herself who seems to have eliminated whatever she thought was too sensationally amorous or revealing.[33] From Gissing's diary, now in the Berg Collection, the record of his early years in London, when he lived with Helen Harrison, was at some stage cut out, probably by Gissing when he wanted to show the diary to Gabrielle Fleury without letting her know about his first marriage.[34] All this means that Gissing's papers, as published, have to be read with caution as only a partial record of a writer whose more important experiences he and others attempted to conceal. It would be naïve to accept uncritically documents that had been so patently doctored. Meanwhile, important material remains unpublished, and of this Gissing's diary and his letters to publishers and agents are of particular importance.[35] The availability of family papers, while the professional ones remain unpublished, has tended to reinforce the popular view that Gissing was more interesting as a person than as a writer.

It is of course primarily, if not exclusively, as a writer that George Gissing must be approached in a critical study such as this one. That the difficulties Gissing had with publishers during his lifetime contributed to the messy situation we inherit seventy years or so after his death is clear. Before Gissing's alien art was understood in his own country, before he had any chance of being appreciated by more than a minority of readers, new types of novel were written which made the nineteenth-century novelist seem old-fashioned before, in the case of

Gissing, a just appreciation of his work had been arrived at. A critical book is not as useful as a new edition of his novels, but it is hoped it will help.

A critical book will help to establish the essential characteristics of Gissing's work, as well as determining on a more basic level what he wrote and how he wrote it, but it is fair to ask, nonetheless, what difference the knowledge will make. Were Gissing's novels available in the bookstore in well-edited editions, and if readers were not prejudiced against him by pseudo-biographers, would he in any sense appear in a better light? Is there a good or interesting novelist partly concealed behind his own publication experiences?

The answer can only be a strong affirmative. Gissing's better novels, *The Unclassed, The Nether World, Born in Exile, The Odd Women* and *The Whirlpool,* are certainly as interesting as anything written by Mrs Gaskell, or Arnold Bennett, or H. G. Wells. Rejected would be Rebecca West's assertion that Gissing does not consist of 'separate works of art' but rather 'one long cry of social protest', as well as Angus Wilson's extraordinarily contorted opinion that, because he was a misfit, Gissing wrote novels for the art of which 'he was in many ways so ill-equipped'. Gissing's novels are not all of a piece: some of them – *The Unclassed, Thyrza, New Grub Street, Born in Exile, The Odd Women, The Whirlpool* and *In the Year of Jubilee* – are much better than the others. Furthermore, as it is hoped this study will demonstrate, he was experimental, and experimental in an interesting way. Extravagant claims will perhaps never be made for a writer who is so entirely unmetaphorical and in a sense, then, so unimaginative. Yet if we could attend one by one to his books, as he actually wrote them, he would be re-established as an interesting social realist, a naturalistic writer who knew parts of English life better than many of his contemporaries, and a pre-Freudian psychological novelist who explored, albeit in a manner that has dated, tense or awkward relationships between socially alienated individuals. He deserves a fair hearing.

2
'Tableaux Vivants': the Composition and Revision of *Workers in the Dawn*

GISSING'S first published novel, *Workers in the Dawn*, was written between 1877 and 1879, severely revised in the winter of 1879–80, published in the spring of 1880 and revised again in the early 1890s for a second edition which, however, did not appear until 1935. According to the publisher, only a few copies of the three-volume first edition were sold, while the two-volume second edition published by Doubleday Doran and edited by Professor Shafer is also rare.[1] Despite this rather daunting situation a chapter will now be devoted to *Workers in the Dawn*, both because it is intrinsically interesting and because it provides the perfect example of a cluster of questions that will be of concern throughout this book. These questions concern the novelistic problems Gissing set himself and the ways in which, in successive books, he tried to solve them.

Gissing arrived in London in 1877 determined to be a novelist. Whether because of discussions he had had during his year in the States, or because while there he had been impressed by French novelists like Sue, Georges Sand, Henri Murger, and Balzac, or because of private assessment of the English novel which had made him realize he had to carry the matter beyond Charlotte Brontë and George Eliot, it seems extremely likely that from the outset he had a sense of the type of novel he would have to write.

Such a novel would be contemporary in interest, anti-Romantic in attitude, unevasive in its treatment of the realities of urban life, unmetaphorical in style and experimental in its method in more or less the same sense as that intended by Zola in *Le Roman expérimental*.[2] This is a remark made with hindsight, based on knowledge of how in fact Gissing developed as a writer. His literary alliances in 1879 are not the main point. He did in fact read a lot of French fiction in the Boston Public Library; he did have to liberate himself from the examples of Charlotte Brontë and George Eliot; and though he disavowed a knowledge of Zola and turned out to be unlike him in many important respects, it is obvious that initially his approach to the problem of writing a novel was quite similar.[3] The point for the moment is that, while Gissing had a strong sense of the type of novel he would write, he did not have a very clear idea of how he would write it. Essentially Gissing taught himself to write a modern novel – one appropriate to the last two decades of the nineteenth century – by trial and error. In *Workers in the Dawn* he creates the most immense difficulties for himself, which he only in part resolves; it is extremely interesting, though, to see how he attempts to resolve them.

The world which Gissing creates in *Workers in the Dawn* is inhabited by paupers, beggars, drunks, prostitutes, thieves, as well as by thinking and respectable artisans. The hope for the future lies with the latter group, especially if their good sense and common decency can be rallied to the socialist cause. The physical world which these characters inhabit is the London slum. Outside this environment are middle-class characters who are represented as caring about the world in which they find themselves. Gissing makes links between the two sets of characters and here, as in later novels, much depends upon whether links between working-class and middle-class characters are credible to the reader. In the case of *Workers in the Dawn* the linking device is at first a plot line that has the main character, Arthur Golding, involved with a working girl, Lizzie Clinkscales, and an educated girl, Helen Norman. This arrangement immediately exposes one of the difficulties Gissing had to overcome, because a love relationship between two of the characters has little to do with the social circumstances of the rest of humanity. Romantic love and social realism for Gissing turned out to be incompatible: only when he negated romance by showing his characters as alienated from each other was he able to locate a story about people in the actual world he wanted to describe. If he does not solve it, he at least comes to grips with this problem during the writing and revision of *Workers in the Dawn*.

The characteristic mode of *Workers in the Dawn*, as of much of his later work, is visual. There is a double emphasis. First, the physical environment is described, not with brilliant, often violent metaphor as in Zola, but directly, plainly, factually: place is described as seen by the narrator and, by implication, by the character. This turns out to be extremely important in early Gissing because the identification of a character with place, based on the character's own knowledge, thoughts, and words, is rarely stressed: what is stressed is a sense of alienation from place, based upon what the reader is obliged to see through the narrator's eyes. This is a question of technique. Few could match Gissing's knowledge of urban life in 1880; in the novels, however, certainly in *Workers in the Dawn,* it is described from without not from within. It will be seen later that this insistence upon place regarded from without is a feature of Gissing's nihilism that determines the type of novel he is able to write. Secondly, characters themselves are imagined visually, as if there were thought to be some correlation between physical appearance and behaviour. Gissing thought there was such a correlation, so the technique of set-piece description can also be seen as part of his overall nihilism; if a character's behaviour was predetermined by heredity in a manner reflected in the character's physical make-up, does this not impose a severe limitation on personal freedom? Gissing thought it did. It will be seen that this visually conceived sense of alienation is in later novels like *Born in Exile* transferred from the narrator to the characters themselves. But in *Workers in the Dawn* the reader is to a greater extent made to see what the characters themselves do not understand.

A good example of this – and there is really only room for one example in a chapter devoted to revision – is Gissing's description of a Victorian nudist show. Few other writers would have attempted it in 1880; most would have avoided the difficulties Gissing created for himself. The passage occurs towards the end of the novel when Arthur Golding searches for his wife, Carrie, for one last time. After Carrie had left him, his friendship with Helen had prospered, but once Helen realized that he was married he saw that he had no choice but to seek his wife again as duty required. Walking the streets late at night, he was forced to take shelter from a storm.

> At this moment he found himself near a lighted entrance into which several people were hastening, and hither he too repaired, in the intention of seeking shelter till the violent hail was over. It was a narrow doorway, situated in a very shabby back street, and, as he entered, he found himself in front of a second door, on which was a large placard, exhibiting the words, 'Tableaux Vivants'. Hearing the sound of music within, he pushed the door open, and entered a moderate-sized room, lighted only by a jet of gas suspended from the low ceiling. Standing and sitting about the room were some thirty or forty men, engaged in watching the entertainment. Their eyes were directed to a small elevated platform, of circular shape, which was placed immediately under the gas-jet, the rays from which were concentrated upon it by means of a large shade. On the platform, which kept slowly revolving to the sound of melancholy hand-organ, stood two women, at first sight apparently naked, but in reality clothed in tight-fitting tissue of flesh-colour. The fact that one was in the act of offering an apple for the other's acceptance rendered it probable that the group was meant to represent Adam and Eve. As the platform revolved,

the two engaged in a slow pantomime indicative of conversation. Such was the entertainment, watched in silence, only broken now and then by a coarse laugh or a whispered comment. Of course it was meant to be vicious, and certainly was indecent in character; but surely not the severest moralist could have devised a means of showing more clearly the hideousness of vice. The cold, bare room, swept through by a gust from the street whenever the door opened, the wailing hand-organ playing a waltz in the time of a psalm-tune, and with scarcely a correct note, the assemblage of gross and brutal-featured men whose few remarks were the foulest indecencies, the reek of bad tobacco which was everywhere present, the dim light, save on the revolving platform where the shivering wretches went through their appointed parts – surely only in England, where popular amusement is but known in theory, could so ghastly an *ensemble* attract a single spectator.

But to Arthur it was no opportunity for moralising.[4]

This last remark presumably means Gissing understood that the scene was not relevant to the character, though in some not clearly stated way it was supposed to be relevant to the reader. He was searching for a connection between environment and behaviour which he later came to see did not exist. But for a while he thought it did and for some years characteristically related human action to its physical location.

It also took Gissing some years before he could make his style wholly economical, which meant not just keeping his eye on the object and avoiding metaphor, but also eliminating the stilted language of phrases like 'Their eyes were directed to' and 'hitherto he repaired' and 'from which were concentrated upon it by means of'. Similarly, he had to write a number of novels before the impact of emotive, loaded words like 'hideousness', 'foulest', and 'brutal-featured' was at least reduced. Nowadays such words so much imply a moral judgement that it is quite difficult to accept the idea that for Gissing they were accurate descriptive words. Certainly Gissing places his realistic portrait of urban life in jeopardy by allowing himself, as author, to moralize about his character's experiences, which is another way of saying that the young novelist, when he wrote *Workers in the Dawn*, had 'point of view' problems which remained to be solved in later novels. That these problems were solved it is hoped will become clear in later chapters, but in the passage just quoted the shift in point of view, quite apart from the moralistic tone, creates an unhappy type of aesthetic distortion. Arthur Golding enters a room. Gissing comments on what is to be seen there. Then the reader is told that Golding did not have time for the thoughts that Gissing allowed himself. The reader waits therefore to discover Golding's reaction, but he does not get it. Golding takes Carrie away, finds her a room and immediately begins to talk about the way they might be reconciled. As he does so, he accepts Carrie's experiences as suffering and does not, at least openly, think of them in the same terms as his earlier 'debauch'. The heavy comment in the passage quoted above thus seems not just unnecessary but also aesthetically inappropriate. As a result phrases like 'the hideousness of vice' become mere melodrama and the reader concludes that the author has no clear idea of what he means when he uses the phrase.

The problems Gissing experienced while writing *Workers in the Dawn* were a consequence of the free rein he at first allowed himself, particularly in the early months before the novel took its final shape in August 1879. He did not yet understand the need for strategy, for calculation, for compromise. He wrote freely, relatively speaking, without discipline and as yet unresponsive to the demands of the form it took him so long to master. He said as much himself in the much-quoted letter he wrote to his brother Algernon shortly after publication:

> The book in the first place is not a novel in the generally accepted sense of the word, but a very strong (possibly *too* plain spoken) attack upon certain features of our present religious and social life which to *me* appear highly condemnable. First and foremost, I attack the criminal negligence of governments which spend their time over matters of relatively no importance, to the neglect of the terrible social evils which should have been long since sternly grappled with. Herein I am the mouthpiece of the advanced Radical party. As regards religious matters, I plainly seek to show the nobility of a faith dispensing with all we are accustomed to call religion, and having for its only creed a belief in the possibility of intellectual and moral progress. Hence it follows that I attack (somewhat savagely) the modern development of Ritualism, which, of course, is the absolute antithesis of my faith.
>
> In doing all this, I have been obliged to touch upon matters which will only be sufferable to those who read the book in as serious a spirit as mine when I wrote it. It is *not* a book for women and children, but for thinking and struggling *men*. If the readers can put faith in the desperate sincerity of the author, they will not be disgusted with the book; otherwise it is far better they should not read it.[5]

A letter of this kind is no more than a starting point. Gissing's family in Wakefield expected a novel, a novel of a conventional kind, not a violent attack upon aspects of life they themselves took for granted. It is not surprising, therefore, to find him justifying himself to them, since he knew very well what they would accept and not accept. They were devout church-goers, staunch believers, good people whose lives were guided by duty and a sense of propriety. They knew they were like most people whom they knew. Ignorant of politics, ignorant of the social turmoil of the cities, ignorant of suffering that was not the responsibility of the sufferer, they were in no sense prepared for Gissing's harsh portrait of urban life. Throughout his life, Gissing was to point out that aspects of his work which upset people were in fact not revolutionary, indeed not as revolutionary perhaps as he would have liked, but were rather the commonplaces of the *avant garde* that in other places were fully accepted, not in Wakefield or in the thousand replicas of Wakefield up and down the country, but in London, Berlin, Paris, Boston and New York.

To look simultaneously at a lengthy quotation from *Workers in the Dawn* and a letter of Gissing's about it is to confront immediately one of the main questions of Gissing criticism. The passage about the 'tableaux vivants' shows that Gissing was still learning how to write: the letter shows that he was prepared to defend his book as an attack on the social issues of his day. At first it might seem as though his ability to write well and his lifelong concern for social issues are separable, so that a critic could legitimately attend to what Gissing has to say about contemporary life (and come to the conclusion, for example, that he is an extremely interesting, second-rate writer) or alternatively make narrow literary judgements about his success as a novelist (and conclude, perhaps, that many early novels have only documentary value). This separation is not in this book accepted as a legitimate critical strategy. Instead it is argued that as Gissing arrived at a more sophisticated understanding of the social problems of his day, so his skill as a novelist developed as well. In particular, it is argued that as he became preoccupied with relationships between people, especially masculine–feminine relationships, and the tensions between society and the alienated individual, so his sense of what could be done with the novel form became more sure. This development, as the discussion continues, will place words like 'realism' and 'naturalism' under strain, because as Gissing experimented with various fictional possibilities, so the sense in which he was a 'realist' or a 'naturalist' altered. Certainly he was always, identifiably, a late nineteenth-century realist in his rejection of romance and idealization; in his obsession with the observed details of life; in his creation, for the reader, of fictions made from contemporary actualities; and in his complete avoidance of metaphor or of other forms of reference that might have invalidated his nihilism. On the other hand, he did not have a programme. As a social realist he had to learn as he went along, and in the case of *Workers in the Dawn* he did this by thinking about its length.

Workers in the Dawn was inordinately long because, in effect, it at first consisted of two novels. Gissing changed his mind about the novel in the course of writing about it, developed the second part in a way not anticipated in the first, and either did not bother or more probably did not have time to make the necessary corrections to the early chapters. He may not have seen that such changes were needed. In 1879 the bothersome thing about the novel was chiefly its length. Since Gissing had seen the book rejected by at least four publishers before sending it to Remington, and since even Remington asked him to reduce it, there is no escape from the conclusion that Gissing knew he had to shorten the book considerably even to publish it at his own expense. Yet, his concern about the length of the book did not mean that *anything* could be cut. The type of cut Gissing made, as revealed by the manuscript, is also of great interest in that it reveals the extent of Gissing's awareness of his own problems. At this early stage in his career, he aspired to combine what he had learnt from Charlotte Brontë and George Eliot (about novels whose structure derives from the slow inner growth of intellect and sensibility in the main characters) with what he had learnt about social and psychological realism from Continental novelists, particularly the French. He had yet to discover how to make such a novel, and how to incorporate within its fabric both psychological and social insight, and *Workers in the Dawn* reflects his confusion. The confusion, however, is instructive. A detailed study shows that some of the deletions from the manuscript were beneficial, in that authorial intrusion and a certain amount of padding were reduced, while other deletions are to be regretted, because they were only made to appease the taste of the publisher.

Later, most likely in 1890 or 1891, Gissing improved the first edition text, or was persuaded to improve it, by removing some of the anomalies between the first half, representing the story as Gissing had first conceived it, and the second half, which to a much greater extent takes its shape from the force of a single character, Carrie Mitchell. Thus, while the manuscript reveals what Gissing was obliged to delete for moral as well as pragmatic reasons in 1879 in his first encounter with the Victorian publishing world, by the time he again revised the book that problem had been forgotten, and he was able to attend to problems of structure and balance on the basis of his experience during the whole of the 1880s – a period in which he had written nine or ten novels and at the same time consolidated his knowledge of Continental literature. Were the revised novel ever to be published, it would show how Gissing, between publishing the book for the first time in 1880 and revising it in the early 1890s, had come to terms with his craft.

First, then, we shall look at the making of the first edition text. Behind the first edition, as mentioned already, is the well-preserved autograph manuscript, now in the library of the Academic Center at the University of Texas. The manuscript, as corrected, corresponds almost exactly to the text of the first edition, but is interesting in its own right since the equivalent of some 70 MS. pages were deleted by horizontal strokes of the pen – Gissing's pen – across the page, in a fashion unlike his usual method of deleting and equally unusually *after* pagination. Furthermore, some pages are missing from the MS., which is otherwise paginated consistently and continuously throughout. Since the MS. was used by the compositors, as is clear from the fact that it not only corresponds to the printed text but also carries the compositors' names, fingerprints and printers' marks, and since the missing page numbers would suggest that the pages were removed after the book had been submitted and perhaps after it had been accepted, it would seem that the deletions were made at the same time and that, whether Gissing made them willingly or not, they resulted from discussion between author and publisher.

The physical evidence of how the novel was first composed is important when considered in conjunction with his later revision of the novel. But before that second revision is discussed, there is more to be said about the nature of the deletions from the MS. The immediate reason for the deletions from the MS. was length: it consisted of 728 pages before the deletions were made. Yet what should be deleted? The retentions or rejections are almost bound to indicate something of the author's purpose and help in an understanding of the author at work. It has been suggested that because Gissing was obliged to shorten the novel, almost anything might have been sacrificed, but detailed consideration produces no evidence that this first revision was an act of mere desperation.

In the case of *Workers in the Dawn*, detailed consideration of the retentions and rejections is of considerable interest simply because it is Gissing's first novel, a novel whose various elements, once developed, were to become the strong features of his later work, but it is an approach fraught with some danger since a great deal that might have been deleted, was not. Gissing said as much himself: 'On reading the proofs of *Workers in the Dawn* I am dissatisfied with much, and see how greatly I might have improved my work, had I taken more time with it.'[6] On the other hand, in a letter written little more than a week earlier, he had implied that the novel had a consistency and coherence for him despite its length: 'Remington wanted me to reduce the book seeing that it would be vastly larger than the average novel of the day; but I told him this would be impossible save by re-writing it, and so the printing goes ahead.'[7] As already mentioned, the deletions from the manuscript are not only of interest because, having been made by Gissing himself, they show his artistic priorities when he made them: they are also interesting because Gissing cut out passages likely to offend the reader or distract him from the main drift of the story.

Some of the passages deleted were digressions, for example a page or two about the educational significance of Vasari's lives, which in the original was really little more than Gissing talking to himself. Extended discussion between some of the characters had the effect of a digression, which reduced momentum; in this category Arthur Golding's father's alcoholism and death, the suicide of Hannah Clinkscales' first husband, and the drift of Lizzie Clinkscales to a life of prostitution were superfluous horrors, as it were, which detracted from the story by making it melodramatic. They were eliminated. A number of cloying, overwritten passages of 'high sentiment' were likewise deleted.[8] All of these were changes which any author might have made during the writing of a novel and little significance is to be attached to them.

More interesting are passages which may have been deleted because they were judged offensive. Seeing *Workers in the Dawn* through the press was Gissing's first experience of the English publisher and his moral standards. Later he had unsatisfactory encounters with Bentley and with Chapman & Hall. Though the evidence is not conclusive, it is difficult to avoid connecting the deletion of certain passages from *Workers in the Dawn* with Gissing's later feeling that complete artistic integrity was impossible in England. On 3 June 1886, for example, he wrote to Thomas Hardy: 'The misery of it is that, writing for English people, one may not be thorough; reticencies & superficialities have so often to fill places where one is willing to put in honest work.'[9]

The passages in question have never been published, so a few of them will be quoted by way of example. Of Mrs Whiffle's gradual destruction under the strain of childbirth, the narrator's original comment had been:

> Of course it never occurred to her that every additional child she brought into the world rendered life so much the harder for every member of an overgrown community, and that perhaps only indirectly, meant increase to the statistics of the prison, the brothel, the lunatic-asylum, the dead house. No, there was always the consolation present with her that she had more children than her neighbours.[10]

Almost any publisher in 1880 would have objected to these sentences, unguarded as they were by qualification or metaphor. To explain the way in which Michael Rumball became a suitable companion for the young hero of the novel, the narrator had said: 'he had yielded himself entirely to the dictates of a reprobate mind, had become a prominent figure on the turfs, and was in short on the highway to destruction when a sudden accident stepped into his rescue.'[11] The accident was that he blinded himself in the right eye with a beer bottle when he fell off a wagon and, as a consequence married the servant girl in a pub where she nursed him back to health. 'He was at bottom an honest, good-hearted fellow, and Arthur Golding might have fallen into far worse hands than his and Ned Quirk's – say, for instance, into those of a bishop or any other highly-salaried servant of the state.'[12] Once again this is gratuitous comment by the narrator, relevant to the overall theme of the novel but distinctly callow because not realised in a convincingly dramatic way. These, surely, are the words of the angry young man who has yet to learn how to incorporate such sentiments into the fabric of his fiction.

The explanation of the difference between the virtuous and high-minded Helen Norman and the pragmatic, cynical approach of her friend, Maud Gresham, had originally been one of direct parental influence:

> Essentially, Maud Gresham's philosophy was at one with her father's. Firstly she had grown by degrees to look upon abstinence from evil as, upon the whole, more practicable than, and therefore preferable to positive exertion for good; and then, in the second place, she had serious doubts as to the possibility of doing good in the world, even if one were ever so much disposed to it.[13]

An interesting example this, because Gissing was deleting from *Workers in the Dawn* an idea which informs all his later work, without exception. Maud was one of the prototypes for a whole gallery of inwardly resigned, essentially pessimistic characters, none of whom believes that positive or wilful action on their part could have any meaning. In other words, the force of Gissing's nihilism was already apparent. For Maud Gresham a good action was an impossibility. What one sees in Maud – and this deleted passage is just a very blatant expression of the sense of character which pervades the novel – is a character who wants her life to have meaning but knows, with conviction, that it cannot.

Of Arthur Golding's initial hesitation about approaching Carrie Mitchell directly 'to offer her what help he could' and of his vain attempt to exclude 'all ignobler feelings' from 'the sentiment which called into play the highest energies of his intellect', Gissing had first written:

> The explanation of his state of mind is sufficiently obvious. All that fierce energy of sensual emotion, which in most young men of his age has already become dulled by cheap gratification, was now for the first time wakening within him and subduing him with forces he had never really felt and knew not how to subdue. All that license of the imagination, which a life of healthy activity, both of body and mind, had hitherto held within bounds, now broke loose from restraint and wrought its utmost will.[14]

Equally interesting, because here too, one sees the young author approaching directly the question of sexual motivation that was to frustrate him throughout his career. The triteness of the phrasing is unimportant. What is important is the directness with which the novelist tries to write about the conflict between 'the fierce energy of sensual emotion' and the same character's conventional sense of honourable behaviour. It will be seen that Gissing learnt to be evasive on this subject, perhaps because of this and other similar experiences, but that he did not abandon the insight, as books like *New Grub Street*, *Born in Exile* and *The Odd Women* demonstrate. In *Workers in the Dawn* he had quickly brought himself to the threshold of an understanding of non-moral motivation but for the moment was prevented from proceeding.

It must be acknowledged that this list of deletions is selective and that other less interesting passages were omitted, presumably just to shorten the book. That granted, it seems more than likely that the ones quoted here do in fact represent a classic confrontation between author and public taste – or at least public taste as imagined in the publishing world. After the fire in which John Pether was killed, when Arthur Golding, separated from Carrie Mitchell, tried to obliterate his past, the first edition statement that 'perhaps it will be better to render no detailed account of the few days which followed',[15] replaced a description of Golding going to the theatre for the first time in his life.

> On leaving the Theatre he was heated, flushed, out of himself with excitement. Never had he less inclination to return quietly home; the evening seemed only just beginning for him. As he paused in the doorway of the Theatre, looking in each direction, wishing he knew where more excitement was to be found, he suddenly felt a dainty arm slip within his, and a musical voice address him with a most familiar greeting. Half-alarmed he looked down, & saw that it was a pretty looking girl who had thus claimed his acquaintance. Nothing would have been more *apropos* . . .[16]

It is not difficult to imagine a Victorian publisher or publisher's reader thinking that for Golding to marry Carrie Mitchell was bad enough, for her to have 'friends' and take to the bottle was cutting close to the bone, and that for him to be picked up by a prostitute when he ought to have been in agony over the breakdown of his marriage was altogether objectionable and beyond the limits of decency and common sense.

In each case the passages quoted above are from a longer episode, the whole of which was deleted during the revision of the manuscript. Gissing improved the book by shortening it, though the first-edition text is still too long. Perhaps he also weakened it, however, by blunting the edge of imaginative perceptions and by flattening, as it were, passages that otherwise would have been of greater interest. The counterclaim that these passages were eliminated because they were authorial statements has little weight: the whole novel is written from the point of view of the author and there are hundreds of authorial statements as eligible for exclusion as these. More plausible is the notion that Gissing, having had difficulty in getting the book accepted, removed passages, or was required to remove passages, that were likely to attract unfavourable attention.

Workers in the Dawn is just yet another Victorian three-decker that was directly moulded by the supposed moral attitudes of its potential readers. Had Gissing been given better advice about this first book, his whole career might have been different. At all events, it turned out that even in his best novels he succumbed to the need for euphemism and evasion, as in *New Grub Street,* and accepted editorial interference just for the sake of getting a book published, as in the case of *The Whirlpool.* To prefer the manuscript to the first edition on the grounds that Gissing would have published the deleted passages had Remington allowed him to do so must remain, of course, debatable, however interesting, but it would presumably be legitimate, even desirable, to include in any new annotated edition *some* of the manuscript passages omitted from the first edition, particularly those excluded for moral rather than literary reasons.

So much for the first-edition version of *Workers in the Dawn,* which is what most readers nowadays must read if they read the book at all. Gissing did, however, revise the novel, either completely or in part. In this chapter it will be argued that Gissing carried the revision as far as was necessary; that the revision had to do with a basic structural flaw in the first-edition text; that a study of the manuscript reveals how this flaw came to be there in the first place; and that a study of the second-edition emendations shows how Gissing attempted to patch up the first-edition text by removing major inconsistencies in the design of the book. If this is true, we shall have an example of a genetic or manuscript study that has a direct bearing on the critical understanding of the novel in its final form. But before this can be argued it is necessary to review the evidence.

The second edition of *Workers in the Dawn* was published by Doubleday Doran in 1935 (though not as valuable on the secondhand market as the first edition, this two-volume version is also extremely rare). Professor Shafer edited the novel from a copy of the first edition that had been corrected by Gissing himself (now in the Beinecke Library at Yale) and it seems reasonable to suppose that the annotated copy, then in the possession of Mr and Mrs Frank Capra, had been prepared for the one-volume edition proposed by Lawrence & Bullen in the early 1890s. This would have been one of the revisions already mentioned in chapter I. When Gissing switched from Smith, Elder & Co. to Lawrence & Bullen for the publication of *Denzil Quarrier* and *The Odd Women*, Lawrence & Bullen attempted to obtain the copyright of Gissing's early work so that it could all be republished in revised, one-volume editions. With *The Unclassed*, 1895, and *The Emancipated*, 1893, they succeeded; Chapman & Hall claimed to have made a loss on the first, and Bentley said the same of the second. (Thus it is the second edition of both books that provides the definitive text.) During the same period, Gissing also corrected or revised first-edition copies of *Isabel Clarendon* and *Workers in the Dawn*. In the case of *Isabel Clarendon* the corrected copy is in the Alexander Turnbull Library in Wellington, New Zealand, and the changes made by Gissing are mentioned by Pierre Coustillas in the Harvester Press reissue. This leaves *Workers in the Dawn*. Without doubt, it too was revised in the early 1890s. (Gissing, incidentally, had made similar revisions for two Smith, Elder novels, i.e., the second edition of *The Nether World*, 1890, and the second edition of *Thyrza*, 1891.) There is no evidence to show why Lawrence & Bullen did not proceed with new editions of *Isabel Clarendon* and *Workers in the Dawn*. Perhaps the abortive negotiations with Smith, Elder had demonstrated that a collected edition was impossible. Perhaps Gissing himself had come to disapprove of republication, after looking at the books again. Nonetheless, whatever commercial or practical factors may have been at play, the corrections Gissing made to the first-edition text of *Workers in the Dawn* are of considerable critical interest. They amount to a total deletion equivalent to eighty first-edition pages and represent repairs to the mutilated text as Gissing was at first obliged to publish it.

Because these corrections and deletions were made to the first of the three volumes only, Professor Shafer assumed, quite fairly, that the process was incomplete and therefore chose to indicate the deletions that were to have been made by means of footnotes, without actually removing any of the first-edition text. In his Introduction, Shafer stated: 'Inasmuch as the revision was never completed, I have not printed the revised text of Part I; but every alteration made by Gissing has been recorded in a series of footnotes identified by the letter "G". It will be seen at once that Gissing's principal object was to shorten the novel, though other changes made by him are not without interest.' Shafer's caution was natural, particularly since he had not seen or did not record having seen the manuscript; nevertheless it is obviously the revised version of the novel that ought to be the basis for critical discussion, whether the process of revision had been completed or not.

These changes to the first edition text may be listed briefly. First, Gissing eliminated many of the merely tart reflections on the Church that had remained in, even after the revision of that manuscript. A parenthetical remark on the adequacy of Norman's stipend – 'that treasure upon earth which the clergy doubtless prize merely as a type of the heavenly treasure which will one day be theirs' – is the kind of gratuitously sour remark that goes.

Secondly, he further shortened the descriptive passages, removing mawkish passages that had little relation to the main story. In the example which follows the parts he deleted are in square brackets:

> But the good people of Whitecross Street are thirsty as well as hungry, and there is no lack of gin-palaces to supply their needs. Open the door and look into one of these. Here a group are wrangling over a disputed toss or bet, here two are coming to blows, there are half-a-dozen young men and women, all half drunk, mauling each other with vile caresses; and all the time, from the lips of the youngest and the oldest, foams forth such a torrent of inanity, abomination and horrible blasphemy which bespeaks the very depth of human – aye, or of bestial – degradation. And notice how, between these centres and the alleys into which we have peered, shoeless children, slip-shod and barehoaded women, tottering old men, are constantly coming and going with cans or jugs in their hands. Well, is it not Saturday night? And how can the week's wages be better spent than in procuring a few hours' unconsciousness of the returning Monday.
>
> The crowd that constantly throngs from one end of the street to the other is very miscellaneous, comprehending alike the almost naked wretch who creeps along in the hope of being able to steal a mouthful of garbage, and the respectably clad artisan and his wife, seeing how best they can lay out their money for the ensuing week. The majority are women, some carrying children in their arms, some laden with a basket full of purchases, most with no covering on their heads but the corner of a shawl.

[But look at the faces! Here is a young mother with a child sucking at her bare breast, as she chaffers with a man over a pound of potatoes. Suddenly she turns away with reddened cheeks, shrinking before a vile jest which creates bursts of laughter in the bystanders. Pooh! She is evidently new in this quarter, perhaps come up of late from the country. Wait a year, and you will see her joining in the laugh at her own expense, with as much gusto as that young woman behind her, whose features, under more favourable circumstances, might have had something of beauty, but starvation and dirt and exposure have coarsened the grain and made her teeth grin woefully between her thin lips.

Or look at the woman on the other side, who is laughing till she cries. Does not every line of her face bespeak the baseness of her nature? Cannot one even guess at the vile trade by which she keeps her limbs covered with those layers of gross fat, whilst those around her are so pinched and thin? Her cheeks hang flabbily, and her eyes twinkle with a vicious light. A deep scar marks her forehead, a memento of some recent drunken brawl. When she has laughed her fill, she turns to look after a child which is being dragged through the mud by her skirts, being scarcely yet able to walk, and, bidding it with a cuff and a curse not to leave loose of her, pushes on stoutly through the crowd.]

One could find matter for hour-long observation in the infinite variety of vice and misery depicted in the faces around. It must be confessed that the majority do not seem unhappy; they jest with each other amid their squalor; they have an evident pleasure in buying and selling; they would be surprised if they knew you pitied them. And the very fact that they are unconscious of their degradation afflicts one with all the keener pity. [We suffer them to become brutes in our midst, and inhabit dens which clean animals would shun, to derive their joys from sources from which a cultivated mind shrinks as from a pestilential vapour. And can we console ourselves with the reflection that they do not feel their misery?]

Well, this is the Whitecross Street of to-day; but it is in this street rather more than twenty years ago that my story opens. There is not much difference between now and then, except that the appearance of the shops is perhaps improved, and the sanitary condition of the neighbourhood a trifle more attended to; the description, on the whole, may remain unaltered.

It was about half-past ten on a Saturday night, towards the close of November.[17]

A general proposition that will be made in this book is that, as Gissing became more interested in people and their relations with each other, and less interested in the simple determinism in which people are a function of social conditions, his social conscience diminished and his sense of social alienation increased. Here one sees the process beginning. He started off by wanting to say something about the people of Whitecross Street only to find he had nothing to say. The implication of responsibility in the 'we' of the deleted sentences is inconsistent with the idea of a neutral observer. Here, then, Gissing is feeling his way out of a difficulty, or at least revising a somewhat intractable early work in the light of his greater expertise of the 1890s.

Thirdly, he removed an inappropriate, perhaps autobiographical metaphor. In the first version, Helen Norman's parrot and the drawing of a parrot, which Arthur made in Mike Rumball's pet shop and then gave to Lizzie Clinkscales, were both made to represent his ambiguous feelings for the two girls, his gesture on behalf of Lizzie being confused with his as yet unarticulated feelings for Helen. In the revision, the parrot episode was eliminated, as indeed Gissing almost invariably eliminated casual or accidental symbolism.

Fourthly, the negative attacks on characters who were not 'workers in the dawn', but quite the opposite, and who were not needed for the second part of the novel, were for the most part eliminated. There is still, in the revised novel, a carping criticism of the 'haves' as opposed to the 'have nots', but a better balance has certainly been achieved. The space allowed to Mr Gresham, Mr Waghorn, the senior Mr Golding and Mr Whiffle was severely reduced while Mr Norman's part in the novel is altogether reduced, as indeed became possible as soon as the emphasis changed from a study of the factors affecting a young man growing up, to a study of a young man's disastrous marriage.

Finally, Lizzie Clinkscales disappeared. Why? The answer turns out to be interesting, because it shows Gissing moving away from the novelistic formulation he had inherited in an attempt to find something more appropriate to his sense of things in 1880. This is put vaguely on purpose. When Gissing started the novel he may have had a set plan which he tried to implement, but if so the evidence reveals that in writing the novel he encountered a difficulty which he had not anticipated at the outset. For as long as the novel chiefly concerned 'workers in the dawn', and was predominantly a critique of contemporary English urban life, it was reasonable for Gissing to imagine a situation in which the main character, Golding, might either opt for social commitment and at the same time marry a good-hearted 'daughter of the people', Lizzie Clinkscales, or withdraw from a social predicament which he could not influence and marry Helen Norman, who represented art, culture and refinement.

The introduction of the much stronger character, Carrie Mitchell, relatively late on in the novel, invalidated this simple equation. The two characters, Lizzie Clinkscales and Carrie Mitchell, belonged in different types of novel, Lizzie Clinkscales having elements of warm caricature that made her almost a character out of Dickens, while

Carrie Mitchell, much more directly – even harshly – realized and drawn, belonged much more with the new social realism. There was a clumsiness, besides, in Gissing's having his hero know these women equally well. Significantly, the proletarian figure was abandoned, as indeed was consistent with Gissing's weakening interest in the social protest element of his book as first written. She ought to have been abandoned in the first edition text as well, as one can see from the fact that the point at which Gissing introduced Carrie Mitchell into the novel (a point identifiable in the manuscript) was also the point at which the revision for the second edition ends. A brief review of the evidence will bring the implications of this into focus.

Gissing was close to finishing the novel in the summer of 1879. On 5 August of that year, he told his brother Algernon: 'At present I have three weeks' or a month's hard work before me in which I hope to finish my novel.'[18] Even though the novel is not referred to by name in this letter, mention of a mortgage chapter ties it firmly to *Workers in the Dawn*. About a week later, he wrote to Algernon again: 'Ten days' work will complete it. It will make a volume about the size of *Shirley* in your edition.'[19] As far as one can tell, he worked steadily at the novel between 20 August, when he told Algernon that he had just finished the twenty-eighth chapter (information of considerable critical significance, as will be shown later) and 3 November when the book was finished: 'It consists of 46 chapters, of some 450 MS. pp., and will I fear, make three good volumes.'[20]

Although Gissing said he had finished the book, there is a problem. The MS. at the University of Texas in fact consists of 709 pages.[21] Only a few explanations are possible. Gissing may have written 46, not 28 chapters and 709 not 450, pages by 3 November; or 450 pages and fewer chapters; or 46 chapters and 709 MS. pages which for the sake of describing the book to Algernon he took to be the equivalent of 450 book pages. The novel as we now have it consists of 47 chapters: 46 is close and it is difficult to think of Gissing hitting upon the figure by accident. Perhaps, then, the '450' was the error? If so, further speculation would be possible, since 450 does have significance. The 28 chapters mentioned on 20 August would have amounted to about 450 MS. pages. Volume II, chapter 13, begins on MS. 441. In a single-volume novel, this would have been chapter 28. The chapter heading on MS. 441 shows that Gissing changed his mind, not once but several times.

Chapter 13 of Volume II is in fact the first serious chapter about Arthur Golding's relationship with Carrie Mitchell, who is mentioned for the first time on Shafer II 54 and MS. 410. Arthur Golding, the hero or principal male protagonist, had of course been in the novel from the beginning, but it seems remarkable that Carrie Mitchell, who replaces all the other female characters in importance, should only have been introduced at this late stage. Up to this point, there was nothing in the novel to predetermine the outcome of their meeting; his marriage to her could have been happy or unhappy. It became unhappy and the decision evidently resulted in a certain amount of rewriting, including the insertion – perhaps at an early stage of composition – of four chapters.

The circumstantial evidence, in other words, supports the hypothesis that Gissing wrote roughly 450 pages before introducing one of his main characters, that having done so he either at the time or later shortened the first part in order to balance the story, and that he made these changes too quickly for there to be time for a genuine assessment of whether the Carrie Mitchell part of the story was consistent with what had gone before. Gissing had to modify the story as far as Helen was concerned, for example, but superficial modification was not the same as ensuring that the early characterization of Arthur Golding was consistent with the attitudes he adopted in his crisis with Carrie Mitchell. Because Gissing failed to make changes, the necessity for which stares one in the face (i.e. the changes that he made later), one is forced to the conclusion that he finished the book in a hurry and that the Carrie Mitchell episode absorbed all his energy.

This is seen clearly when one considers the way in which Gissing developed the relationship between Arthur Golding and Carrie Mitchell. To look fairly closely at the powerful and psychologically absorbing development of this relationship, as written in the manuscript and retained through the revision, is to understand why Gissing had to alter the early part of the novel, but not the rest. First mention of Carrie Mitchell occurs in Volume II, Chapter XI. She was a mantle-hand and the landlady's niece. Almost immediately came the formal description typical of Gissing's early books.

> She was very pretty, if not positively handsome, tall, with dark hair which she arranged in a tasteful way, and dressed in black which seemed to indicate mourning. Though her beauty was of a somewhat sensual type, and her features betrayed no special intelligence or good humour, Arthur felt strangely attracted to her for all that.[22]

This immediately alters the basic conception of the novel. In the first version, Arthur Golding in effect had to decide between democratic involvement with ordinary people (Lizzie) and a more aloof commitment to art and philanthropy (Helen). Now the conflict becomes one between the ideal of beauty (Helen) and the actual experience of sexuality (Carrie). No wonder a thorough revision became necessary. Golding fell in love with Carrie before they had even spoken to each other and quickly forgot Helen Norman. When Mark Challenger discovered that Carrie was to be evicted because pregnant, Golding was overcome with compassion and secretly paid her rent. In Chapter XI, entitled 'Love or Pity' Gissing dispassionately portrayed the confusion of motive in Arthur Golding, his hero. Whereas his love for Helen had been a 'devotion of the spirit' and 'a sentiment which called into play the highest energies of his intellect, the noblest impulses of his heart to the exclusion of all ignobler feeling', once he had met Carrie his senses

> had sway over him. His blood coursed hot through his veins, his pulses throbbed. One moment he burned with vehement anger at the unknown author of the poor girl's troubles, becoming conscious of a depth of resentful ferocity in his nature, the existence of which he would not have believed; the next, his being seemed to melt with excess of passion, as he thought of Carrie's beautiful face and form, and dwelt with unutterable tenderness upon the vision of her tear-reddened eyes, her pale cheeks, her feeble step. He suffered physically; it were as though some force were straining at his heart strings, making him pant for breath.[23]

Passion in Gissing means physical desire. Golding's suppressed erotic longing was expressed in the contemporary clichés of pity and self-abasement, since in order to rationalize his desire and at the same time justify the lack of decorum in his breaking the social barrier between person and person, he imagined the as yet non-existent relationship in chivalrous terms which, though useless and absurd, were the only ones available to him. He would justify getting to know the girl by helping her. And the desire to help was not less real because it concealed a repressed eroticism. Gissing subsequently showed that the failure of Golding's marriage with Carrie Mitchell could be traced back to Golding's first thoughts about her. Once Golding had made the arrangements to pay her rent, he 'flung himself on his bed for a few hours' rest, his whole frame aglow with tremulous delight. To be able to have served that poor, pale-faced, yet beautiful girl, and to have done so, moreover, at the cost of some sacrifice, was a joy of almost fierce intensity.'[24]

Just as Arthur Golding was confused about the reasons for his interest in Carrie Mitchell at a time when he was theoretically devoted to Helen Norman, a confusion of motive that Gissing in one sense managed well, so Gissing, the novelist, was not altogether sure in his handling of the subject that obviously preoccupied him. At one point, for example, when Carrie Mitchell had left the house, had had her child, had been found at Christmas with the child dead in her arms, and had been rescued by Arthur Golding and Mark Challenger, Golding then having the practical problem of providing for her, Gissing castigated the reader, or the world at large, for lack of understanding.

> He was troubled, moreover, to discover some plan by which he could make an offer of assistance with suitable delicacy and then install Carrie in her room without fear of endangering her reputation; the latter, especially, being a task which the fearful and wonderful complication of our social delicacies and pruderies renders always somewhat difficult. The world is so very slow to believe that connections other than of a certain kind can possibly exist between young people of different sex who see each other in private; it is so easy for corrupt imagination to picture situations completely familiar to themselves, so extremely difficult for them to conceive the existence of virtue and self-respect.[25]

Passages of this kind meant that even though Gissing restructured and greatly improved the novel in the course of revising it, problems remained that he did not solve until he had more experience. Gissing did not at first realize the restraints and controls necessary for effective third person narrative, failed to distinguish himself from himself as narrator and failed to let the characters speak for themselves in a consistent fashion.

Gissing failed to show the relationship from the point of view of the girl. Indeed, she is seen by the reader only as she was seen by Arthur Golding: turned away from the house during a Christmas party, sheltering in a porch-way near the Prince of Wales Theatre with her dead child, walking with Golding under their one umbrella in a rainstorm, returning home with a girl friend from a spree in Oxford Street when he thought she was in her room, drinking in a pub in Huntley Street. But from the point of view of the man, Gissing did show that the mess into which Golding got himself was psychological. He was not really an emancipated person despite the terms in which he thought about himself. On the contrary, he was a puritan. He retained a prim morality that was an absolute obstacle to his ever living naturally with an uneducated, 'sensual', good-natured girl like Carrie Mitchell. When they argue, the two of them, about Carrie's freedom to come and go as she pleases just before they were to be married, Golding adopts a patronizing tone consistent with his general attitude.

> In his attempt to exalt her nature above the level on which it had hitherto moved, he, the democratic agitator, the ardent sympathizer with the most miserable of poverty's victims, waxed quite aristocratic in his conversa-

tion. In his heart he would rather have seen Carrie fall into the most complete snobbishness on the subject of riches and rank than continue at rest among the sympathies with vulgar life with which she had grown up.[26]

Gissing evidently knew what he was doing. He emphasized the extent of hypocrisy and self-deception in Golding as it became the cause of the breakdown of the marriage, a breakdown made manifest in Carrie's inability to learn, as well as in her drinking and her prostitution. Some critics have written as though Carrie were the cause of Golding's difficulties. This is not in fact how Gissing presented the matter, least of all in the novel as it was eventually restructured. As a matter of fact, when one comes to know Gissing well, one realizes that this enigmatic, ironic strategy in which alienated characters are played off the one against the other is characteristic of him. He becomes the master of the muddled relationship, and what happens here to Golding and Carrie Mitchell clearly anticipates *The Unclassed*, *Thyrza* and *Born in Exile*.

The foregoing discussion has been designed to show that Gissing could not afford to keep Lizzie Clinkscales as well as Helen Norman, when he introduced (in 1879) a third important character, Carrie Mitchell; that being able to identify the point at which Carrie Mitchell was introduced helps one to understand the structural inadequacy of the first-edition text; that there was a logic to the later revision of the novel (in the 1890s) which obliges one to take the revision seriously (especially the elimination of Lizzie Clinkscales) and to adopt the second edition (of 1935) as the copy-text; and that the difference between the first, bowdlerized edition and the second, revised edition constitutes a clear illustration of the way in which Gissing was developing as a novelist, inasmuch as there is a tension in *Workers in the Dawn* between two interests which he cannot immediately reconcile: his interest in alienation and the breakdown of relationships between people and his interest in the physical environment and the social conditions that much of the population had to endure. Could he bind both of these into the one novel? *Workers in the Dawn* is interesting as a first novel because he attempted to do exactly that. In the work of the next decade, he experimented with other versions of the same thing, first veering towards a naturalistic treatment of social conditions of which individuals were a function, then moving away from naturalism in a later emphasis upon individuals alienated from a social life with which they had no meaningful contact whatsoever.

Two minor matters must be mentioned at this point, at least to clear the air and to prepare the way for the later chapters. Critical consideration of Gissing must be based upon the right text: *Workers in the Dawn* provides a good example of a novel which has usually been considered in the wrong – that is to say, the unrevised – version. This is of greater importance than what Gissing thought about the matter himself. For example, just after finishing *The Emancipated* he wrote to Eduard Bertz about his earlier work: 'Heavens! how it must have brought back old days, to re-read *Workers* and *The Unclassed*! Not for any consideration would I open those dreadful books! All I have ever written seems to be apprentice-work; I fear to examine it.'[27] These remarks, though often quoted, can be quite deceptive. Gissing may have feared to examine *Workers in the Dawn* because of its association with those early days when he and Bertz had been impoverished, struggling writers, but a few years later he did in fact examine it and examine it with more than casual interest, as has been demonstrated. Secondly, at this stage in the discussion, bibliographical or textual questions seem more important than biographical ones. It may well be that *Workers in the Dawn* was converted from a rather leisurely, rather theoretical descriptive novel about social conditions in London into a fiercely imagined account of a marriage because of the deterioration of Gissing's own first marriage while he was writing the book in 1870. The time at which Carrie Mitchell was introduced into the novel is indeed crucial from a biographical point of view;[28] it is not crucial from a critical point of view, however, since what happened to Gissing's marriage in 1879 has nothing to do with how a reader might respond to the revised text in 1894 or thereabouts. Such, at least, is the assumption which will inform the critical discussion of Gissing's other novels in the chapters which follow.

3
1880–5: 'By Indirection Find Direction Out': Gissing's Apprenticeship

GISSING's first novel, *Workers in the Dawn*, had been published in 1880. Five years later came *Demos*, written in 1885 and published in 1886. *Demos*, in turn, was quickly followed by *Thyrza* (1887) and *The Nether World* (1888). Whereas *Workers in the Dawn* had not been a successful novel, either commercially or artistically, but was rather a portfolio of ideas which Gissing was to explore, test, utilize, develop through the whole of the decade which followed it, *Demos* (published anonymously) only five years later, was a powerful work which, despite faults and lapses, had the unity of imaginative purpose which *Workers in the Dawn* had lacked. In terms of immediate popular impact, *Demos* was to be Gissing's first success, a limited success admittedly, but a genuine milestone for a writer who was only twenty-eight. He evidently learned a lot during the comparatively brief period of five years between publishing his first and beginning to write his fifth novel; throughout this period he thought a lot about the art of fiction, worked hard, read intensively and continued to write as much as he could, given the fact that he still supported himself by the private tutoring in Latin and Greek which took several hours of each day.

During the years which separated *Workers in the Dawn* and *Demos*, (discussed in chapter 4) Gissing wrote at least four novels: 'Mrs Grundy's Enemies', which was accepted by Bentley but never published; *The Unclassed* (1884), in many ways a brilliant novel and the one from this group which has best stood the test of time; *Isabel Clarendon* (1886), first written in three volumes then reduced to two; and *A Life's Morning* (1888), which was written before *Demos* although not published until a few years later. He had started but failed to complete at least one other book, tentatively called 'A Child of the Age'.[1] The three published novels that appeared during this period of apprenticeship were not all good books; in fact only *The Unclassed* justifies extended discussion. Less ambitious than *Workers in the Dawn*, more directed towards the solving of specific novelistic problems that had not been resolved in the first work, they were in many respects lightweight creations by comparison with what followed them. Only in the very activity of writing did Gissing discover how to write his own kind of novel, as indeed only gradually did he plumb and find ways of making the most of his own subject. In this chapter, *The Unclassed* is taken seriously because it so clearly shows the progress Gissing made, technically, between his first novel and the three London novels to be discussed in chapter 4, while (later in the chapter) the much slighter books, *Isabel Clarendon* and *A Life's Morning*, are discussed, though as digressions from the main stream of development.

Gissing was living a necessarily simple, but nonetheless stable life while he wrote these four novels. He had separated from his first wife and was living by himself in Chelsea: 'There is only one place in the world wherein to live', he wrote, after more than a year at the same address, 'and that is *Chelsea*'.[2] His letters give hints of his wide reading, hints only, for later events show that he was familiar with works not included amongst those he recommended to his brothers and sisters. Yet even in the letters to Wakefield there is an assurance of culture that evidently had a wide foundation. He recommended books like Morris' *Earthly Paradise*, a poem 'abounding in the quaintest archaisms'; Ruskin's *Unto this Last*, which Gissing liked as a 'contribution to – or rather onslaught upon – Political Economy'; Landor's *Imaginary Conversations*, for its 'perfect prose'; and Scott's *Redgauntlet*, for the romantic situations of which he must 'try to find parallel kinds in modern life.' Gissing kept up the habit throughout his life: he was always reading and always recommending books to his friends and family. In the early 1880s he read a lot of German, and to his brother, Algernon, particularly recommended Eckerman's *Conversations with Goethe*, 'a most delightful book'. Meanwhile his sister, Margaret, was reading Schiller under his direction, after which he would have her 'follow up with a Goethe – a still diviner man'. In accepting responsibility for his brother's and sister's education, he took it granted that they should read both German and French works, preferably in the original. Gissing himself continued to read Latin and Greek authors daily, just as he continued to dream of the 'gloriousness' of seeing Italy, Sicily and Greece, Rome, Athens, the Ionian Islands – 'countries where every spot of ground gives off as it were an absolute perfume of reminiscences and associations'.[3] Equally influential, or perhaps even more influential, was his first encounter with Turgenev in 1884, an author whose cosmopolitan and nihilist attitudes later helped Gissing find his most mature fiction. 'I have just got from Germany translations of five or six of Tourguéneff's novels. They are published in the *Universal Bibliothek* at 3d. a volume!'[4] This was an important milestone. But only one of many: it was during this same period that he had come to terms with Schopenhauer.

Because we are accustomed nowadays to reading many literatures in translation and because foreign books are more readily available, it might seem at first sight that Gissing's experience was quite similar to that of any other educated and reasonably inquisitive person. Not so. Not many Englishmen were reading Schopenhauer and Turgenev in 1884. In any case, it is worth insisting, a little, on the breadth of his reading if only to retain within the discussion of his fiction a number of obvious facts: first, that Gissing was above all a literary man – that is, was someone whose insights, whose experience derived as much from books as from life; secondly, that his literary experience included contemporary European fiction, probably to a degree that few other Englishmen could match; thirdly, that his austere, sinewy, undecorated, unmetaphorical way of writing was a considered style; fourthly, that it was in his foreign reading that he found a strong justification for his own social and intellectual attitudes, at least to the extent that it becomes absurd, for anyone who knows anything about Gissing's daily thinking life, to write him off as a naïve fellow the shape of whose works was determined by his early traumas. We have much more to cope with a knowledgeable writer who, for better or worse, was aware of what he was doing.

He was also aware of some of his own artistic shortcomings, which he tried to rectify, while in London, by reading magazines, going to galleries and attending concerts. Perhaps with *Isabel Clarendon* already in mind, he made several visits to the Academy to see Rossetti's paintings, interested himself in art generally through visits to other galleries like the Grosvenor, and about a year later, made the for him startling remark in a letter: 'So I get music, without which it is difficult to manage.'[5] In 1885, the music was 'Scotch songs' *[sic]* at a dinner party, musical Sundays at the house of 'some Jewish people' and 'Bucalossi underneath . . . though he only plays Valses'. Still, humdrum as this may be, Gissing was always eager to extend his knowledge, something which his later books show he did successfully, for he was not so stupid as to be interested in the art of fiction and not be interested in the arts themselves. Interestingly it is quite a bit later, in *The Whirlpool*, that he gives expression to Schopenhauerian ideas of music that had probably developed in London in the early 1880s. At any rate, it is wrong to think of Gissing condemned to a life of drudgery and hardship. The five-year period was important for him because between *Workers in the Dawn* and *Demos* he became informed about what was going on in London, knew what intellectuals like himself were thinking about, read the same books, pondered the same ideas, and enjoyed himself in the process.

Nor were Gissing's pleasures confined to art and literature. On Sundays, a day on which he rarely worked, oppressed as he always was by memories of the Wakefield sabbath, he would go on steamer trips to Putney, Richmond, Kew, and Kingston and when the weather became warmer rowed on the Thames, sometimes staying on the river until nightfall.[6] He benefited also from Frederic Harrison's friendship and trust, dined at the house, taught his boys, joined the family on picnics and was given charge of his pupils when Harrison's wife was ill. Particularly when he had separated from his wife in 1882, Gissing tackled the Victorian task of improving himself in body and mind with great earnestness and with his usual energy.

This was a period in which Gissing was able to work with vigour and determination. Life was not uniformly black, as some have insisted:[7] indeed there have always existed strong counter-statements, like that written by Frederic Harrison. After Gissing's death, Harrison wrote to H. G. Wells in order to identify the 'Mme George Gissing' from whom he had received a card announcing Gissing's death (actually, of course, Gabrielle Fleury, not Mrs Edith Gissing[8]), and in the course of a short correspondence with Wells attempted to rectify some of the stories that were already in circulation.

> I am amused to read the various myths which his young admirers and readers are putting about. They are mostly mere romances. George Gissing passed through a year or two of acute pressure and dreadful suffering – for which he alone was responsible. To the age of 18 he had a perfectly comfortable, easy, successful, and even brilliant life, with every prospect of a fine career. That he threw away and smarted horribly for some years. At 22 he introduced himself to me. I made him tutor to my sons. He spent every morning in my house – he dined at my table with my sons and my wife and myself daily, came to our evening parties, and was in every sense one of our friends. I introduced him to John Morley, then Editor of the *Pall Mall Gazette*, and got Morley to employ him on the paper. This Gissing abruptly declined. I got him numerous pupils in excellent families, when my sons went to school. I sent him in charge of my family to a beautiful house on Ullswater during the autumn of 1884, which he enjoyed greatly.[9]

Gissing was in relatively comfortable circumstances, in other words, when he began *The Unclassed* at the beginning of 1883. He was then twenty-five years old, earned enough money from his pupils to leave him time to write at the rate of about a novel a year, occasionally sent money home to Wakefield, gave his wife an allowance of a pound a week through a solicitor, and would from time to time indulge in minor luxuries such as having some of his books bound. They were indeed minor luxuries and he grumbled ceaselessly. The 'morning's drudgery' of teaching detracted from his real work. He was soon having trouble with Bentley over 'Mrs Grundy's Enemies', which had been accepted on Boxing Day 1882. He had fits of profound depression, allowing himself to be overwhelmed, temporarily, by loneliness and self-pity. On the whole, however, life did not treat him as badly as people have claimed or as in his worst moments he claimed himself. To give just a single example of the way in which critics have enjoyed dwelling on the bleaker side of Gissing's existence, and by doing so have predetermined many readers' response to his books, one can mention Jacob Korg's remark about Gissing's not objecting to the small payment he received from Chapman & Hall for *The Unclassed*, because 'he was so accustomed to genuine failure'.[10] This is surely an unjustified exaggeration. Not many writers have three novels accepted for publication by the age of twenty-six and a young writer disappointed by the reception of his first book cannot be said to be *'accustomed* to failure'.

On the contrary, Gissing was confident he was on the side of the angels and his determination then and later was absolutely remarkable. This can be seen in his reaction to Bentley's handling of 'Mrs Grundy's Enemies'. Bentley offered £50 for it, less than two years after the publication of *Workers in the Dawn*. Not unnaturally Gissing was jubilant.[11] The book had earlier been rejected by Smith, Elder, but not because it was thought badly written. If Gissing's report to his sister is to be trusted, the firm's reader had said: 'It exhibits a great deal of dramatic power and is certainly not wanting in vigour, but in our judgement it is too painful to please the ordinary reader and treats of scenes that can never attract the subscribers to Mr Mudie's Library'. To which Gissing added sardonically: 'Of course I could have told them all that'.[12] A young author does not necessarily feel that he had failed when he offends the powers-that-be, for his disappointment over the rejection is balanced by the fact that he sees how reactionary the other party is. He sent the book to Bentley and had to wait about two months for a decision. At Christmas 1882, when the book was accepted, his morale must have been high indeed.

R. A. Gettman, in *A Victorian Publisher: A Study of the Bentley Papers*, has given a succinct account of what happened to 'Mrs Grundy's

Enemies' after it was accepted. He showed that Bentley, personally, must have recognized the strength of the book,[13] that the printing of it began almost immediately, that when Bentley became alarmed by certain passages on seeing them in proof, he tried to rescue the book by having Evelyn Abbott, of Balliol College, suggest cuts and changes, and that Abbott, too, recognized the novel's merits. Gettman quoted a letter from Abbott in which he said: 'I still think the work is striking. The best of all that I have read for you. I should be sorry if the success were spoiled by want of care'.[14] It would be quite superfluous to repeat Gettman's account of the matter, but there is point in drawing attention to the timing. Gissing had no reason to suppose that his book was in danger; he believed that it was being printed. At issue, therefore, in the spring of 1883 was only the extent to which the publisher would allow him to be outspoken. He wrote to Algernon about it. Bentley had asked him 'to soften certain features in some of the description and dialogue'[15] and Harrison had told him to 'give way'. Less than a week later he wrote to Algernon again. 'No great progress to report. The printers, however, have put on a spurt, and will, at this rate, finish Volume II by end of week . . . I had much rather Bentley dictate desired changes, than run the chance of altering things which perhaps he would permit to stand.'[16] In this way, he acknowledges, obliquely, the arrangement that had been made with the publisher, at the same time showing he was not unduly upset by the delay.

Gettman concluded that 'it is not clear when Bentley informed Gissing of his decision not to publish "Mrs Grundy's Enemies".'[17] Since Bentley kept the type standing for four years and did not sell the paper he had bought for the novel until 1887, and since Gissing himself was at work on the revision of the novel in 1884, it would seem fairly certain that, at least while he was writing *The Unclassed* during 1883, he had no real reason for supposing that 'Mrs Grundy's Enemies' would never be published. This being the case, Gissing's next book, *The Unclassed*, must to some extent constitute a response to difficulties implicit in the creation of credible fiction out of unpalatable social material, which means *The Unclassed* can most usefully be seen, not as a backing away from but as a confrontation with novelistic problems which at that time few other novelists had been able to solve. Or rather, if some novelists *had* managed to solve the problem, it was in the special sense of having cannily contrived to refer indirectly to matters which, referred to directly, would have been unpalatable to the average reader. The evasions and euphemisms of Meredith's later work, as well as the very structure and fashioning of important novels like *The Amazing Marriage* and *One of Our Conquerors*, demonstrated that he at least took this problem seriously. That much the same can be said of Hardy is well-known. The same forces that made Mudie take Meredith's *The Ordeal of Richard Feverel* off his circulating-library list in 1860 also caused a magazine editor's censorship of *Tess of the D'Urbervilles* more than thirty years later. These were the novelists whom Gissing admired and respected. With them he learned by experience that to use a popular form for the treatment of unpopular subjects was by no means easy. He had to learn *how* to write a novel in which the novelist's vision and the reader's expectations were reconciled. The loss of 'Mrs Grundy's Enemies' and the writing of *The Unclassed* were important parts of this learning process. The young Gissing could not afford to be down-spirited in 1883, for his commitment to novel writing was complete. Having fashioned his private life appropriately, he had one novel in print, one in the press, and one in progress. After telling Algernon about his fight against prejudice, he said: 'Never mind: I have that which never fails one – confidence in myself. The day will come when I shall smile at the recollection of these initial difficulties. Preserve this letter, and look back on it in the year 1890!'[18]

In summary, then, Gissing continued to work at those themes and preoccupations he had identified as his own in *Workers in the Dawn*. Throughout the period 1880–5 he searched out, sometimes successfully, sometimes unsuccessfully, *artistic* answers to the *artistic* questions posed by his first book. His interests did not substantially alter, though he tried at first this approach, then that. During the brief spread of years that can fairly be called a period of apprenticeship, one can see within it two phases: the 'innocent' phase in which Gissing continued to work at the material of *Workers in the Dawn* (i.e. in 'Mrs Grundy's Enemies' and *The Unclassed*), and the 'experienced' phase when he felt obliged temporarily to take other people's opinions into account, however unsatisfactorily (i.e. when he wrote *Isabel Clarendon* and *A Life's Morning*). But whether this distinction between two apprenticeship phases is acceptable or not, what is certain is that during this formative period his interest in socialism weakened while his belief in himself as a certain type of artist remained steady. He remained close to the thematic material he had introduced into *Workers in the Dawn*, but the treatment of that material was more in terms of individuals than of movements. This preference had important practical consequences.

One consequence can be seen clearly if one jumps ahead to Gissing's response to his family's negative comments on *The Unclassed*.

The family had evidently expected that George's second novel (second to them) would be compatible with the great literature he recommended they should read: instead, they received a novel that made few concessions to the ideal and undermined their ideas about Romance. Like more than one or two literary critics after them, they thought the opinions of Waymark, the main character, were Gissing's own. He had to write to his sister, Ellen, to correct this misconception.

> You evidently take Waymark's declaration of faith as my own. Now this is by no means the case. Waymark is a *study of character*, and he alone is responsible for his sentiments . . . If my own ideas are to be found anywhere, it is in the practical course of events in the story; my characters must speak as they would actually, and I cannot be responsible for what they say. You may tell me I need not have chosen such people: ah, but that is a question of the artist's selection.[19]

This is a letter which needs to be read by anyone new to Gissing, because in it he is so forthright, assured, definite. He says that *The Unclassed* cannot harm those who misunderstand it but will 'be enjoyed by those who are, like myself, purely neutral'; that his intellectual standpoint (criticized by Ellen) does not preclude 'human goodness'; that he writes as he must, as his imagination dictates, not because he bears society a grudge ('I – I assure you very earnestly – I am in anything but a parlous state'); and that, from his intimate acquaintance with 'Balzac, Tourguéneff, Dumas, etc.', he knows that he is not doing anything startling but is simply a part of the modern movement. He was exceptional, he said, only because he drew his characters 'more *faithfully* than any other English novelist would.'

In other words, whatever others might say, Gissing saw himself purely as a novelist, a literary artist, a writer who thought about what he was doing and had positive ideas about his contemporaries and this explains the apparently surprising fact of his curt refusal of John Morley's offer of a journalistic career.[20] This does not mean that he had solved his problems, for all that *The Unclassed* is such a good book. It means that he was aware of his problems, an all-important consideration for anyone trying to come to terms with his development as a novelist. In particular – and to anticipate the more detailed discussion of *The Unclassed* – he had the problem of motivation, a question which any novelist must confront who does not accept the values of the society in which he writes. Gissing's characters do not behave as many of his readers would have behaved; nor do they make the judgements about other characters that would satisfy the average reader's sense of values;[21] nor do they fashion their lives in a way that is consistent with conventional morality, as likely to be perceived by the average purchaser of the book. Why? Of the several possible answers to this question there is one which, though true, would scarcely sustain a whole writing career, i.e. that Gissing observed and recorded urban behaviour without necessarily understanding it. It is true that his attitude to motivation was based in part upon observation: he knew, had seen for himself, that in the 1880s people behaved in ways vastly different from what old-fashioned moralists might expect, so there was a documentary element to his 'faithful' depiction of what he had observed. It is not true, though, that he could manage in novel after novel without understanding how his characters would relate to one another – i.e. without a thought-out idea of what motivated them. This was particularly the case as he moved away from a socialist view of life, a movement that is marked by the progression from *Workers in the Dawn*, where he allows some characters a legitimate socialist idealism, to *Demos*, where he denies it. If the desire to improve society is not a legitimate motive (and in a novel is not accepted by the novelist as a motivating force sufficient to sustain the action), what then? Gissing found congenial answers to this question in Schopenhauer, whose works gave validity (at least temporarily) to Gissing's pessimistic notion of characters existing with limited freedom and limited powers of self-determination in an amoral world.[22]

Gissing, then, when he came to write *The Unclassed*, was in the process of changing his ground. The ardent, angry young writer who had mounted an attack on Victorian institutions in *Workers in the Dawn* and 'Mrs Grundy's enemies' and who had seen himself as a concerned individual, sincerely worried about the issues of the time, even to the extent of attending socialist meetings, gave way to the more detached, *fin-de-siècle* writer who more and more delegated the responsibility for moral and social opinions to his characters, concentrating increasingly on the contemporary world as seen through their eyes or in the context of their lives, not his own, a shift of emphasis which progressively made the documentary subservient to the psychological, as will be seen. In *The Unclassed*, Waymark puts aside his novel because he needs money to stay alive. He becomes a rent collector and thereby obtains first-hand knowledge of the London slums. The issue of social exploitation is raised through the character (not the narrator) and the reader to a much greater extent sees only what the character sees. The social problem is not dodged, but Gissing's focus has shifted significantly, as indeed occurred in rewriting *Workers in the Dawn*. In as far as the social conditions of urban England were, in his novels, irremediable, it was logical for a writer who could not turn away from those conditions to take as his proper subject the psychology of social alienation. *The Unclassed* is a strong move in that direction.

Another way of putting this would be to say that Gissing persistently regarded himself as an artist, because art was in opposition to life, because being an artist meant not being committed to ideas, programmes, policies, because indeed the detachment was absolutely essential to the artistic act itself. So he writes to his brother: 'how I laughed the other day on recalling your amazement at my theories of Art for Art's sake! Well, I cannot get beyond it. Human life has little interest to me, on the whole – save as material for artistic presentation.'[23] What needs to be understood, as far as the art of fiction is concerned, is that an art-for-art's sake approach immediately presents the novelist with a whole set of new problems concerning structure and motivation. All very well to say that human life is 'material for artistic presentation', if that means, as it did for Gissing, that human life will not be seen in the light of moral, political or social prejudice, but that still leaves unresolved the problem of how the thing will be done. Although it is true that Gissing during this apprenticeship period tended to make remarks that threw Art and Life into opposition, and indeed incorporated the same opposition into his novels, as he does in *The Unclassed*, the art-for-art's sake component of such statements needs analysis, because even a writer who regards people as phenomena to be studied must in the end have characters who act, think, speak, relate to each other and so on, characters who cannot be regarded only in static terms, whose actions and motives, indeed, need explanation at least within the context of their own self-awareness. Take, for example, one of Gissing's well-known statements from this period:

> I am by degrees getting my right place in the world. Philosophy has done all it can for me, and now scarcely interests me anymore. My attitude henceforth is that of the artist pure and simple. The world is for me a collection of phenomena, which are to be studied and reproduced artistically. In the midst of the most serious complications of life, I find myself suddenly possessed of a great calm, withdrawn as it were from the immediate interests of the moment, and able to regard everything as a picture. I watch and observe myself just as much as others. The impulse to regard every juncture as a *situation* becomes stronger and stronger. In the midst of desperate misfortune I can pause to make a note for future use, and the afflictions of others are to me materials for observation.[24]

Period-piece, Pateresque statements of this kind mean that Gissing did not have a thesis, a programme, a set of ideas to propound, or anything like that; rather that the particular type of art he would attempt would be that which belonged characteristically to the end of the nineteenth century in Europe, the art of distance, detachment, alienation. If this is the case, analysis brings us once again to the central questions: regarded distantly, do people's lives have a shape that credibly can provide a novel with its structure? Regarded from a detached, clinical, neutral, sociological point of view, have people's desires, thoughts, actions have more significance than as a function of their social circumstances, and, if the answer is even a partial affirmative, can a positive type of motivation be attributed to them, or can they be seen only in terms of alienation – alienation from themselves, from each other, from the world in which they live? These questions remain crucial for Gissing the artist, but it is time now to look more closely at his second published novel, *The Unclassed*.

The novel concerns a small group of people who knew each other at school and chanced to meet again when they were older. Ida Starr attacks Harriet Smales at school for calling her mother a prostitute, so providing Harriet with a motive for revenge later in life. Waymark, at first a teacher, meets Maud Enderby at a different school and a nervously 'emancipated' friendship continues after they have both left. Without much fuss, Gissing established the necessary nucleus of characters.

Only the minimum of contrivance was needed to bring the group together. Waymark, an aspiring novelist, advertises in the newspaper for a potential friend with like interests and by this means meets Julian Casti, an aspiring poet, who had grown up in the same family with Harriet Smales. Harriet later tricks Julian into marrying her. Waymark, meanwhile, abandons his school-teaching job, goes to his dead father's friend for help, and becomes a rent collector in the slums in the hope that he will be able to write his novel in his spare time. At about the same time, Waymark meets Ida Starr, or rather is befriended by her after an episode outside a theatre when he gave money to a prostitute. The connection between all the major characters in the book is that they are people whom Waymark knows: an art mistress whom he met in his first job (Maud Enderby), a chemist's assistant (Julian Casti), Harriet (Julian's wife), Ida Starr, a pure-hearted prostitute who, ostensibly for neither sexual or mercenary reasons, picked him up outside a theatre, and Woodstock, property owner and old friend of his father. The simple linear treatment that Gissing utilized in *Workers in the Dawn* is thus avoided. These characters meet naturally, are made to meet naturally, and constitute, such appears to be Gissing's aim, an urban group whose relationships with each other are not predetermined by wealth, occupation or class. This type of urban group was to be Gissing's 'subject' for at least a decade. *The Unclassed* is his first thought-out attempt at a treatment of it.

He could not manage entirely without contrivance. After all, he was attempting to do without many normal types of social motivation: the desire for position, marriage, wealth and so forth. So he permits himself two crucial coincidences. The first is that Julian Casti, whom Waymark met by chance through an advertisement, should have grown up with Harriet, who was at school with Ida Starr, whom Waymark also met completely by chance. Had Waymark known that Ida Starr had known Harriet, he presumably would not have brought them together when Julian Casti's marriage began to deteriorate. The second crucial contrivance was that the Woodstock for whom Waymark worked as rent collector was Ida Starr's grandfather. On this coincidence not too much is made to depend, since in the final analysis the same ends could have been achieved by different means. Nonetheless, the element of coincidence in *The Unclassed* is a measure of Gissing's difficulties with plot, for too much contrivance of this kind is not compatible with reproducing artistically a world that is regarded as 'a collection of phenomena'.

The Unclassed was made to depend upon the opposition of two sets of values: the supposedly established or official values of Victorian society and humanistic values of contemporary agnosticism. Waymark's friendship with and engagement to Maud Enderby represents the one, his relationship with Ida Starr represents the other. This opposition is sustained throughout the book and is often treated explicitly. In Chapter xxi, for example, when Waymark discovers that for his sake Ida has stopped being a prostitute and has returned to an earlier job in a laundry, he tries to work out for himself, as honestly as possible, his present feelings for the two women whom he has come to know well. Waymark's friendship with Ida, a non-sexual friendship, had grown into an easy intimacy in which personal honesty and the avoidance of humbug were crucial. Forced by circumstance to acknowledge this friendship seriously, he thinks about it in the following terms:

> Could he believe her capable of yet nobler ideas; could he think that only in reverence of the sanctity of love, and without regard to other things, she had acted in this way; then, regarding her as indeed his equal, he would open his heart to her and speak somewhat in this way. 'Yes, I do love you; but at the same time I know too well the uncertainty of love to go through the pretence of binding myself to you forever. Will you accept my love in its present sincerity, neither hoping nor fearing, knowing that whatever

happens is beyond our own control, feeling with me that only an ignoble nature can descend to the affectation of union when the real links are broken?' Could Waymark but have felt sure of her answer to such an appeal, it would have gone far to make his love for Ida all-engrossing. She would then be his ideal woman, and his devotion to her would have no bounds.

Waymark did not dare to suggest living with Ida outside marriage because he could see that she had made a deliberate attempt to change. 'On the other hand, to offer to make her his legal wife would be to do her a yet greater injustice, even if he had been willing to so sacrifice himself. The necessity for legal marriage would be a confession of her inferiority, and the sense of being thus bound would, he well knew, be the surest means of weakening his affection.'[25] Naïve or not, sentiments such as these had rarely been expressed openly in Victorian England. Something of the strength and weakness of Gissing's early work is here in a nutshell. The weakness is that he retains the Victorian cliché even when describing something supposedly un-Victorian. An equal relationship between man and woman outside marriage is a 'noble idea'. A reason for living with a man, without wishing to be married, is the 'sanctity of love'. A willingness to let the relationship continue without formality would make her an 'ideal woman'. These are Waymark's clichés, of course, not Gissing's, for Gissing still has his tongue in his cheek; even so it is evident that the emancipated character has yet to free himself from the language of the world he rejects.

On the other hand, there is also evident strength; passages such as this one must have startled many of Gissing's readers by their frankness and lack of evasion. Waymark is considering marriage to a former prostitute. He thinks marriage might be an injustice to her. To marry her would be a sacrifice, whereas living with her outside marriage would preserve his integrity and the integrity of the relationship. In any case, 'whatever happens is beyond our own control'. No wonder Bentley rejected the book.[26] To an established publisher like Bentley even the language was suspect. It may not have been inappropriate for Waymark, *in propria persona*, to talk like this, but Gissing's ascription of the ideas of 'nobility' and 'sanctity' to a character whose thoughts, to a conventional reader, must have seemed utterly depraved would necessarily have seemed perverse, as indeed from the point of view of a straight-laced reader it was. To a large extent Gissing had transferred from the narrator (who voiced opinions that sounded like Gissing's) to a set of characters (whose encounters implied similar anti-bourgeois ideas), the responsibility for the action of the novel whose internal ironies were now, amongst other things, structural. The irony is in this case expressed by a resolution of the plot which is not in any real sense a resolution of the predicament in which the characters found themselves.

Waymark's feelings about Maud Enderby follow those about Ida Starr immediately.

> In the case of his feeling towards Maud Enderby there was no such doubt. Never was his blood so calm as in her presence. She was to him a spirit, and in the spirit he loved her. With Maud he might look forward to union at some distant day, a union outwardly of the conventional kind. It would be so, not on account of any inferiority to his ideal in Maud, for he felt that there was no height of his own thought whither she would not in time follow him; but simply because no point of principle would demand a refusal of the yoke of respectability, with its attendant social advantages. And the thought of thus binding himself to Maud had nothing repulsive, for the links between them were not of the kind which easily yield, and loyalty to a higher and nobler nature may well be deemed a duty.[27]

Here again there are strengths and weaknesses. Maud is the Helen Norman of *The Unclassed*. Gissing loads the dice heavily against the 'higher and nobler nature', since while Waymark is engaged to Maud and before he has acknowledged to himself his feelings about Ida, an entirely new part of the action, concerning another generation of Enderbys, has been developed. In a set of Ibsen-like revelations, Maud discovers that her parents are still alive, that her father until he embezzled money from a disaster fund had been a clergyman, and that her mother was a flighty social creature currently have an affair with one of their friends. Because of Maud's religious upbringing in the care of her aunt, her deeply ingrained conviction that all pleasure is sinful, and her fear of admitting to herself that her affection for Waymark is in part sexual, she identifies her own feelings with her mother's promiscuity and feels blighted by what Gissing here, as elsewhere, calls a 'contagion of the spirit', that is, the inability to control the physical and emotional forces that threaten the character's resignation to circumstance. Gissing's satire on religious, middle-class respectability is now contained in the deliberate melodrama of the Enderby episode. Appearances are not to be trusted. The prostitute is in fact a good woman and the life of the respectable middle-class girl is built upon a lie.

The weakness (or what at first seems a weakness) of the strategy Gissing adopted is that, while allowing himself the almost doctrinal contrast between Maud and Ida, and then more particularly in attributing Maud's lapse into religiosity to the sense of sin that overwhelms because of its hereditary implications, the author failed to relate the Enderby episodes to the main story in any integral way. Though it seems, for example in the chapter referred to above, that Waymark is making a choice, in fact Maud leaves London without telling him why and eventually releases herself from her engagement without revealing the actual reason. Had Waymark known the reason, Maud would have been a more genuine, less 'ideal' person for him. But he did not know. In other words, Gissing stopped short when he might have created a genuinely psychological situation, the dramatic implications of which derived from the characters' full knowledge of circumstance. One makes this kind of remark with diffidence, though, because it means that Gissing stopped short of writing a different type of novel – one depending for its movement on the characters' full knowledge of their circumstances. Gissing's habit of letting narrator and reader know more than his characters is a function of his deterministic world view: *of course* things happen to people which circumstance does not permit them to understand, says the determinist. So it is quite proper to have a type of fiction in which this insight is expressed.

At the same time, we see here – in another sense – a typical Gissing strategy. The book in part is about the sense of sin. Sin, for Waymark, in the passage noted by Gladstone when he first read the book, 'has been a word without significance for me'. Sin for Ida Starr, the sometime prostitute, is a moral repugnance from which she can free herself by her own decision, represented in the novel by her night swim: this is the humanist solution, as it were. Sin for Maud is the sin of the parent, an overwhelming hereditary burden, expressed in *The Unclassed* in the contemporary idiom of instant heredity.[28] Gissing lets the characters explore these ideas for themselves, most notably in that explicitly Schopenhauerian chapter entitled 'The Will to Live',[29] where Waymark presents himself to Maud as a sincere agnostic committed to the 'doctrine of philosophical necessity' ('Let us live whilst it is called today') and Maud, in listening to him, experiences the bittersweet of a 'tumult of emotion' in which 'the completeness and persistency of love' was felt to be the 'testimony of her soul's loss'.[30] It is exactly at this juncture, incidentally, that Gissing has Waymark, in an apparently unpremeditated action, propose to Maud: 'the gathering emotion of the hour had united with opportunity to decide his future', says the laconic narrator of a character who felt 'relief' to have committed himself but 'discontent' to have become an accomplice in 'the respectable make-believe that takes the form of domestic sentiment'. Consistent with Gissing's nihilism is a crucial episode seen by the character as 'no result of deliberate decision'.

Consistent, equally, is his ending the chapter with the characters apart, each thinking his own thoughts, already diverging. Psychological insight is expressed therefore by means of confusion and half-truth, not by full awareness, and the strength of this novel derives from Gissing's play or irony, that is from a structure appropriate to the world in which the characters are made to live.

To go back over the ground, two aspects of the novel seem to characterize the strategy Gissing adopted in *The Unclassed*. As far as the first is concerned, Gissing did succeed in creating, as he told Algernon when he finished the book, 'not a social essay, but a study of a certain group of human beings'.[31] A feature of this study was that, as the characters think out the meaning of their existence (which is the context in which sin is regarded), the point, for the reader, now rests much more in juxtaposition, contrast, irony, even satire than in the mere words of the narrator, as was the case in the unrevised *Workers in the Dawn*. This will characterize Gissing's dramatic method through many books. The second aspect is the relative insignificance of the plot, something which was inevitable for a writer who did not observe plots in contemporary life and who felt sure that meaningful sequences of events were unlikely. To appreciate Gissing it has to be accepted that an integration of plot and character would not have served his purposes, because what he wrote about were the disintegrations, breakdowns, fractures of contemporary life where his kind of character, the Waymarks and Ida Starrs, have an existence that is fortuitously meaningful to them in their private world. Gissing always denies his characters the full power of self-determination: he sets himself the task of managing without romantic heroes. Sometimes he allows his characters a limited awareness of their lives, as here, in *The Unclassed* and in the 'naturalist' novels which follow: *Thyrza, Demos* and *The Nether World*. Sometimes he allows his characters a greater awareness of the intermesh of their own lives, as in *Born in Exile*. The emphasis of the first type of novel tends to be deterministic in a social sense: the emphasis of the second determinist in a psychological sense. In either case, it is Gissing who is doing the allowing or, rather, it is Gissing who in not allowing complete resolutions insists upon his decadent, *fin-de-siècle* world view. For it is a form of decadence, this, to build fictions that depend upon partial awareness, frustrations, necessary denials and cancellations, just as it is decadent so to structure a novel that the characters are seen to have no chance of solving the problems they confront. But what is seen may be, as it is in *The Unclassed*, an extremely powerful portrait of what it felt like to be alive but rootless in the contemporary Britain of the 1880s. In

Bentley's opinion, Gissing was too successful:

> I send you a copy of the report which has been sent to me. You will see what the reader says about the heroine who is a prostitute being represented as good & noble and pure.
>
> Though we know in this unfortunate class that there are many with kindly instincts yet the nature of the life tends to deaden & in time destroy the good originally present. It does not appear to me wholesome, to hold up the idea that a life of vice can be lived without loss of purity and womanly nature. I confess that I am of the opinion that the realistic treatment of such a subject works for evil as well as good, & possible more for the former.[32]

In retrospect, Bentley's reader seems wide of the mark on so many counts. When one thinks about the compact, economical, revised version of the novel, one feels not that Gissing created a heavy atmosphere by dwelling on an evil side of London life, but that he softened his 'realistic treatment' by the development of the action. What in 1884 seemed harsh, ninety or so years later seems sentimental. While it is true that the novel concerns a wife who tricks her husband into marrying her without love (Harriet), a property owner (Woodstock), whose failure to forgive his daughter led partly to the suffering of his granddaughter, and a young girl (Ida), who lapsed into prostitution as an alternative to respectable slavery as a domestic servant, these main actions and the often melodramatic incidents associated with them are balanced by what, for Gissing, was remarkably serene writing.

At the heart of the novel are two strong friendships, between Waymark and Julian Casti and Waymark and Ida Starr. There is nothing 'depressing' about either. With Casti, Waymark has those long, half-reflective, half-intellectual discussions about art and life that so characterize Gissing's men in all his books. They are real friends, meeting on a footing of equality, without reference to position or wealth. They help each other as they can. With Ida Starr, Waymark is also on a footing of emotional equality. In defiance of convention, he visits her rooms to smoke, chat, talk books while she relaxes in her dressing gown, simply refusing to accept the values by which other people would judge such encounters. Quite apart from the fundamental serenity of these two friendships, the novel is full of episodes that are far from pessimistic in their impact: Ida's garden party for children, a sunny romance between Sally Fisher and Mr O'Gree in which caricature is fortunately resisted, and the Sunday expedition to Richmond with its uncomplicated pleasures of food and talk and music. 'As regards the *tone* of the book, I myself, after reading anything', said Gissing to his brother, 'always say: "Now does this convey the impression that the author is human in his emotions, or the opposite?" and I am very conscious that the tone of the present work is intensely human, strong with genial emotion'.[33]

Although Bentley, in his letter of refusal, said tersely that 'it is not for want of talent that I feel obliged to decline your work, but the nature of the story itself'[34] and although many thinking readers were probably unwilling to go further in praise of the book than Gladstone when he classified it as a 'novel of the didactic and speculative class',[35] at least one contemporary reviewer managed to identify features that made *The Unclassed* extremely interesting at the time and were to remain as components of the Gissing novel for at least a decade. A long unsigned review appeared in the *Evening News* for 25 June 1884.[36] 'Mr Gissing', said the reviewer, 'original in this as in other respects, shuns sentimentality and courts the serious consideration of the difficult moral problems his subject supplies, and we are bound to say that this confidence in his own power to deal successfully with exceedingly delicate materials is justified by the result now before us'. This reviewer realized that *The Unclassed* was remarkable for being 'absolutely free from either pruriency or prudery'; that the study of character was never 'superficial' but at times was 'really penetrating'; that the study of Waymark's feeling for Ida Starr and for Maud Enderby 'simultaneously' would 'interest the psychologist as well as the ordinary reader'; and that there was a 'terrible realism' in Gissing's treatment of the slums or what the reviewer calls 'the life that festers and decays morally and physically in the rookeries which, in large numbers, are still the disgrace of London'. The review was not completely favourable (Gissing's treatment of Christianity was a 'travesty') but at least the author's concerns were identified fairly. What the reviewer failed to understand, however, was that given these concerns Gissing had been obliged to write a different type of novel. Thus the final sentence of the review, to the effect that with 'a more complete power of seeing' Gissing 'might have made a permanent and valuable work of art out of the materials that have been employed in *The Unclassed*', does not exactly fit the mark, since what Gissing needed was the greater skill – particularly skill in ironic counterpoint – that was later to characterize novels like *The Odd Women* and *The Whirlpool*.

For the sake of later discussion, it is important to notice that, despite the successful balance of the social and the psychological in *The Unclassed* and despite the brutal picture of what exploiting the need for shelter means, Gissing in order to concentrate on Waymark's circle of friends moved the locale away from the slums. By doing this, he avoided one of the problems posed in *Workers in the Dawn*, the problem of the relationship of people to place, reduced the novel's scope to achieve a greater immediacy of action, and postponed his encounter with the demands of naturalism where place would have to be seen, not as a background, but as an integral part of life. Gissing had not abandoned the idea of writing a novel which would be *both* a psychological portrait of a group of unclassed people and an uncompromising, detailed treatment of urban life, for the three novels discussed in chapter 4 are all attempts to achieve the synthesis. After writing *The Unclassed*, however, he wrote fairly quickly two weaker novels that add little to his reputation and constitute a hesitation, though a brief one, in his career. Perhaps this hesitation was the result of public comment on *The Unclassed*; whether it was or not, Gissing only recovered his stride when he wrote *Demos*, two years later.

It was suggested at the beginning of this chapter that Gissing wrote *The Unclassed* in an innocent frame of mind, not doubting that Bentley would publish 'Mrs Grundy's Enemies' and not anticipating public reaction to his story about a prostitute. All that changed in 1884, when he learned that he would have to revise 'Mrs Grundy's Enemies' himself if he wanted it published and that he was having to defend *The Unclassed* even to his friends, including close friends like Frederic Harrison, who called the character of Waymark 'mere moral dynamite'.[37] People who had not read and perhaps had never heard of *Workers in the Dawn* until they saw the title on the titlepage of *The Unclassed*, now realized that the quiet, bookish, well-mannered, correctly dressed tutor was in addition a complex, even dangerous person: an intelligent man who put himself to trouble to disturb their peace. For who else, within the atmosphere of troubled talk about Darwin, would have devised a story in which the middle-class daughter collapses as a human being because she thinks she has inherited her mother's immoral tendencies, while the working-class daughter grows as a human being because she learns she can free herself from the hereditary influence of a mother who was a prostitute? The balanced irony of the book could scarcely be missed by anyone who read it, for Gissing had in fact transposed into fiction, successfully, what he had called 'his passionate tendency of revolt'. *The Unclassed*, for 1884, was in a sense too successful, too powerful a book and for the moment he turned away from it. We shall see that this turning away was to be only a temporary deviation. He later returned to the technique of ironic counterpoint, as in *The Odd Women*. He retained a burning interest in the social phenomenon of hypocrisy, as *Born in Exile* demonstrates. And, despite protestations to the contrary, he continued to have at least some interest in *The Unclassed*, for he was prepared to revise the novel ten years later.

Chapman & Hall, when the firm published *The Unclassed*, became Gissing's first real publisher. Naturally affected by the criticism of the book, he attempted to write one they would find acceptable. In this way it came about that he wrote in quick succession the two novels, *Isabel Clarendon* and *A Life's Morning*, which have so little to do with the main line of his development as a novelist. The fact that *Demos* was first mentioned in June 1884,[38] the month in which *The Unclassed* was published, and that serious work on it began in August 1885, or perhaps even earlier, is sufficient evidence that Gissing had little energy to spare for the other two novels. *Demos* is the natural successor to *Workers in the Dawn* and *The Unclassed*, and *Isabel Clarendon* and *A Life's Morning* are intervening potboilers.

The first version of *Isabel Clarendon* was written during the winter of 1884–5, as the frequent references to it in the letters show. 'The task of getting into the fictitious world one has created always costs agony',[39] he told his brother on 18 September 1884, in a remark which presumably indicated that he was just settling down to real work on the book. He worked on through the winter until late in March. Having moved to his new flat near Baker Street, and having 'toiled incessantly', he reported that his new book (which was still called 'The Lady of Knightswell') was at last finished. But George Meredith, acting in his capacity as Chapman & Hall's reader and literary adviser, decided that it would have to be rewritten and its length reduced. This did not mean, as Korg said, that *'Isabel Clarendon* was written expressly for Meredith': it means that Meredith insisted on the revision and then still advised Chapman that the book was not worth much. Actually Meredith's real influence was somewhat different. It was shortly after this that Meredith told Gissing to return to his London subjects, so that in point of fact *Demos*, not *Isabel Clarendon*, resulted – only in part, of course – from Meredith's advice. At all events, Gissing spent the greater part of June and July 1885 rewriting the book in two volumes, renamed it *Isabel Clarendon*, and in a letter to his brother written on 9 August announced that he had finished.

> Tonight I finish *Isabel Clarendon*. I have done my best to make the story as realistic as possible. The ending is as unromantic as could be, and several threads are left to hang loose; for even so it is in real life; you cannot gather up and round off each person's story. But this time I believe the work to be good. Yesterday I wrote for nine hours, and at last in that peculiar state of

excitement in which we cannot see the paper and pen, but only the words. I kept choking and had my eyes painfully moist. I don't think the result of this can be worthless.[40]

Even at that point, however, it is possible that his labours had not ended. Retrospectively he entered in his diary the dates of July–September 1885 for the writing of *Isabel Clarendon*, so it could be that the slight disturbance in the MS., a fair copy of this second version of the book, represents further work done either before or after he had resubmitted it to Chapman & Hall.

Isabel Clarendon is the story of a moody, 'unclassed', bookish and poor young man who, before finally settling down as the manager of a book shop in Norwich, suffers the agony of a vast infatuation for the fairly wealthy, middle-class widow whose name became the title of the book. When Pierre Coustillas discussed this story in the Introduction to the Harvester Press photographic reprint of the novel,[41] he argued that it had 'a richness of which no stock has yet been taken, for its scarcity has inevitably stemmed the curiosity of critics and, if fresh peeps at *New Grub Street* or *The Private Papers of Henry Ryecroft* have been taken in recent years, *Isabel Clarendon* still awaits a systematic and coherent examination'. Coustillas' interesting introduction remains the principal favourable notice of the novel, an introduction to which readers interested in Gissing must remain indebted.

Yet it is difficult to accept the high claims he makes for a book which is loosely written and episodic, and which entirely lacks those characteristics which give Gissing's other novels their power. Not only are the characters presented without real motivation, but the book as a whole lacks momentum, because the plot has little energy or forward movement. Bernard Kingcote happens to meet Isabel Clarendon and Ada, the illegitimate daughter of Mr Clarendon. They, the two women, are trapped by Mr Clarendon's will by which his money was to go to Ada, when she came of age, not to Mrs Clarendon. Kingcote does not know about this. Nor does Ada know about the romantic attachment or pseudo-engagement of Kingcote and Mrs Clarendon. And Kingcote, on his side, knows next to nothing about Ada's own pseudo-engagement. Gissing's tendency in his early books to create situations in which characters are allowed very little knowledge of each other's real motives has already been noted. Here the tendency is carried to a ridiculous extreme. Though some of the other characters in the novel are not uninteresting, their relations with each other, in the terms of the novel, are so arbitrary and trivial that melodrama, unalleviated by humour or irony, is the result. A psychological novel in which the characters never really get to know each other is a travesty indeed.

Nor is it only the lack of momentum, the melodrama, and the arbitrariness that mar *Isabel Clarendon*. In style, the novel is frequently meretricious and shallow. 'He held the door open, and she swept gently past; Robert smiled, so pleasantly did her grace of movement affect him. There are women who enter a room like the first notes of a sonata, and leave it like the sweet close of a nocturne; Isabel was one of them'.[42] Lapses of this kind are all too frequent. In invention, there are equally disastrous lapses as when Kingcote, having travelled from London to see Isabel, observes her with Robert Asquith while concealed in the shrubbery and takes this as cause for the break between them, even though he did not hear, or may not have heard, what was said. Gissing gives the characters no chance to recover: Isabel and Kingcote are never reconciled. In characterization, Gissing's snobbery is rather too frequently exposed, as when, out of the blue, Gabriel, Kingcote's friend, tries to persuade him to accept the Norwich book shop: 'Please to remember', Gabriel remarked, 'that I am an artist, and that you have certain pretensions to culture. I did not imagine we ever talked on any other basis'.[43] This is the device by which Gissing glosses over the quite arbitrary disposal of his main character, if device it can be called.

Finally, Gissing resorts to evasions, which (for reasons which have already been given), he may have felt necessary but which, nonetheless, leave one with the feeling that he chose on this occasion to pander to the worst side of public taste. Thus the situation in which Kingcote is drawn to Isabel while the reader can see perfectly well that his real ally or soulmate ought to be Ada, the plain but intellectually interesting girl, is actually the same as Arthur Golding knowing both Helen Norman and Carrie Mitchell in *Workers in the Dawn*, and Waymark knowing both Maud Enderby and Ida Starr in *The Unclassed*. Gissing during this first decade had a penchant for triangular situations consisting of one man and two women, the one intellectual, the other sensual. Here the sensually attractive woman is Isabel Clarendon but, presumably because of the middle-class setting and the novel's 'polite' tone, Gissing so suppressed the issue that it is difficult to know what he really meant. For example, when Isabel asked Kingcote to visit her Norwich hotel, he instantly realized her power over him:

> Nay, she had worse power than that. From the long-sealed chambers of his heart came a low cry as of a reawakening life, life which would fain be free again. The sweat stood on his forehead as he crushed down the tenderness,

the passion which he had thought dead. The sight of her handwriting, after so long, had given back to him the dreadful power of seeing herself, her features, her beautiful form. He flung himself by the bedside, and smothered his face; the striving of the old spirit drew groans from him.[44]

Compared to *The Unclassed*, this is insipid stuff. The sexual desire is repressed by romantic, melodramatic euphemisms: 'worse power' (why worse?) 'dreadful power', the cries and groans. Perhaps Gissing could not do without the euphemism. He was obliged to utilize the idiom that was available to him. But all in all he shows that, at least in this novel, with its polite atmosphere and bourgeois setting, he is incapable of developing his own theme, except by reference to Kingcote's fits of jealousy, so that the reader must remain indifferent to the question of whether or not Kingcote's friendship with Isabel Clarendon is likely to prosper. The question of sexual relationships, which in *The Unclassed* Gissing approached without inhibition, is here evaded. Nothing matters in a novel in which so little is at stake.

A Life's Morning is even more of a pot-boiler than *Isabel Clarendon*, so much so that Jacob Korg's plot summary almost does it justice. According to the *Letters*, Gissing started to write *A Life's Morning* in August 1885,[45] though in his diary he later noted that it had been written between September and November of that year. Despite the fact that Smith, Elder liked it, there were snags to be overcome including, according to Morley Roberts,[46] the request that Gissing should rewrite the ending. Eventually, after a delay which saw the publication of a number of other novels, Smith, Elder allowed it in effect to be 'carried' on the relative success of *Demos* and *Thyrza*. It was published in serial form in the *Cornhill* in twelve, monthly instalments during 1888 and in book form on 15 November 1888. By that time Gissing himself had virtually forgotten it. Probably as soon as it was written and certainly by the time it was published, Gissing recognized it as one of his weaker works. He never revised it and the first edition therefore provides the only text.

Since a main part of the purpose of this book is to demonstrate the development of Gissing's skill as a novelist, a purely negative critical discussion of *A Life's Morning* – for such it would have to be – would do little good, since the novel, one of his weakest, is so clearly a deviation from his true course. Both the plot, depending simply and improbably on moral blackmail, and the characterization, which is weak even in the case of Emily Hood, whose motives are obscure and whose fate is insignificant, are of the kind that might have been invented by Jasper Milvain's sisters in *New Grub Street* and then rejected even by them.

Emily's realization that the ideas of art and beauty she treasured in her innocence had little to do with the realities of existence is rendered shallow by the device which requires her to reject the person she loves because of her father's crime.[47] Gissing failed to make anything of this situation, for the kind of novel *A Life's Morning* might have been was still outside his range. Nor was he in this instance attempting to extend his range. It was not set in London; it was not a treatment of urban or slum life; it was not in any profound sense about the displaced intellectuals who people most of Gissing's early work; and it was not, except in an extreme sense, a novel which expressed social concern. *A Life's Morning* was outside Gissing's limits at the time it was written. It could be seen, perhaps, as a precursor, a pallid precursor, of the type of novel that Gissing was to write in the mid-1890s, but even in that different context it would scarcely deserve extended discussion.

Whereas *Workers in the Dawn* was a private, secret book, unknown by many people in 1880 and later rejected, so it would seem, by Gissing himself, (he did not list it in his *Who's Who* entry, for example) the four novels that have been discussed briefly in this chapter represent Gissing's first real encounter with the Victorian public and the Victorian publisher. The three published novels had been written in the calendar years 1883–5. If one labels these the years of apprenticeship it is chiefly because Gissing tested, during this period, both himself and his public, or the public, to discover what was possible for him. He discovered that he could not write the 'polite' three-decker of the kind that, because unobjectionable, would be automatically serialized in a magazine, and that he had been right when he had told Frederic Harrison that his feeling for 'artistic excellence' meant accepting as a fact his 'passionate tendency of revolt'. He learnt, however, not to give this tendency free rein. In other words, the writing of these four novels made him apply his mind to the problem of how to be true to his own conception of the novel and yet get his work published. The result was the series of books discussed in the next three chapters.

In chapter 2 the extensive revision of *Workers in the Dawn* was taken to be a token of Gissing's serious artistic purposes. When the opportunity presented itself, he revised the novel in the light of his greater experience. Although Gissing at some stage began the revision of *Isabel Clarendon*, probably for the proposed collected edition of Lawrence & Bullen that never materialized, he never really had a chance to republish it. The same applies to *A Life's Morning*, though perhaps for different reasons.[48] *The Unclassed* is different because it held its own during Gissing's lifetime, despite the author's confused feelings about a novel which reminded him of his early days. In 1886, when he sent a copy to Hardy, he said he himself would not dare to read it again: 'it is too saturated with by-gone miseries of every kind. Fortunately you will read it without unworthy prejudice. I suppose it is inferior in most ways to my later book *Demos* – immature, in fact'.[49] These sentiments he expressed again three years later in a letter to Eduard Bertz: 'Heavens! how it must have brought back old days, to re-read *Workers* and *The Unclassed*! Not for any consideration would I open those dreadful books! All I have ever written seems to be apprentice work; I fear to examine it'.[50] But despite the disagreeable associations with his early years in London, he did examine *The Unclassed*. As was mentioned earlier, he revised it for Lawrence & Bullen in 1894, remarking to Bertz that he still found it odd that people should be reading the book.

Odd or not, the book was seen to be an important milestone in the development of the novel, apprentice work certainly, but nonetheless important, as Gissing himself had implied in his letter to Hardy when he said that 'reticencies and superficialities have so often to fill places where one is willing to put in honest work'.[51] In the revision of 1895, when he reduced the novel to two-thirds of its former length,[52] he made it 'less crude and absurd'[53] in form and at the same time, in a new preface, urged the modern reader to read it as narrative pure and simple without bothering about the romanticism which Gissing thought still marred the book.[54] It is worth noting, in passing, that both Hardy and Meredith were affected by the novel, Hardy by the first and Meredith by the second edition. In his dry way Hardy referred to it as an 'interesting present':[55] interesting indeed, for the connection between *The Unclassed* and *Tess of the D'Urbervilles*, two tales of pure women, is quite obvious. Meredith was sent a copy of the second edition, perhaps just in time for the parallels between *The Unclassed* and *Lord Ormont and His Aminta* to be of interest: at least in one instance, the women swimming in the sea to purify themselves of their past, the similarity seems too close to be accidental.[56] Of course there is no need to search out a correlation between what Gissing thought about the novel and what contemporary novelists thought about it. For them it was a significant step towards the type of fiction they wanted to write: a fiction that would be less evasive, less dominated by non-literary considerations. For him it was a significant step in the development of his craft, a stage in his learning what type of social realism he might, with greatest authenticity, write. In these, as in other respects, *The Unclassed* remains one of the most important of his early works.

The remarkable thing about Gissing as he worked through this apprenticeship period was his incredible determination. No man could write books as different as *The Unclassed* and *Isabel Clarendon* without thinking a great deal about the factors that made them different. With these thoughts about the art of fiction in mind, he wrote *Demos*: during the next few years he would explore the possibilities of a social realism in which the individual was invariably subservient to his environment.

4
Experiments in Naturalism

THE strong surge of energy that had allowed Gissing to write *Workers in the Dawn*, 'Mrs Grundy's Enemies', *The Unclassed*, *Isabel Clarendon* and *A Life's Morning* continued unabated through the decade. In 1885, Gissing was still young. He still supported himself partly by tutoring. He still read widely and worked hard. He still lived in London, by himself for most of the time, though there were family visits and one of his pupils for a while lived with him in his little flat near Baker Street. It will be seen that towards the end of the 1880s he began to travel abroad and that, roughly at the same time, his feeling for his characters' environment also altered. When he wrote *Demos* (1886), *Thyrza* (1887) and *The Nether World* (1889), he was preoccupied with their physical environment; once he had published *The Nether World* he veered away from the strictly conceived, determinist correlation of character and physical environment that makes the word 'naturalism' such a tempting label for it. Gissing was always in some measure a determinist and always interested both in the forces that affected or determined his characters' lives from outside and in the negotiated freedom from those forces that characters might in small measure find for themselves.

In *Demos*, *Thyrza* and *The Nether World* the forces that determined the characters' lives were physical and economic. Gissing had come to be fascinated intellectually and imaginatively with place, habitat, environment. Though his interest in programmes of social reform had already begun to weaken,[1] he nonetheless remained absorbed by what was a new subject, the little-known, little-studied areas of London such as Lambeth and Clerkenwell which as places for people to live were for all practical purposes out of control – out of control in the sense that large numbers of people lived in relatively small areas of the city without benefit of social services or amenities. Gissing had looked at the physical environment of these people, had studied it closely as an acutely interested, but detached outsider. He had likewise listened to people speak (without necessarily talking with them) and so became more skilful at reproducing their characteristic speech in his novels. It has already been mentioned, but can reasonably be stressed once more, that Gissing's outsider's view of these urban areas was essentially visual: his considerable knowledge came not from sharing the lives of urban working people but from his looking at them as part of social phenomena which many, probably most of his contemporaries preferred to ignore, whilst by the same token he was obeying the instinct of the social realist when he created for his characters environments that were in their myriad detail faithful to this knowledge.

The exterior physical world as opposed to the interior moral world was his new subject. The detailed description of the physical environment, in this period of his writing life, was more than the drawing-in of the background to the characters' lives: it was integral to Gissing's whole conception of the novel, because his characters' behaviour had to a large extent become a function of place. Unreasonable to expect freedom of action, moral self-determination, marvellous transformations of character from people whose everyday lives were so moulded by physical and economic pressures that they could scarcely endure, let alone influence or control. A more sensible view of the matter was that, while a few people might escape these environmental pressures by moving away from them, most people had to resign themselves to circumstance. To the extent to which Gissing in these three novels asserted the powerful determinist notion that individual freedom was chimerical because all behaviour was in some sense determined by environment, so one feels justified in resorting to the specifically late nineteenth-century term 'naturalism'. Naturalism is the social realism of the determinist. In a fairly consistent way, Gissing so shapes these three stories that a conscious resignation to the circumstances of existence constitutes the full measure of a character's freedom. And in each novel, their overall view of things is reinforced by the fact that the characters' attempts to escape their environment are made to fail.

In the shaping of each story Gissing continues to depend upon the considerable difference between what the characters and what the narrators are allowed to know. Gissing goes to considerable trouble to create a credible physical environment for his characters, for the characters are by and large made to accept circumstances as they find them. Thus there are few conversations in these novels about change. Just as the characters do not talk about emigration, revolution, parliamentary reform, or social movements, so they never talk, either, about painting a room, repairing a window, making a dress or saving money for some future non-essential purchase. In other words, they are not at all imagined as people who might influence their own lives. On the contrary, they are imagined in Schopenhaurian terms, pessimistically. Characters are either resigned or not resigned to the circumstances of existence. The circumstances of existence are unalterable. If the character is not resigned to circumstances, he must inevitably suffer, as Clara Hewett suffers in *The Nether World*. If the character is resigned to circumstances, he may hope to endure with dignity what fate has outrageously ordained for him. In this vision of life, the rebel will be less emancipated than the ordinary person who has adapted himself to his environment, for Gissing now sees life in popular Darwinian terms where Schopenhaurian resignation and individual adaptability to physical circumstance are compatible with each other. This sense of what life is like becomes so strong that it to a large extent replaces normal motivation: characters are rarely motivated by greed, avarice or ambition, or indeed by any desire for a realizable material end, for desire is foolishness. Nor, at this stage in his career, did Gissing have any other ideas about what made people behave as they do: he needed Freud but had to manage without. (Freud's first generally accessible book was to be *Studies in Hysteria*, 1895, though for the man in the street he remained unknown until the twentieth century.) Thus his art, though it already raised questions of a psychological kind, kept for the moment its essentially visual quality, just as it continued to depend for its effects upon the narrator's identifying what the characters themselves could never understand.

The novelistic formulation which is being discussed here, a formulation which essentially rests upon an insight into character and environment which was peculiar to Gissing, at one and the same time gave these naturalistic novels their strength and involved the author in further difficulties. The strength had to do with public acceptability. Recall, for example, Mallard in *The Emancipated*, who (though in a later novel) might be taken as a prototype, as it were, for many characters in *Demos*, *Thyrza* and *The Nether World*. He tells Miriam Baske that a free person is 'not only freed from those bonds that numb the faculties of the mind and heart, but is able to control the native passions that would make a slave of her.'[2] For Gissing, resignation to circumstance did not involve promiscuity, sensuality, abandonment, emotional or sexual freedom; it meant the self-respect that goes with self-control. This residual puritanism gave his working-class novels an acceptable 'right-wing' flavour. Gissing was able to draw attention, as it were, to the realities of slum life and so to a degree engage the sympathy and interest of the contemporary reader, without creating dangerous or revolutionary characters whom the reader would find threatening. The 'further difficulties' created by Gissing's way of writing about contemporary London had to do with plot. How to contrive an interesting plot and characters invested with a plausible psychology, a set of motives and desires with which the reader could identify, if such a high premium was being placed upon passive acceptance of circumstance, and more generally on the dominance of environment over character? Problems of motivation become critical for Gissing and it will be seen that he eventually turns away from mere pessimism in order to probe more deeply into the psychological make-up of his characters. This will be discussed more fully in a later chapter. Meanwhile, we can make do with the rough rule of thumb that, for as long as Gissing's emphasis was upon the pressure of environment, he had to manage with makeshift, not always very convincing plots, simply because a plot – a plot of any kind – implies a meaningful relationship between events which naturalism in its very essence denies. It is not surprising, then, that *Demos*, *Thyrza*, and *The Nether World* are weak on plot at least in the conventional sense of the word.

Gissing realized that the constraints upon personal liberty were most crippling for women, so in each of these early novels there are women characters, or at least one woman character, who tries to free herself from 'those bonds' of upbringing, religion, parental influence, class distinction, poverty or wealth, and ignorance 'that numb the faculties of the mind and heart'. For this purpose Adela Waltham in *Demos* made a conscious effort to understand politics, in particular socialist politics; Thyrza Trent in *Thyrza* attempted to achieve independence by means of music; Clara Hewett in *The Nether World* ran away to become an actress. The chief instrument of feminine emancipation, however, was education. Helen Norman in *Workers in the Dawn*, Maud Enderby in *The Unclassed*, Miriam Baske in *The Emancipated*, Marian Yule in *New Grub Street*, and both Sidwell Warricombe and Marcella Moxey in *Born in Exile*, all attempted to achieve independence of personality by reading, that is by educating themselves. Ideas of personal freedom not associated with culture are almost entirely absent from Gissing's early work. This stress upon individuality achieved through education or self-education is quite distinct from the original constraints. Whatever the constraint, the end is always the same. Thus Adela Waltham needed to escape from her middle-class upbringing, while Thyrza needed to escape from her working-class upbringing. Miriam Baske needed to escape from wealth, Thyrza Trent from poverty. Living was seen either as frustration or as assertion. The self might be frustrated by circumstance: that was a defect not of social but of personal values. The self might overcome circumstance: that was a victory which permitted the values of the sensitive and serious agnostic to be expressed. Later in this chapter, Clara Hewett in *The Nether World* will provide the ultimate example of Gissing's powerful and uncompromising attitude to this need for escape.

Gissing saw his male characters in the same light. Korg complained that Gissing could not make up his mind about whether heredity or environment played a greater part in shaping his characters' lives.[3] How could one make up one's mind? And why should one? The Gissing men sought a destiny of self-fulfilment, in and despite a class-structured society, sometimes held back by themselves, by their own make-up, sometimes by circumstance, by factors (including other people) outside or beyond their control. Whatever happened to them, the reader was to regard them in a different light from those who never attempted to be free and those who did not understand that there was anything at stake. Thus Mutimer in *Demos* and Egremont in *Thyrza* both attempted to free themselves from class, the one from his working-class background, the other from the Oxford education that tied him to the establishment. The downright failures are not so very different. Reardon in *New Grub Street* aspired to the independence enjoyed by Mallard in *The Emancipated*: his failure was a failure against circumstance which, in his case, happened to be partly from his own character, partly an unfriendly and unaccommodating publishing world. In Gissing's naturalistic novels, Gilbert Grail in *Thyrza* provides the archetype of sensible resignation to circumstance based upon a thoughtful appreciation of the limits of possibility.

Demos, which was the first of the naturalistic novels, is seen in this chapter as an early experiment in the form, which Gissing to a greater extent mastered in *Thyrza* and *The Nether World*. It is an important novel because of Gissing's vivid portraits of working-class characters, like Mutimer's mother and Emma Vine, and of working-class occasions, such as the crowd scenes, and because Gissing, more than in *Workers in the Dawn*, allows his characters and situations to speak more (though not yet completely) for themselves. He is still learning his craft. As for the characters, they resemble similar characters in other novels. There is the intelligent, sensitive, at first idealistic working man, here called Richard Mutimer, a character clearly related, imaginatively to those thinking artisans in *Workers in the Dawn*; the educated, worldly-wise man, Hubert Eldon, with private means, a distant relation of characters like Harvey Rolfe; the honest, plain, unambitious and virtuous working girl, Emma Vine; the sensitive, thinking woman, Adela Waltham, like so many Gissing women emancipated in her thoughts but not her behaviour; the example of the established middle-class, Mrs Waltham; and the representatives of the unthinking mass of ordinary folk, including the members of Richard Mutimer's family. Must these characters be trapped by position, upbringing, heredity, class, is the question that Gissing in effect asked when he brought them together.

As though to answer this question, Gissing created a situation in which the class barrier was temporarily bridged by matrimony. Richard Mutimer, a self-educated demagogue, theoretically but sincerely committed to socialism, unexpectedly inherited a fortune and immediately spent it on the establishment of a socialist industrial community, with Robert Owen's 'New View of Society' as a model.[4] He is represented as having talked, thought, and read a great deal about how the lives of working people might be improved, even transformed. Adela Waltham who, unknown to her mother, was already on the road to emancipation from her upbringing, who was predisposed to socialist ideas because of the example of her brother, and who had been warned off by her mother from the only marriageable man she knew, responded in her ignorance to Mutimer's rugged idealism and married him. Mutimer ought to have been able to escape his background. He had the desire, the opportunity and the money. He could escape from the confines of class. Adela Waltham should have been able to escape from hers. She too could escape from class. What possibilities for human beings would there be if such escapes, migrations, changes, unions were always doomed to failure? Was it in the nature of things that they were doomed to failure?

Having created this situation Gissing tested it by the contrivance by which Adela discovered a copy of the old Mutimer's will in the church pew in which he died, a will which revealed that the estate had not, after all, been left to Richard Mutimer. The reader already knows that Adela married Mutimer without loving him in order to demonstrate her ability to support the ideas in which she believed – a course of action she felt free to pursue since there seemed no chance of marrying the person whom she actually loved. Both characters were vulnerable because both had acted without conviction. When the will was brought to light, Mutimer alienated his wife by his reluctance to give up the money. In this way, the idealism of each character is exposed. Neither was in fact capable of freedom from the values that had been inherited and acquired.

An unsympathetic reader might well say of *Demos* that Gissing maliciously placed the characters in a situation in which they could be exposed, not by themselves, but by him. Adela, in particular, was not given much chance to be loyal to her ideals. A sympathetic reader might, on the other hand, see Gissing as exploring the possibilities of emancipation from class and not blame him absolutely for this relative failure in the contrivance of a plot that would make manifest credible tensions between people and environment.[5] Gissing here is confronting but not completely solving one of the naturalist's main problems, i.e. preventing characters dominated by environment from appearing merely as the novelist's puppets. Early parts of the novel, especially the episodes which concern Emma Vine, make the reader feel that the environment matters, that behaviour is a function of place, that the Mutimer family behaves as it does because of its circumstances, and that the economics of place determine the expectations of the brothers, but later on the reader realizes that the plot which actually unfolds has a romance structure independent of place, so that the relationship between the two parts, the parts represented by the Mutimers and the Walthams, seems arbitrary. Incidentally if this account of the reader's response to *Demos* is correct, one might venture the following theoretical observation. If Gissing in a later book, tightens the plot so that the characters are more controlled by environment, less by contrivance and authorial manipulation, he will move towards a coherent type of naturalism. If he turns instead towards the psychological questions he has broached but not fully treated, here the question of what would have happened to Mutimer and his wife if circumstance had not directed their lives, he will in effect be moving his fiction towards the psychological realism represented by novels like *Born in Exile* and *The Whirlpool*. But this is theory. That this is a problem can be seen clearly in *Demos* when Gissing allows the ironical detachment of the narrator to weaken the narrative account of how the characters become involved with one another.

In the case of Mutimer, Gissing's initial portrait of him was so harsh that only someone as naïve as Adela Waltham could have been taken in. In Chapter V Gissing described Mutimer's study, for example, and then his books:

> The one singular feature of the room was a small, glass-doored bookcase,

full of volumes. They were all of Richard's purchasing; to survey them was to understand the man, at all events on his intellectual side. Without exception they belonged to that order of literature which, if studied exclusively and for its own sake – and here it was – brands a man indelibly, declaring at once the incompleteness of his education and the deficiency of his instincts. Social, political, religious – under these three heads the volumes classed themselves, and each class was represented by productions of the 'extreme' school. The books which a bright youth of fair opportunities reads as a matter of course, rejoices in for a year or two, then throws aside for ever, were here treasured to be the guides of a lifetime. Certain writers of the last century, long ago become only historically interesting, were for Richard an armoury whence he girded himself for the battles of the day; cheap reprints of translations of Malthus, of Robert Owen, of Volney's 'Ruins', of Thomas Paine, of sundry works of Voltaire, ranked upon his shelves. Moreover there was a large collection of pamphlets, titled wonderfully and of yet more remarkable contents, the authoritative utterances of contemporary gentlemen – and ladies – who made it the end of their existence to prove: that there cannot by any possibility be such a person as Satan; that the story of creation contained in the Book of Genesis is on no account to be received; that the begetting of children is a most deplorable oversight; that to eat flesh is wholly unworthy of a civilized being; that if every man and woman performed their quota of the world's labour it would be necessary to work for one hour and thirty-seven minutes daily, no jot longer and that the author, in each case, is the one person capable of restoring dignity to a down-trodden race and happiness to a blasted universe.[6]

In the sentences which follow, Mutimer failed what for Gissing was the crucial test: he knew nothing of literature, least of all poverty. As P. J. Keating has said: 'The main point Gissing is making about Mutimer is that he is an incomplete human being, he is tainted by his class background to such a degree that the positive qualities he possesses are destroyed by the negative qualities he is incapable of correcting'.[7]

Earlier, however, Keating had quoted part of the passage given above, had remarked correctly that 'Richard Mutimer is to be out of place in upper-class society because he has not read the right books',[8] and then said 'that the obvious conclusions are shirked'[9] by Gissing, presumably meaning that if social conditions caused Mutimer's difficulties he ought not to be satirized for them and that a man is not to be written off simply because he fails to join a small, educated, emancipated elite. Here is one of the points, by the way, at which Gissing critics tend to divide. On the one hand are those interested in novels as social history, whose knowledge of nineteenth-century England convinces them that, since *Demos* is almost an accurate account of working-class conditions, it would have been a better novel if it had been completely accurate, something which would have been possible only if Gissing had adopted the right criteria for judging a character like Mutimer. Gissing's disposal of Mutimer as a working-class character who fails to transform himself into something else is unsatisfactory for such critics, who feel it would have been better for Gissing to portray contemporary social conditions without satire. On the other hand are critics whose instincts lead them to take these novels as they are and not imagine what they might have been. Such a reader finds it easier to compare one novel with another, than to relate a book like *Demos* to social conditions which the reader knows about independently. Perhaps these two types of response are not incompatible, though perhaps, too, the time has not yet arrived for reconciliation between the two approaches.

Demos actually succeeded in a modest way with the contemporary reader because of the reactionary stance Gissing appeared to adopt, but it maybe fails, when regarded in retrospect, because of the discrepancy between Gissing's sympathy with working-class life, which is manifested particularly in the fine portrait of Mrs Mutimer, Richard's mother, and his heavily destructive treatment of the main character.

The discrepancy was perhaps in part caused by Gissing's uncertainty of purpose as he rescued himself from the mistake of having written *Isabel Clarendon* and *A Life's Morning*. In October 1885, for example, he told his sister: 'Meredith tells me I am making a great mistake in leaving the low-life scenes; says I might take a foremost place in fiction if I pursued that. Well, the next will in some degrees revert to that, though it will altogether keep clear of matter which people find distasteful. I shall call it *Demos* and it will be rather a savage satire on working-class aims and capacities.'[10] In the following month, in a letter to his brother, he reverted to the same theme: 'I fear I have erred greatly in leaving my special line of work.'[11] Evidently he still felt the wounds inflicted by the public, his publishers and his friends after the publication of *The Unclassed*. He therefore proceeded cautiously. 'It will deal with Socialism and the working classes, and from a very conservative point of view. I mean to give three months to it, and to make it worth reading and worth having written.'[12] One might speculate, in other words, that the savage satire on working-class aims and capabilities, made manifest in Gissing's treatment of the Mutimer family, was over-compensation, that Gissing did not know quite how to do it, and that *Demos* was a trial run for the two more evenly sustained novels that were to follow, *Thyrza* and *The Nether World*. When he wrote them, he managed to do without the satire and the right-wing aloofness that weaken *Demos*.

Gissing was an experimenter not a theorizer. When something went wrong, he tried again: *Demos* can usefully be seen as one of a series of attempts to write a naturalistic novel. Perhaps he could have engaged in a theoretical discussion of what worked and what did not work in *Demos*, but perhaps he embarked upon *Thyrza* with only a vague sense that something of a different kind had to be attempted. What were they, though, the theoretical problems implicit in *Demos*, as Gissing might have been aware of them? In theory, the naturalistic novel should have a contemporary theme and be set in the present; its many characters, not one of whom should be allowed the prominence of a Romantic hero, should represent a recognizable urban population occupied in a variety of ways with the normal affairs of existence; and there should be an insistence upon place as one, if not the only, determinant of behaviour. Actually, the naturalist starts with place and the people who happen to live there, rather than with people first and only incidentally the place in which they happen to live. To say that the naturalistic novel 'should' have these characteristics is only to say that such a novel would have coherence, a certain internal consistency, a type of artistic integrity. Linda Nochlin has given a good recent account of what is involved.[13]

Of course Zola was the theorist contemporary with Gissing, especially in *Le Roman expérimental*, where he stressed the importance of seeing the individual within a social context, so that the novelist needed an objective social 'overview' in which the relationships of people could be observed and described impartially and the dynamics of social organizations portrayed without romantic distortions. Zola's book was broadly based upon a distinction between fatalism and determinism, where the latter term was used scientifically. It was better to understand than not understand the forces that determined the way people lived.

> Nous montrons le mécanisme de l'utile et du nuisible, nous dégageons le déterminisme des phénomènes humains et sociaux, pour qu'on puisse un jour dominer et diriger ces phénomènes.[14]

This large purpose was linked in Zola's mind, at least when he wrote *Le Roman expérimental*, with the assumption that the human being could also, like society, be studied objectively, even medically, and that was important for the novelist to understand how the individual worked – worked, that is, in the physiological or neurological sense. Gissing would have agreed with this, as will become even more clear in a later chapter. But the point being made here is not that Gissing knew of Zola and imitated him, but that Gissing perfectly understood the cultural forces that brought a person like Zola to write *Le Roman expérimental* and that, in England, with a full appreciation of the issues at stake, he was simultaneously working at English solutions to the questions about contemporary fiction that Zola raised. By 'English' is meant here solutions which Gissing hoped would work in England despite the deeply felt moral sense that informed English public life. Although Gissing found it prudent to tell Frederic Harrison that he had not read Zola when he wrote *Workers in the Dawn*, by 1885 it would have been impossible for him to be unaware of Zola's work, not least because of the Vizetelly case. (Vizetelly was one of the avant-garde publishers of the 1880s and had been sent to prison for publishing Zola's novels in unexpurgated English versions.) Nonetheless, it must be emphasised that Gissing was not the kind of novelist who wrote to a prescription; rather we call *Demos*, *Thyrza* and *The Nether World* naturalist novels because, in retrospect, we can see that they share certain characteristics, satisfy certain requirements, and because there is a progressive development in Gissing's technique.

In *Demos*, Gissing only partly satisfied the theoretical requirements of even his own austere, non-metaphorical type of naturalism. He built the novel around a contemporary theme – the question of class mobility – but somewhat spoilt his treatment of it by lapsing into satire of his own chief character. He demonstrated the folly of idealism in his main character, but allowed the reader, through the agency of a plot too dependent upon mere accident, to see them rather in that older Romantic convention in which people with will and desire either succeeded or failed in living not to the world's but to their own standards. And thirdly, he permitted too much mobility. Both Mutimer and Adela Waltham leave for a large part of the book the places which, in a pure naturalist novel, would have defined them. Gissing started with but failed to sustain the relationship of person and place. This is not to say that he failed to write an extraordinarily interesting, and indeed challenging, book. The modest contemporary success of *Demos* was well-deserved. At least he had found a way of writing about people like the Mutimers and the Vines. On the other hand, Gissing had not yet found the novel that would have to be written, or at least which he would have to write, if he wanted to write about the immediate, urban, working-class world on its own terms, without satire and without condescension. Perhaps *The Nether World* is Gissing's most successful book in this respect, but in his next novel, *Thyrza*, he moved much closer to solving the theoretical difficulties implicit in *Demos*.

Thyrza[15] is not *about* social reform. Nor does it put a theory on trial. It is as wrong to see *Thyrza* as a fictional discussion of social issues as it would have been wrong to fail to see that at the heart of *Demos* was an inter-personal or psychological 'subject' which co-existed with a depiction of contemporary life. One of the characters in the novel has a theory of social reform, at least to the extent that he wants to do something useful with his life. At the beginning of the novel, before the reader knows the main action is to be set in the London district of Lambeth, this wealthy young man, Walter Egremont, tells his friends in Cumberland – the Newthorpes and their friend Paula Tyrell, who happens to be staying with them – about a scheme they immediately dismiss as the idealist project of a young Oxford graduate troubled by the conscious of the rich. 'What I should like to attempt', he tells them, 'would be the spiritual education of the upper artisan and mechanic class'.[16] Most of the characters in the book are members of this upper artisan and mechanic class. Egremont has decided to help them, motivated by the same thoughts and feelings as compelled Helen Norman in *Workers in the Dawn* and Ida Starr in *The Unclassed*. His problem was to bridge the class gap in some useful way, without condescension and without being merely patronizing. Helen Norman had met the problem by good works: she had founded a night school. In *Thyrza*, Gissing put Egremont in a similar position.

Lambeth was chosen for Walter Egremont's enterprise because his father had a factory there, because in the factory there was a foreman he knew called Bower, whom Egremont expected would name a group of suitable men likely to benefit from a course of lectures on English literature, and because the father of a patient of another friend of Egremont, Mrs Ormonde, happened to live there too. (The reader discovers later that his name is Bunce.) Egremont consciously wished to avoid the pitfalls of a holier-than-thou approach. 'It seems to me that if I can get them to understand what is meant by love of literature pure and simple, without a thought of political or social purpose – especially without a thought of cash profit, which is disasterously blended with what little knowledge they acquire – I shall be on the way to founding my club of social reformers'.[17] There is nothing to suggest that Gissing identified either with Egremont's zeal and idealism or with the cynicism of the professional politician, Dalmaine, whose support for popular education to counteract foreign competition is mentioned even before Egremont makes his own confession of purpose. Gissing once again chose to write a book on a topical subject: the subject then made its own demands upon his imagination. Egremont believed he *ought* to address himself to the social circumstances that his family's business in Lambeth had forced him to know as a reality of life. Why he believed this, why anyone believes it, is unclear. The idea that a person might be troubled by class distinction, especially that a person who enjoyed the privileges of wealth might be troubled by it, was Gissing's subject. What would happen if such a person stepped across the class barrier? Such is the situation that *Thyrza* tested.

There is an important structural difference between *Demos* and *Thyrza*. In *Demos*, Mutimer moves out of his urban environment; Adela Waltham moves out of her rural, middle-class environment, though she later returns to it. In *Thyrza*, the greater part of the action occurs *within* an urban locality, except for the beginning and the end of the novel. The main part of the novel, that which is located in Lambeth, has in this sense a much greater integrity than the equivalent parts of *Demos*. At the same time, Gissing still found it useful to create a context for the main action by depicting, at the beginning and at the end of the novel, that other world from which some of his characters came. Some critics have argued that even if *Thyrza* is an improvement on *Demos*, *Thyrza*'s structure still shows Gissing's inability to be wholly responsive to the urban environment that was his main subject.[18] Be that as it may, the new structure is part of Gissing's experiments in naturalism, part of his interesting attempt to find an imaginative formula that worked for him. For this reason, it is worth looking at the way in which Gissing, at the beginning of the novel, anticipated the balance of forces that was to be its main point. And it is Chapter II which, on many counts, needs the closest attention.

The first part of the chapter is concerned with Egremont's decision to work with the poor, the second part with his proposal to Annabel Newthorpe. Throughout the novel, social ideas and attitudes are confused, intermixed and contrasted with personal aspirations and feelings. In the second chapter, however, Gissing proceeds with caution. He underlines the fact that much that is to happen in the book will be dependent upon the development of Egremont's character. 'Success depends upon my personal influence', says Egremont. 'I may find that it is inadequate.'[19] Gissing emphasizes, too, the cool reception Egremont's statement received from his listeners: they talked about the weather and went to bed. In the pages which follow, Gissing makes clear not only that Annabel understood, before the main action had even commenced, Egremont's streak of insincerity but also that his having his life 'consecrated to a worthy end', as she politely put it, had little or nothing to do with her turning down his proposal of marriage. This scene is crucial, as any reader who knows the novel well will appreciate; the reader would have felt quite differently about Egremont had he simply seen him arriving in Lambeth with the hope of doing good. His failure could have been less the result of his own character, more the result of circumstances that defeated him. Furthermore, Egremont's eventual failure would to a much greater extent have constituted an attack on a 'widely supported theory of social reform'. As it is, the reader knows in advance that Egremont's desires are confused, idealistic, human (as Adela Waltham's had been in *Demos*), and that he is therefore not simply the mouthpiece of a set of ideas. The conclusion of the book confirms the importance of what Walter Egremont and Annabel Newthorpe said to each other in Chapter II. Indeed, their final conversation – the conversation that ends the novel – was really a continuation of what they had talked about four years earlier on the shore of Ullswater. On that early occasion, when Egremont left the Newthorpes to go to London, the rain 'fell in torrents'; over Beachy Head, at the end, the clouds cleared disclosing 'a restored twilight'. In such a light Gissing's more perceptive characters have to make their way.

They had to make their way in an imperfect world in which class differences could not be reconciled. In this world, the recreated world of late nineteenth-century urban England, people were held apart by fundamental differences of wealth, privilege, and attitude. Such were the facts of existence and the individual, however sensitive his social conscience, was powerless to confute them. Thus the all-encompassing idealism that informed Egremont's actions at the beginning of the novel had to give way to a limited understanding of human capability, a compromise with existence, a merely human ethic. But only after Walter Egremont, and the reader, had visited Gissing's Lambeth.

The closed society in a small part of Lambeth that Gissing created for the purposes of the novel was heavily populated. In fact it was crowded. The crowds filled the small spaces available, crammed themselves into the pubs, milled about on Lambeth Walk. On most days of his life, a person could meet and would naturally meet most of the people he knew. Only seldom did he know someone whom his neighbours did not know. Most people lived in single rooms: it was a vast step for Jo Bunce to move with his two children from one room to two.

Gissing had to stretch his imagination to comprehend the fact of Lambeth: he was not writing from experience of his own. Most of his readers either did not know that whole families lived in single basement rooms on next to nothing or thought that a man with a family could change the circumstances of his life by his own efforts. They were as incapable of comprehending the fact that the whole of a man's life might be determined by forces outside his control, as of appreciating the feelings and attitudes that went with a realization of this fact. It was difficult for a middle-class reader to accept that a man might not be responsible for his own actions: the middle-class world was constructed upon the premise of moral responsibility. Thus, to see Lambeth in an 'objective' not a moral context was an effort of the imagination that was at first beyond them. At first it was beyond Gissing. After all, his contemporaries did not know how to come to terms with industrialization, poverty, urban growth, disease, and people in large numbers. Similarly Gissing did not at first know even how to describe what he saw. Perhaps it is partly because of the imaginative effort involved in this attempt that the group of characters drawn in *Thyrza* are presented so compassionately.

In the progress of the novel, the characters were drawn one by one from the crowd and the reader has the feeling that they are not exceptional, but representative, the group shown being a microcosm of a particular social order. For Gissing's anti-Romantic purposes the number was important. There was the thirty-five year old Gilbert Grail who worked in a soap and candle factory from 6 a.m. to 7 p.m. each day for forty shillings a week and whose idealism, because of the pressure of environment, was 'the haunter within' – 'a spirit ever straining after something unattainable';[20] Luke Ackroyd, his friend from the north of England, whose 'rough comeliness' and 'intelligence' were matched by 'a good deal of self-will and probably a strain of sensuality',[21] and for whom 'being in love was, to tell the truth, a matter of vastly more importance than all the political and social and religious questions in the world';[22] Totty Nancarrow, a Catholic, nineteen years old and living by herself in Newport Street, 'for all the world like a lad put into petticoats'[23] and known for her love of 'marmalade and pickles' and disdain of mere necessity; Jo Bunce, widower, locksmith and militant atheist, whose 'spare frame' and 'hollow cheeks which suggested insufficiency of diet' did not conceal the 'manliness in his appearance' and with whom 'familiarity revealed a sensitive significance in the irregular nose, the prominent lips, the small severed chin and long throat';[24] Bower, a foreman at the factory in which Grail and Ackroyd worked, whose wife kept 'The Little Shop with the Large Heart', one of the social centres and meeting places of the group; Mary Bower, aged nineteen, a moralist and regular in her attendance at Chapel, including to other people's disgust the mid-week Special Prayer meetings; and Lydia and Thyrza Trent, twenty-one and seventeen respectively at the beginning of this book, living together in the Grail's house, sleeping in the same bed, working in the same hat factory, and the closest of companions since the death of their father several years earlier. These people never left, never had left and never expected to leave their own locality. They were as much confined by locality as the villagers in Hardy's *The Woodlanders*.[25] What they experienced, felt, thought, was therefore shared by the people constituting this universe. In creating this confined, credible world Gissing was as successful here as in any of his books at depicting the physical environment which any reader could see would necessarily impose a pressure upon those who lived there.

There was no recourse to the sensational zoom lens. When attention was drawn, in the development of the plot, to a particular person, the others were not thrown out of focus. The emphasis upon Thyrza Trent or Walter Egremont did not make the others disappear. To permit Egremont to join the group, Gissing imagined a social idealist who temporarily drew together a few of the characters: Bower, Grail, Bunce and Ackroyd attended Egremont's first lectures. Yet life went on in Lambeth whether there were lectures or not, as the reader is made to feel.

Life had mainly to do with survival, work and relations within the group. Love, the chief relationship, was circumscribed by the lovers' deeply ingrained sense of economic and social necessity; far be it from them to defy fate. Ackroyd was in love with Thyrza. Lydia was in love with Ackroyd but concealed the fact because of Thyrza. Grail was in love with Thyrza but concealed the fact because of poverty, illness and despair. When Thyrza refused Ackroyd, he turned to Totty Nancarrow. She told him to stop drinking. Time passed. During the four-year span of the novel, the characters reached limited understandings with each other, as it were in the natural course of events: Totty Nancarrow went to live with Jo Bunce when he moved; Lydia Trent and Luke Ackroyd came to know each other and were reconciled. Gissing succeeded in catching the sequences of ordinary moods and aspirations, insights, deceptions, arguments, clarifications, honesties and dishonesties. It is within this context, not from an outsider's point of view, that the story of Thyrza is told.

Thoughtful, intelligent and sensitive, she was permitted modest social mobility by means of the device by which, in love with Egremont, she literally left Lambeth to be found almost immediately by Mrs Osmonde who trained her in the manners of the middle-class, treated her with respect and put her on the road to independence by encouraging her to become a singer. Gissing had contrived an ironical situation in which Egremont wished to remove class barriers by working in Lambeth, while Thyrza in fact left Lambeth to avoid the predicament of being loved by Grail, the man downstairs, while she herself loved someone whom, because of her lack of social attainment, she could not expect to marry. No one in the novel really believed that the class barrier could be breeched, unless it was Egremont – and he only believed it for a brief period of time. Thyrza did not, though she desired it. She was different from the other people of her immediate neighbourhood in that she had a reason to leave it; she had a motive for desiring more than she could reasonably expect; she had the capability, so the reader is shown, to respond to something better than the life she normally would have had. Her desires were not fantasies or dreams because, from outside her world, Egremont had come to her. Thus, for Gissing, she represented the legitimate study of human potential in a restricting environment. What was the fate of a sensitive person in such a case?

Gissing was not the only novelist to have appreciated the advantages of showing the differences between brothers and sisters, or in this instance sisters, who had grown up in exactly the same environment.[26] The Victorian social determinist could not help but be interested to know how people with the same background turned out differently. But while the relationship of heredity and environment remained so puzzling, how to explain the differences? The difference between Lydia and Thyzra was striking. Lydia, the sister who was to be defined by her environment, was at peace with it and indeed knew nothing else (so that she *could* not aspire to anything outside her own world), appeared first in Chapter III and Gissing permitted himself his usual set-piece introductory description:

> There was a footstep in the shop – firm, yet light and quick – then a girl's face showed itself at the parlour door. It was a face which atoned for lack of regular features by the bright intelligence and the warmth of heart that shone in its smile of greeting. A fair broad forehead lay above well-arched brows; the eyes below were large and shrewdly observant, with laughter and kindness blent in their dark depths. The cheeks were warm with health; the lips and chin were strong, yet marked with refinement; they told of independence, of fervid instincts; perhaps of a temper a little apt to be impatient. It was not an imginative countenance, yet alive with thought and feeling – all, one felt, ready at a moment's need – the kind of face which becomes the light and joy of home, the bliss of children, the unfailing support of a man's courage. Her hair was cur short and crisped itself above her neck; her hat of black straw and dark dress were those of a work-girl –

poor, yet, in their lack of adornment, suiting well with the active, helpful impression which her look produced.[27]

A twentieth-century reader is perhaps not surprised that a girl who lacks education, whose parentage is obscure, and who lived in one room with her sister, may be shrewd, refined, and 'alive with thought and feeling'. Not so the reader who could have borrowed *Thyrza* from Mudie's circulating library in 1888. Such a reader would have felt that these characteristics or qualities could only be the result of 'improvement', education, training.

In attempting to establish and sustain a credible balance between his treatment of Lydia and his treatment of Thyrza, Gissing once again confronted the question of whether a person could in fact escape from his own background. If a person could, then the fictional interest would lie in the particular way in which a person freed himself. Gissing very rarely allowed this to happen. The rationale of a naturalist novel would disappear if a person could easily break with his own background: there had to be *some* relationship between person and place; indeed, in ninety-nine instances out of a hundred, there had to be a necessary relationship. On the other hand, if a person could not escape from his background, several questions had to be answered. First, if the main part of the story was to be the meeting of a wealthy, free-thinking, philanthropic, Oxford undergraduate and a sensitive, working-class girl who was 'bettering' herself by becoming a singer, why bother to show her background at all? She had, after all, left it. Secondly, if Lydia, Thyrza's sister, was an example of someone at one with her environment, what explanation could be given for someone who did not accept it? What was the meaning of not accepting the place in which you lived? In the popular Darwinian sense, there ought to have been a concordance between person and place. For the naturalist also? What, then, was the meaning of emancipation for such a person?

For the time being, Gissing's answer to this important contemporary issue was implied in his fashioning of the plot, which from his point of view represented a strong rebuff of the romantic expectations of any reader who thought that Egremont and Thyrza might have married. In a romance, the beautiful young girl would have been carried away from her hideous environment to begin life anew. In a naturalist novel, to begin life anew is impossible. However you may have been fashioned by heredity and environment, you necessarily remain what you are. Magical transformations are ruled out. Gissing therefore has Thyrza return to Lambeth, where without love, but with considerable trust and respect, she marries Gilbert Grail, staying within her class, within her environment. Once again it must be noted that, in order to resolve the main action of the novel in this way, Gissing prevents Egremont and Thyrza from facing up to their own situation. They do not talk to each other; that is, when their predicament is at crisis point they do not talk. They do not even meet. If they had met and talked and been allowed to work out the implications of their own situation, they could have acted independently and made themselves exceptions to the determinist norm either defying convention or by going somewhere else – by breaking the bond of environment. That Gissing realized a major issue was at stake is clear from the novels he wrote in the 1890s, where he has sets of characters confront the very question which he allows Egremont and Thyrza to avoid. This in itself is enough to show that *Thyrza* was powerfully conceived in the naturalist mode – which is not to say, of course, that Gissing's avoidance of the psychological interests of his own story will meet with general approval.

It is interesting to notice that when Gissing revised the novel for Lawrence & Bullen's edition of 1891, he underscored the difficulty implicit in his handling of *Thyrza*. Here is further evidence of the fact that Gissing was aware of what he was doing, was conscious of the internal artistic and imaginative demands of his own fiction, and was willing to re-work a novel, if the occasion arose, in order to achieve consistency. During the period between his first writing the book and his revision of it, he had learned much more about contemporary thinking in the fields of medicine, psychiatry, and neurology. He had read Maudsley and Ribot.[28] In particular, he was intimately conversant with the fashionable theory that any atypical behaviour, whether of an extreme kind as in the case of madness or genius or of a common kind as in the case of unsocial behaviour superficially caused by alcoholism, would in fact be susceptible to physiological descriptions of a kind that would make moral comments superfluous.[29] This suited Gissing. It was easier for him to think a person's relationship with his environment was through the agency of an inherited nervous system, which might be healthy or unhealthy without the responsibility being in any way his, than to suppose that the springs of action lay in the character's will, he, the character, having the moral power in some way to determine his own fate. Indeed, Gissing gave this theme robust treatment in *The Nether World*, a fact which demonstrates conclusively that he read Maudsley at that time. In the first edition of *Thyrza*, he gave a hint of what he had in mind by laying some stress on Thyrza's congenital heart condition. She was physically different from the others, so naturally she behaved differently. It is interesting to notice that Gissing gave this additional prominence when he revised the book.

Her heart condition apart, Thyrza in the first edition was different from other people in Lambeth because she aspired to things unknown to her and beyond her environment as did, pessimistically, Gilbert Grail. Thyrza was idealized and Gissing must have thought that he could afford the suggestion that she was at odds, at least slightly, with the locality in which she lived. In the revised version the more sentimental features in the portrayal of Thyrza were brought under control. Her face, in the first edition, 'was not a morbid physiognomy, yet it impressed one with a sense of vague trouble',[30] while of her eyes it was said: 'imagination dwelt in them and seemed ever busy with things remote from the workroom and the dull street'. Gissing deleted this lapse: the street was anything but dull: Thyrza did not regard it as dull; nor did anyone else. The drift of the book was to show Lambeth as the interesting and, indeed, essential locale for a certain type of action. Dreaming about an escape from a place others accepted needed an explanation of a more fundamental kind.

The other change is more startling. In the second edition the sentence reads: 'It was a subtly morbid physiognomy, and impressed one with a sense of vague trouble'. Again, an internal contradiction is removed and in the process the quality of the whole paragraph is altered.

> It was not easy to recognize her as Lydia's sister; if you searched her features the sisterhood was there, but the type of countenance was so subtly modified, so refined, as to become beauty of rare suggestiveness. She was of pale complexion, and had golden hair; it was plaited in one braid, which fell to her waist. Like Lydia's her eyes were large and full of light; every line of the face was delicate, harmonious, sweet; each thought that passed through her mind reflected itself in a change of expression, produced one knew not how, one phase melting into another like flitting lights upon a stream in woodland. It was a subtly morbid physiognomy, and impressed one with a vague sense of trouble. There was none of the spontaneous pleasure in life which gave Lydia's face such wholesome brightness; no impulse of activity, no resolve; all tended to pre-occupation, to emotional reverie.[31]

In this way, by saying that Thyrza's make-up was 'morbid' but 'subtly' so, Gissing prepared for the ambiguities of Thyrza's behaviour, for the contrast between her practical and impractical side, the unresolved tensions between dreaming and common sense. She had common sense enough to refuse Ackroyd. She was susceptible to the repressed passions in Grail; without knowing why, she agreed to become engaged to him. By nature she was faithful and honest; yet, again without knowing why, she felt compelled, in the weeks before her marriage, to search out Egremont. Forced to realize that she ought not to marry Grail if she did not love him, she ran away. She left Lambeth. To this point in the novel Gissing had provided a sufficient, if not an overpowering, explanation of motive and situation, of a kind that was compatible with his profound sense of the confined environment of Lambeth. To say this is to stress the kind of novel *Thyrza* is. No more. Whether or not it might be regarded as successful would depend of course upon how Gissing resolved the problems he had set himself.

Before the crux of the novel can be discussed, a further word must be said about Walter Egremont. He is to be distinguished from the Establishment figures in the book, like the Tyrells and the Dalmaines: he was trying to free himself from their life, from their kind of life. That is to say, he ought to be distinguished from them, although Professor Korg, for example, entirely glosses over his position, his character, and his situation. 'A wealthy young idealist named Walter Egremont decides to educate the working people who are the raw material of reform'.[32] Similarly, Mabel Donnelly described Egremont as being at the 'apex' of the novel's class structure.[33] Actually Egremont, though wealthy, felt 'a gap between him and the people born to refinement who were his associates',[34] was moodily nostalgic for the time he had spent with his father who had been an oil-cloth manufacturer in Lambeth, and by the time the action of the novel commenced experienced a 'temporary distaste for the society in which he had always found much pleasure'.[35] In a crucial passage, totally characteristic of Gissing, Egremont is made to think of himself as *déclassé*, without a home, alienated from both societies. 'What if in strictness he belonged to neither sphere? What if his life was to be a struggle between inherited sympathies and the affinities of his intellect? All the better, perchance, for his prospect of usefulness; he stood as mediator between two sections of society. But for his private happiness, how?'[36] Though he came to the Lambeth world of Paradise Street as an outsider, he was not so cut off from his father's employees that his feelings about his own position must seem implausible. Furthermore, his position in the novel is strengthened by Gissing's contrast between him and the Dalmaines and the Tyrells. The uprooted thinking man is so much part of Gissing's world, occurs so frequently in other novels, one need not doubt Gissing's emphasis on this occasion, which (again) is not to say that Gissing believed what Egremont believed. On the contrary, Gissing's approach remained experimental. How would such a person as Egremont cope?

How would he behave?

One rather insists upon Gissing's workmanlike, authorly, experimental approach to fiction because of the tendency that certainly at one time existed for critics to extract doctrine and ignore fiction, as for example in Korg's suggestion that 'in *Thyrza* Gissing puts his case against mass education into a speech by a character named Mr Tyrell'.[37] Statements of this kind have distracted large numbers of readers from Gissing's principal concerns. This particular statement, for example, seems to lie behind the remark made by Spiers and Coustillas that has already been quoted: 'Gissing attacks mass education and mass democracy as a remedy for social disorders . . .'[38] Indeed. In point of fact there is nothing to indicate that Gissing associated himself with the seven line quotation given by Korg. The quotation reads:

> The one insuperable difficulty lies in the fact that we have no power greater than commercial enterprise. Nowadays nothing will succeed save on the commercial basis; from church to public house the principle applies. There is no way of spreading popular literature save on terms of supply and demand. Take the Education Act . . . a more intelligent type of workman is demanded that our manufacturers may keep pace with other countries.[39]

The speech of which these sentences are a part is not 'by a character named Mr Tyrell', as Korg claims. It is spoken by Mr Newthorpe who is answering his daughter's question about a man who gave his son, as his only reading matter, atheist tracts.

'But why should the poor people be left to such ugly-minded teachers?' Annabel exclaimed. 'Surely those influences may be opposed?' The conversation was part of the after-dinner talk on the lawn of the Newthorpe's house on Ullswater and provided the context in which Egremont could begin to tell his friends about his own scheme of work. Later, the view expressed by Newthorpe, here given in a cynical, 'philosophical' way as though – as is remarked elsewhere – by a character in Turgenev, is sharply satirized in the person of Dalmaine, the hard-headed politician who says, for example: 'all social reform must be undertaken on strictly commercial principles'.[40] The ironies implicit in the contrast between Egremont, the idealist, and Mr Newthorpe, Mr Dalmaine and Mr Tyrell, the worldly wise, do not have to be thrust into categories: the contrast was not made for the purposes of the social reformer but for the convenience of the novelist. Gladstone noticed this when he noted 'how Dalmaines not Egremonts use the real instruments of good in the world'; that is, he noticed that the question was unresolved by any didacticism on Gissing's part.[41] Within the context of the novel, the reader will not fail to remark that Mr Newthorpe was the character in the book who had consciously and deliberately opted out of the 'modern' struggle for existence, that, though Egremont failed in his project, he married Annabel Newthorpe in the end, that the atheist father who gave his boy burlesques of the Bible to read was Jo Bunce who later married Totty Nancarrow and was not ugly-minded at all, and that the reality of Lambeth – that is, the Lambeth created by Gissing on the page – was far different from what idealists and cynics imagined on the secluded, peaceful shores of Ullswater. What is important about Korg's minor error is that it provides an example of the casual way in which critics have substantiated their preconceptions, not about the books under consideration, but about Gissing's personal attitudes and opinions. So often, as is the case here, the overall structure of a book denies the biographical criticism that has for so long been fashionable.

If the structure of *Thyrza* is to be taken seriously from a literary point of view, and it is an immensely fascinating early novel, discussion clearly has to be based upon the revised text, as C. J. Francis has shown.[42] Gissing reduced the novel in size by the equivalent of 125 first edition pages; the non-functional episode of the Emersons was removed entirely, superfluous dialogue was cut and many of the remarks made directly by the author were eliminated. Thus the second edition is significantly better than the first, as well as being shorter. Some of the faults were not eliminated, however, most notably that dependence upon coincidence at crucial points in the action, and the relative weakness of the Eastbourne episodes in comparison with those set in Lambeth. Nonetheless, the structure of the novel as a whole is made clear enough in the revision: the upper class is contrasted impersonally with the working class, while Lambeth is presented as just as 'real' a place as Mayfair, Eastbourne and the Lake District, and therefore just as deserving of study and understanding.

In this comparison of classes and districts, Gissing's sympathies do not rest with the Tyrells and the Dalmaines. His satire may be arch, but it is unmistakable. 'When Paula had been three or four days wedded, it occurred to her to examine her husband's countenance'.[43] So begins Chapter XXV, which follows a crucial exchange between Ackroyd and Lydia Trent and precedes Annabel's learning about Egremont's disappearance. This is the chapter in which Dalmaine reprimanded his new wife for her frivolity and then ponderously told her about the disappearance of Thyrza. 'Again and again', says

Dalmaine, 'I have to tell you that I never talk nonsense: I am a politician'.[44] Is the reader to take this sort of thing seriously when he has Ackroyd, Lydia, Grail and Thyrza in mind?

Seriously it must be taken, not as the key to Gissing's didactic purpose but as part of his balanced view of the two worlds. Thyrza's and Egremont's, separated as they are not just by class barrier and everything it represented in 1887, but by ignorance of the most literal kind. He had developed considerably since he wrote *Workers in the Dawn*. Indeed he was now able at least to improve upon *Demos*, for the satire here is not destructive. Probably he had realized he did not need heavy irony, sarcasm and invective of the kind that marred *Workers in the Dawn*. *Thyrza* is a vastly better book than *Demos* because, positively, Gissing simply described what he knew, what he had come to know and understand, and because, negatively, the burden of authorial comment, interpretation and moralizing is not nearly as heavy. Moreover, the novel is sound in its overall structure. At the end of it, Egremont returned to Annabel and Thyrza to Grail; none of them had succeeded in breaking away from the conventions that bound them; all had learned much as a result of their trial.

This situation, of social disruption, dislocation, alienation, is typical of Gissing. Time and time again he looked at situations in which people were sufficiently emancipated to regard themselves and their backgrounds critically, but were not sufficiently emancipated to act freely, preferring or feeling obliged to renounce the possibilities open to them. In 1887, Gissing may not have thought out how a man like Egremont and a woman like Thyrza would behave towards each other if they were in fact free to live together without having to worry about social status. He was not ready, then, for the quite different solutions of *The Emancipated* and *New Grub Street*, solutions that were not consistent with the heavily environmental design of *Thyrza*. In *Thyrza* freedom has to be denied. Place, location, neighbourhood have to be accepted. As in the case of *Demos*, this in effect left Gissing with a novelistic strategy that involved a right-wing and puritanical emphasis which permitted acceptance by publisher (Smith, Elder & Co.) and by the publisher's reader (James Payn). *Thyrza* raised political questions, having to do with class mobility and living and working conditions in contemporary London, but not in a threatening or revolutionary way. On the contrary, the reader is left with a confirmation of the social *status quo*: class barriers are not broken; working people must settle for the lives they inherit; so must middle-class people like Egremont.

Similarly, though the novel has a sexual undercurrent, it is not pronounced. The characters at the centre of *Thyrza* do not feel so strongly for each other that their feeling becomes a principal, exclusive driving force. The love and sexuality of Egremont and Thyrza might have been a liberating and therefore a dangerous force, but when he wrote *Thyrza* Gissing could only see the personal but not the social significance of sexuality: he still wrote of passions that had to be kept under control and of sexual feelings that would detract from not add to personality. This extreme caution over political and sexual matters was, in 1887, an essential part of Gissing's vision of the world, an aspect of it which will be discussed again later. When Gissing first wrote *Thyrza* it probably seemed to be an essential fictional strategy. A novelist might have stressed Thyrza's sexuality had she been escaping from her environment, might have made her different from her peer group and therefore capable of unexpected romance if she was to go away with Egremont, could have developed the relationship between man and woman if that relationship was not a function of place, but for as long as Gissing wanted to insist upon a necessary connection between heredity and environment, for as long as he wanted to write a novel about what might reasonably happen in Lambeth, and for as long as he wanted to stress the effect of social conditions or human behaviour, he had to play down the positive motivating force of both politics and sex. This was convenient: a Victorian reader could cope with such a formulation. Consequently, while in a different context this particular set of emphases might be discussed as a strength or weakness of Gissing's early fiction, it at least has to be seen, in any preliminary account, as an integral aspect of his art, as something he had to have, as something the sequence of novels demonstrates he chose to have. It is in this way that one begins to see the distinguishing features of Gissing's naturalism, a type of art which could not be forced upon the Victorian imagination in a merely casual manner.

When Thyrza realized that Mrs Ormonde had been able to prevail over Egremont she returned to Lambeth, having no reason to do anything else, was reconciled to Grail who agreed to marry her, learned almost immediately that Lydia would marry Ackroyd, and accepted, in effect, that what she dreamed of attaining was in practice unattainable. She died before she could be married. Egremont for his part eventually met Annabel by chance; they were reconciled and agreed to marry. From Annabel, consequently, Egremont learned what in a better novel he would have learnt from Thyrza or Mrs Ormonde.

She raised her eyes; they were sad, compassionate, yet smiled. 'She could not have lived. But you are conscious now of what that face means?'

'I know nothing of her history from the day when I last saw her, except the mere untoward circumstances.'

'Nor do I. But I saw her once, here, and I have seen her portrait. The crisis of your life was there. There was your own great opportunity, and you let it pass. She could not have lived; but that is no matter. You were tried, Mr Egremont, and found wanting.'

'Her love for me did not continue. It was already too late at the end of those two years.'

'Was it?'

'What secret knowledge have you?'

'None whatever, as you mean it. But it was not too late.'[45]

Annabel's knowledge that Egremont had lost or been deprived of something does not mean that their marriage without passion is to be regarded as meaningless. Gissing had on many occasions postulated that a marriage to be successful had to be passionless. The other marriages in the book, those of Jo Bunce and Totty Nancarrow, and Luke Ackroyd and Lydia Trent, are also without passion. They are not for that reason mere marriages of convenience. On the contrary, they are based on commonsense, limited expectation, mutual respect and personal honesty. The attitudes of Lambeth prevail: it is Romance that is not permitted an existence. Thus Annabel and Egremont did not, at the end of the novel, aspire to go higher than they could actually go.

The night was thickening about them.

'Shall we go up to the Head?' Egremont asked.

'No higher.'

She said it with a significant look, and he understood her.[46]

Generally speaking, the snag with these early books is that the development of any character whose natural life lay outside the social milieu being described would weaken the book as a whole. Had Gissing worked out the motivation of Mrs Ormonde, and in particular had he allowed the development of a relation between Mrs Ormonde, Thyrza and Egremont based upon their appreciation of each other's motives, it is most unlikely that the reader would have been able to accept Thyrza's return to Lambeth, which seems somewhat arbitrary as it is. Psychological as well as physical movement is virtually impossible in the type of naturalist novel Gissing was attempting. A character might escape from his environment. But if he did, what then? Would not such an escape call in question the whole determinist notion of being trapped by circumstance? And if a person *felt* free of environment, how would he then live? Gissing either did not know or was not ready yet to study the kind of person whose freedom from environment was an aspect of a larger alienation. For the moment he concentrated on the pressures of place. The crossing of class barriers in *Thyrza* had made it difficult for him to write a novel with a coherent plot. In *The Nether World*, therefore, such movement was not permitted; the whole action occurs in Clerkenwell, a part of London to which all the characters belong.

A plot is devised which depends upon an eccentric old man whose life and intentions remain a mystery for the greater part of the book; much appears to depend upon his will by which, before he destroyed it, he had left his money to his granddaughter. The plot only appears to depend upon the contrivance, however, whereas in *Demos* and *Thyrza* the contrivance was essential. In *Demos* Richard Mutimer was tested as a character, first when he inherited a vast sum of money and, secondly, when he lost it again as the result of a discovery of a will. In *Thyrza* contrivance was needed to keep Thyrza away both from Grail, her working-class fiancé, and Egremont, her middle-class lover, for a reasonable period of time. The implausible Mrs Ormonde supplied the need. In *The Nether World*, Snowdon's will merely appeared to influence the lives of the principal characters. In actual fact, the relationships between them, relationships which shift and change somewhat as the book develops, did not so much depend upon exterior contrivance as on their feelings for each other. This was possible in *The Nether World* because all the characters came from the same part of London. In *Demos,* Gissing had to arrange a plausible meeting between Mutimer and Adela. In *Thyrza* he had to bring Egremont to Lambeth in a way that would make a meeting with Grail and Thyrza Trent not improbable. *The Nether World* does not make these demands. The nether world was self-contained. Seldom did people come to it. Seldom did people leave.

In *The Nether World*,[47] Gissing submitted the notion of emancipation to its most severe test. He depicted a physical environment – his model was Clerkenwell – so severe and oppressive that literal escape from it was difficult, spiritual escape virtually impossible. There was no relief. The environment did not positively cause people to be what they were, but the connection between environment and personality was so close that the feelings and thoughts of the characters belonged as much to the locality as to themselves.

This locality was grim, forbidding and precisely drawn. It was the area of the City Road, St Luke's hospital, the Metropolitan meat-market, St John's Lane. From her window much of the area could be seen by one of the characters, Clara Hewett: the 'black majesty' of St Pauls'; the 'surly bulk' of Newgate; 'the markets of Smithfield,

Bartholomew's Hospital, the tract of modern deformity, cleft by a gulf of railway, which spread between Clerkenwell Road and Charterhouse Street'. Clara was looking at the world she had first left, in order to become an actress, and to which she had then been forced to return when a rival disfigured her face with acid. 'Down in Farringdon Street the carts, waggons, vans, cabs, omnibuses, crossed and intermingled in a steaming splash-bath of mud; human beings reduced to their due paltriness, seemed to toil in exasperation along the strips of pavement, bound on errands, which were a mockery, driven automation-like by forces they neither understood nor could resist'.[48] Clara, of necessity, was aloof: most people saw this world at street level. It was a world full of activity and other people and noise. 'Three work girls had just entered and were buying cakes, which they began to eat at the counter. They were loud in gossip and laughter, and their voices rang like brass against brass'.[49] The book is full of details of this kind and plainly put contrasts: the working man's club behind the pub, the gas jets in the room upstairs, the smoke, the banjo, the 'nigger' entertainment, and on the other hand, the single, unfurnished, basement room to which John Hewett was forced to move his whole family. The myriad detail of Clerkenwell life was precisely observed and precisely stated. The invective and moral bombast that marred *Workers in the Dawn* have largely been eliminated. By the time Gissing came to write *The Nether World* he knew his subject inside out.

Because locality was in *The Nether World* described in its own terms, because it is not contrasted with any place, whether better or worse, and because Gissing relied less on the set-piece and more on the continuous description of streets and houses and incidents as they occurred, as they were seen by the characters in the course of the action, the element of satire that characterized *Demos* is here minimal, ordinary things being seen more simply for what they were. There is a mass of detail: the hat factory at which girls are paid piecework starvation wages; the filter factory; the burial club, from which a member absconds with all the funds; the flower factory; the alcoholism and the vinegar drinking; the counterfeit money trade; the pubs and the music halls and the working men's clubs and the debauches of public holidays. For once Gissing did not take away with one hand what he gave with the other. He did not undermine his own description with satire or aloof, moralistic comment. The fact of death was feared: John Hewett's feelings about the burial club are at the centre of existence. Rents, however low, had to be paid: the street oratory was about something immediate and real, by contrast with the idealistic socialism of the earlier novels. Illness for the poor was a multiple tragedy: Gissing showed it, without himself standing between the implication of poverty and his reader. To a much greater extent than before he allowed the facts to speak for themselves. He thus wrote one of his most convincing accounts of an area of London.

One of the high points of this account is Chapter XII. 'Io Saturnalia', in which the rival gangs from Clerkenwell went to Crystal Palace to celebrate August bank holiday. On the same day, in the morning, John Hewett's son, Robert, had married not Clem Peckover, whose desire for him was matched only by a more general ferocity of character, but Penelope (Pennyloaf) Candy, whose fate – after this celebration – was to continue her work as shirt-maker and share a room with her husband in Shooter's Hill.

> Everything was new except her boots – it had been decided that these only needed soleing. Her broad-brimmed hat of yellow straw was graced with the reddest feather purchasable in the City Road; she had a dolman of most fashionable cut, blue, lustrous; blue likewise was her dress, hung about with bows and streamers. And the gleaming ring on the scrubby small finger.[50]

On the same train travelled Jack Bartley, leader of the rival gang, with two pounds ten shillings to spend, so it was rumoured, and suitably resplendent: he 'wore a high hat – Bob had never owned one in his life – and about his neck was a tie of crimson; yellow was his waistcoat, even such a waistcoat as you may see in Pall Mall, and his walking stick had a nigger's head for handle'.[51] When they arrived at Crystal Palace, the vast throngs settled down to a day of British sport:

> Did you choose to shy sticks in the contest for cocoanuts [sic], behold your object was a wooden model of the treacherous Afghan or the base African. If you took up the mallet to smite upon a spring and make proof of how far you could send a ball flying upwards, your blow descended upon the head of some other recent foeman. Try your fist at the indicator of muscularity, and with zeal you smote full in the stomach of a guy made to represent a Russian.[52]

So the day passed in sport, idleness, drinking, until the sun set and the gas lamps within the Crystal Palace were lighted. By then the

> dancing has commenced; the players of violins, concertinas, and pennywhistles do a brisk trade among the groups eager for a rough-and-tumble valse; so do the pick pockets. Vigorous and varied is the jollity that occupies the external galleries, filling now in expectation of the fireworks; indescribable the mangled tumult that roars heavenwards. Girls linked by the half-dozen arm-in-arm leap along with shrieks like grotesque maenads; a rougher horseplay finds favour among the youths, occasionally leading to fisticuffs. Thick voices bellow in fragmentary chorus; from every side comes the yell, the cat-call, the ear-rending whistle; and as the bass, the never-ceasing accompaniment, sounds myriad-footed tramp,

tramp along the wooden flooring. A fight, a scene of bestial drunkenness, a tender whispering between two lovers, proceed concurrently in a space of five square yards. – About them glimmers the dawn of starlight.[53]

The long day ended with a fireworks display; love-making and drinking on the train home; an ambush and a street fight; and the sleep of utter exhaustion.

Gissing did not, unfortunately, resist the temptation to call Bank Holiday Monday a 'panacea', to suggest 'an entire change of economic conditions', or to indulge freely, much too freely, in the emotive words that marred some of his earlier work. He was still obsessed by 'vulgarity' of dress, 'animal' behaviour, and 'deformed' appearances. On the other hand, however uneasy a modern reader may be about Gissing's point of view, the novel as a whole and chapters like this one in particular have an immediacy and power consistent with Gissing's greater skill and the novel's more clearly defined structure.

The novel is about two families, the Snowdons and the Hewetts, and their friends. The very slow forward movement of the story is caused partly by the Hewett's poverty, which is so extreme that just to let life continue is next to impossible, partly by Clara Hewett's desire to escape from her family and from her whole 'background', partly by the appearance of Jane Snowdon's grandfather and his wealth which he secretly intended Jane would later use for 'good works', and partly by Sidney Kirkwood, who was the Grail or Mutimer of the story and who loved Clara, almost became engaged to Jane Snowdon and eventually, after her accident, took up with Clara again. This motive power is not considerable. Gissing did not resort to contrivance to the same extent as in *Demos* and *Thyrza*, so *The Nether World* lacks momentum.

In a sense, *The Nether World* was Gissing's acknowledgement that a fairly drawn, realistic depiction of urban life in all its detail was incompatible, at least for him, with a genuinely dramatic treatment of a psychological situation involving thinking people who are self-aware and self-critical. Since Gissing's interest in locality in *The Nether World* was fully extended – it is his most successful book in this respect and the closest, for instance, to Zola – it follows that the scope for psychological analysis was sharply reduced. As many critics have pointed out,[54] this was because Gissing was not really making a novel out of working-class attitudes. He was ascribing to some people in Clerkenwell a sensibility that most of their neighbours lacked. To do this successfully, without straining the reader's belief in the action, he had to reduce his basic equation about people to minimum terms. In the process of simplification, the inherent vulnerability of his attitude to character at this point in his career was exposed.

All the characters in the book occupied a secular, non-political, confined working world. All were part of a 'system' over which they have no control. Most of them lived at subsistence level. Nonetheless, one can see in retrospect that Gissing's attitude to his characters was an ethical one and that the dividing line between groups was very precisely drawn. In the environment of *The Nether World*, to be a human being meant self-control, restraint, resignation, honesty. Sidney Kirkwood represented this ideal just as Gilbert Grail had done in *Thyrza*. Kirkwood's idea of himself was based upon a cool assessment of what it was reasonable to expect from life (very little), and a determination not to lose self-respect by doing anything rash. To be out of control, passionate, bitter against fate, assertive but assertive without self-knowledge, was to be less than human. Not to know what was at stake, not to know the importance of restraint, was to be merely animal. In *The Nether World*, Bob Hewett, Jack Barclay, Clem Peckover, Mrs Peckover, Joseph Snowdon and Scawthorne were amoral. Ethical considerations were, for them, not real. Gissing's overall attitude to people was here being expressed in minimum terms, in the sense that for him it was not good conduct but emancipation that was at stake. Control, restraint and honesty were freedom from the corruption and meaninglessness of the world in which one found oneself. Jane Snowdon and Sidney Kirkwood represented this twilight, unassuming, unpassionate self-control as, for example, when they so easily came to an understanding about Kirkwood's engagement to Clara Hewett. Jane's friendliness to Kirkwood despite her bitter disappointment, her decency, her willingness to repress her own feelings and her preference for open talk give the understanding they reached its chacteristically Gissing flavour.

In fact the episode gives the novel its tone. It is representative of the way Gissing handled things at this point in his career, but it is also a good example of the point at which Gissing stopped short. Jane Snowdon's self-sacrifice has multiple critical significance. First, the sacrifice meant that a conflict between Jane and Clara was avoided. It is this avoidance of perfectly legitimate clashes of temperament and psychological interest that leaves Gissing open to criticism. Why should Jane not have pressed her own case? Why *should* she be nice to Kirkwood? And why should Gissing so arrange things that Kirkwood did not have to decide between two women, both of whom not only loved him but were known to love him? One cannot say that Gissing ought to have dealt with something he avoided, but the avoidance certainly contributed to the type of fiction to which Gissing at this stage devoted his energy. Secondly, Jane's self-sacrifice was consistent with Victorian concepts about women: her self-abasement was heroic. So Gissing got it both ways: everybody behaved 'properly', where 'properly' means as one would expect lower-class characters to behave if they have not taken leave of their senses, that is, as they would have to behave if the reader has to believe in them, if the fiction was to work, (unlike the Clem Peckovers and Bob Hewetts of the world!). This resignation to fate, to circumstances beyond one's control, and the concomitant belief in self-discipline as an instrument of personal freedom, consistent as they were both with Gissing's classical tastes and his preference for such English writers as Charlotte Brontë, meant that Gissing, as a creative novelist, had boxed himself in, since such complete resignation to circumstances was incompatible with an interestingly active plot development. For this reason the tone of the novel is neutral, low-key, lacking in passion.

Although Gissing had reached an imaginative impasse, his power as a writer had increased, and nowhere is this more evident than in his handling of Clara Hewett, who is cousin as it were to Carrie Mitchell in *Workers in the Dawn* and Ida Starr in *The Unclassed*. Clara Hewett was the person who would not accept her station in life, would not accept the pressures of environment, would not be 'reasonable' and would not, or could not, repress her own personality. She would not, because like Carrie Mitchell and Ida Starr, she was a sensual or, as Gissing would say, 'passionate' woman, for whom mental self-control was virtually meaningless. Gissing had difficulty with such characters. He lacked a language of an appropriate kind. It is as though he wanted sexual motivation to play a strong part in a novel but failed to find the means of achieving it. At any rate, when he described Clara Hewett, there was an odd mixture of the ancient Wakefield Gissing with the new, knowledgeable novelist. Here is one of several crucial passages:

> From that day the character of her suffering was altered; it became less womanly, it defied weakness and grew to a fever of fierce, unscrupulous rebellion. Whenever she thought of Sidney Kirkwood, the injury he was inflicting upon her pride rankled into bitter resentment, unsoftened by the despairing thought of self-subdual which had at times visited her sick weariness. She bore her degradations with the sullen indifference of one who is supported by the hope of a future revenge. This disease inherent in her being, that deadly outcome of social tyranny which perverts the generous elements of youth into mere seeds of destruction, developed day by day, blighting her heart, corrupting her moral sense, even setting

marks of evil upon the beauty of her countenance. A passionate desire of self-assertion familiarized her with projects, with ideas, which formerly she had glanced at only to dismiss as ignoble. In proportion as her bodily health failed, the worst possibilities of her character came into prominence. Like a creature that is beset by unrelenting forces, she summoned and surveyed all the crafty faculties lurking in the dark places of her nature; theoretically she had now accepted every debasing compact by which a woman can spite herself on the world's injustice. Self-assertion; to be no longer an unregarded atom in the mass of those who are born only to labour for others; to find play for the strength and the passion which, by no choice of her own, distinguished her from the tame slave. Sometimes in the silence of night she suffered from a dreadful need of crying aloud, of uttering her anguish in a scream like that of insanity. She stifled it only by crushing her face into the pillow until the hysterical fit had passed, and she lay like one dead.[55]

In this passage the 'degradations' are those things that Clara Hewett was forced to do even to live. They were her own menial occupations as seen by her, not the 'depravities' of *Workers in the Dawn* as seen by Gissing. When Gissing said that 'a disease inherent in her being' was 'corrupting her moral sense', he seems to have used his *Workers in the Dawn,* Wakefield, puritanical language. The implication was that an uncorrupted moral sense would condone 'self-subdual' and make 'unscrupulous rebellion' unnecessary. Yet this language – even in phrases like 'the worst possibilities of her character' – was inappropriate to the main drive of the paragraph, where the emphasis was on the idea that, despite herself, she felt compelled to self-assertion. She wanted to live. She had committed no crime, but her struggle against circumstance made her feel like a criminal. In the event, she did nothing worse than become an actress, entering in the process a more free or more lax moral world. Here is a crux. Gissing, preoccupied with the idea of emancipation, at once believed and did not believe in it. To liberate a person was consistent with his own unsatisfied desires and his knowledge that to live a person had to escape from his environment and his upbringing. Not to liberate a person was consistent, however, with both the demands of naturalism and with his deeply ingrained Wakefield puritanism. Clara Hewett is so powerfully drawn that Gissing's dilemma becomes all the more obvious.

When her career on the provincial stage was brought to an abrupt end, she returned to the twilight, restrained world of Clerkenwell, but the point being made was not that the morality of Jane Snowdon, for example, is preferable, but only that escape from the nether world is difficult. The novel does not impose a redemptive experience upon Clara Hewett, as might have been consistent with a moral view of the action. On the contrary, she retained her animal assertiveness, most particularly when reconciliation with the bland Sidney Kirkwood seemed possible. 'All her vital force setting in this wild current, her self-deception complete, she experienced the humility of supreme egoism – that state wherein self multiplies its claims to pity in passionate support of its demand for the object of desire'.[56] Eventually, marriage to Sidney Kirkwood – to the very person who most made a virtue of resignation to circumstance – was for Clara Hewett a final imprisonment. Life continued and there was no relief. The inherent pessimism of the novel had been successfully reinforced by Gissing's ability to create a character who personified emotional, sexual, human rebelliousness and who was denied by circumstance the possibility of living as a free human being.

Gissing's attitude to the matter was a chilly, dispassionate, realistic one. To explore the situation of *The Nether World* from Clara Hewett's point of view was still beyond, although only just beyond, Gissing's range of interests, and he in fact dismissed her before the reader even knew what was to become of her.

> Poor rebel heart! Beat for beat, in these moments it matched itself with that of the purest woman who surrenders to a despairing love. Had one charged her with insincerity, how vehemently would her conscience have declared against the outrage! Natures such as hers are as little to be judged by that which is conventionally the highest standard as by that which is the lowest. The tendencies which we agree to call good and bad became in her merely directions of a native force which was at all times in revolt against circumstance. Characters thus moulded may go far in achievement, but can never pass beyond the bounds of suffering. Never is the world their friend, nor the world's law. As often as our conventions give us the opportunity, we crush them out of being; they are noxious; they threaten the frame of society. Oftenest the crushing is done in such a way that the hapless creatures seem to have brought about their own destruction. Let us congratulate ourselves; in one way or other it is assured that they shall not trouble us long.[57]

How typical of the Gissing of the 1880s is this passage and passages like it. *The Nether World* as a whole is a sustained and often brilliant depiction of an aspect of contemporary English urban life. Few of Gissing's contemporaries, if any of them, knew in detail this brute consequence of industrialization and population growth. Few wrote about it as well as Gissing did in *The Nether World*. Yet Gissing in 1888 still tended to undermine what he so powerfully created. 'Let us congratulate ourselves', he says. The irony is superficial. If we do not congratulate ourselves, what then? What would be our view of 'hapless creatures' who 'threaten the frame of society' if they were not crushed like Clara Hewett? Having *shown* what Clerkenwell was like,

Gissing then asked a question about it which he could not himself answer, a question which some readers will see as detracting from the immediacy of the novel as a whole, and which other readers will want to have answered. Not only did he ask a question, but he also succeeded, positively, in creating a character in whom 'native force was in revolt against circumstance'. From the fact that Clara Hewett was in fact forced back into the 'frame of society', albeit in one of its least agreeable locations, it is obvious that Gissing's emphasis was still that of the naturalist who looked at people in their social organizations and came to pessimistic conclusions about them. In one sense, it says a lot for Gissing that in these three novels, *Demos*, *Thyrza* and *The Nether World*, he had succeeded in exploring the possibilities of this type of naturalism so thoroughly. And *The Nether World* is after all one of the most powerful urban novels written in the nineteenth century. On the other hand, Gissing was clearly not committed to naturalism entirely. Indeed, the characters who gave him most trouble in the 1880s, because they did not fit into the overall world scheme of the social realist, were the ones he looked at later when he was no longer preoccupied with place. And the breakthrough, the release from naturalism, occurs in *The Emancipated*, *New Grub Street* and *Born in Exile*.

5
The Emancipated and *New Grub Street*

THE winter of 1888–9 was the first long period Gissing had spent away from England since he had returned from North America about ten years earlier. It is not too much to say that his going to Italy was the liberating experience which allowed him to take stock of the position he had reached as a novelist. It was the ancient history associated with the Latin classics that attracted him, convert that he was to the belief in a culture necessarily detached from the everyday. As he absorbed himself in the physical experiences of the tourist and saw for the first time the things he had read about, as his letters partly and the diary largely attest,[1] he at the same time reassessed the position to which he had brought himself as a novelist. Whatever the internal process, he from now on moved away from naturalism in its austerest form and became more interested in the psychological.

Italy was a literary experience. The slums of Naples did not become the equivalent of the slums of London. In fact, Gissing recorded in his diary that his attitude changed as soon as he crossed the Channel. Social conscience was either never aroused or was else appeased by the immensely satisfying knowledge (for him) that, according to the guide books, he saw the landscape as Virgil had seen it. A historical continuity that seemed to be visible in Italian towns and in the archaeological sites within range of his donkey cart distracted him from the personal rootlessness he had written about in England – the rootlessness that he knew himself and had observed in the new, rapidly growing, English industrial cities, particularly London. Because of his comprehensive knowledge of Latin literature and because his reasonably fluent Italian had been learnt through books (he reported difficulty with dialects in Naples!) it was scarcely possible that he would have taken anything other than a literary view of what he saw. He was one of the most exclusively literary men alive. A single quotation chosen from many examples will illustrate how he thought. Halfway through the winter, he wrote home to Nelly:

> The Tiber is an old friend – My life is richer a thousand times – aye, a million times, – than six months ago. Now I can talk with any man as an equal, for I am no longer ignorant of the best things the world contains. – It only now remains for me to go to Greece, & a matter of £50 or £60 will at any time manage that. Then I shall have all the ground work of education. The education itself must be the work of the rest of my life.[2]

Italy was a safe place for Gissing because he *could* take a literary view and did not have to worry about the people around him. Since they regarded him as in fact a foreigner, his private feeling of being permanently alienated was reduced in importance. At least temporarily. He was not an alien in an ordinary sense, so that being educated or 'cultured' did not need explanation. Like many Englishmen before and since, he found it easier to be himself when away from England. He could be more English. The intellectual snobbery of the last sentence of the letter just quoted, for example, was a private sentiment and had no direct influence on his relations with other people. Since Gissing's whole attitude to literature was grounded in the classics, there was no anomaly in his thinking about himself as a literary man in Naples: that was the right place for a man of his kind, at least for as long as he confined himself to ruins and monuments. Of course, when Gissing said that he could talk with 'any man as an equal', he really meant that there were only a few men who *were* his equal, as far as a literary education was concerned, and that he did not know very many of them. Education had become an end in itself and from this point on he was to confess his inadequacy in practical matters with increasing openness and frequency.

His journeys, then, and particularly his first journey in the winter of 1888–9, confirmed in him that he had the right to be himself. There were no revelations. He did not meet people who profoundly affected his life. Rather, he returned to England with increased confidence, knowing that he could hold his own amongst his intellectual peers and fairly certain that he could continue to write. The nature of this confidence shows most of all in a letter Gissing wrote to his sister in the course of an argument about *The Emancipated*. She had criticized the book because she read it as an attack on religion and religious values and because, tellingly, she thought Miriam Baske, the principal woman character, was a portrait of herself. It is worth quoting this important letter extensively:

> It does not surprise me that the spirit of the book is distasteful to you, but I certainly am rather surprised that you find *nothing* to like in it. The general opinion here is that the book makes a great advance on my others.

I myself think that it is the best yet in style & characterization.

Well, you see, we look at these matters, not only from different, but from opposing, points of view. There is no use in expressing oneself harshly; that helps nothing. But the fact is, of course, that my intellectual & moral world have scarcely one point in common with that wherein you live. I am afraid you do not even suspect how true this is. The books I read, & the people with whom I converse, have a view of life which to you is either meaningless, or else highly repugnant; & we, on the other hand, find it impossible to accept a single one of the positions which to you are axiomatic, indisputable.

The one thing that grieves me is the thought that, owing to lack of experience, you imagine me singular in my way of thinking. Whereas the fact is that I only represent the prevalent views of our day. You do not know that, because you are so carefully shut in on every hand; so much so, that you will even shake your head in incredulity at what I say. Yet it is so simple a truth that I wonder at having to state it.

Some day perhaps your opportunities will increase, & then, like Miriam, you will be amazed to find people of admirable personal qualities holding views which seem to you utterly incompatible with such respectability.

In very deed, there is a satiric vein in 'The Emancipated' which, to those conservatives who understand it, will make the book rather acceptable than otherwise. (This you evidently missed.) It comes of the fact that I am able to look at both sides, & to laugh at the weaknesses of both. This is why the conservative organs have frequently spoken of me as if I were of their party. The uncompromising party of radicalism still regard me with doubt; I do not go far enough for them, or at all events do not speak with sufficient intolerance. Now these things being recognized facts, it is a little painful to me that *you* should be less discerning than critics who are strangers to me.

But no, you will not like my future books. I have been waiting until my position with the publishers enabled me to write with freedom. Even you must recognize that hypocrisy in literature, however mild, is not admirable. My part is with the men & women who are clearing the ground of systems that have had their day & have crumbled into obstructive ruin. To those who live in quiet corners of the earth, where those systems still seem solid edifices, & who know nothing of the true state of things in the greater part of the world, we seem mere reckless destroyers. This is an inevitable misconception. Short of ceasing altogether to write, I have no choice but to present myself before your imagination in this distorted fashion.

To be sure, the mistake is for you to read *my* books without at the same time reading other books of the day. Therefore I seem to you isolated.[3]

It will be gathered from these brief but bluntly and confidently written remarks that Gissing's journey to Italy was an event of vast personal importance for him, but that it did not in itself constitute a change of direction. When he returned to England in March 1889 he corrected the proofs of *The Nether World*. During the summer which followed he wrote *The Emancipated*. The two novels that are discussed in this chapter are natural continuations of, and improvements on, what Gissing had been doing before. They are also terminations. In *The Emancipated* he returns once again to the theme of personal emancipation by means of slow intellectual growth and self-education. At least this is true to the extent that the book is written from the point of view of Miriam Baske, who resembles that long line of women characters back to the Brontës whose quietly meditated perceptions permit the novelist to write about the less perceptive as well. Miriam Baske is one of Gissing's most important characters because she represents his cold-headed assessment of what the public would accept. A carefully charted and well-explained process of liberation might be acceptable, and this is how Gissing wrote the book, as though to anticipate the later criticisms of his sister. He never again did quite so much explaining! In *New Grub Street* he returned to the treatment of personal relationships imagined within a larger but clearly delineated social context. In several interesting ways *New Grub Street* is a transitional novel. It was written from a previously rejected draft which he took up one summer when he was uncertain about what to do next; years later he revised it drastically. The version that was published in 1890 thus has strong links with the past and yet prefigures those crisply written, later novels of the 1890s, when Gissing gave a book a tighter structure and wrote less evasively. The revised *New Grub Street* was one of that later group. When he first wrote the novel, however, he was still experimenting with the artistic disposition of thinking characters within a social setting that isolated them. The passages that he later eliminated show the point in his career he had reached. When he had published *The Emancipated* and *New Grub Street* a stage of his career was over. He could not simply re-use the old material for novel after novel as these books, in different ways, show. *Born in Exile* is a different matter. It is in that extremely interesting novel that a real shift occurs – a development that will be discussed in chapter 6.

Gissing mentioned *The Emancipated*, which was at first called 'The Puritan', in letters both to his family and to Bertz in February 1889,[4] began to think about it seriously when he returned to England in March and then, as both the diary and the letters confirm, wrote it rapidly in ten weeks between 3 June and 13 August. His sense that something of a problem had been solved, that he had at last written a novel on one of his own themes that was not calculated to offend anyone, led to his taking it to Bentley on the day he finished it, as though to compensate in some way for the earlier rejection of 'Mrs Grundy's Enemies'. He was so confident that he asked for £250 and so satisfied with the solutions represented by the novel that he accepted Bentley's terms: an advance of £150, a further £50 if 850 copies were sold, and yet another £50 if a thousand were sold. 'This is fair enough,' he told Bertz. 'Hope the book will be published about the end of the year. I intend at present to leave England as soon as proofs are finished. I shall probably go to Marseilles, and then by sea to Athens'.[5]

The Emancipated is a deliberately plotted, deliberately structured novel in which Gissing is at pains to devise a situation in which a character can *reasonably* or plausibly escape the rigid and confining moral system prevalent in Victorian England. The old idea of a mind escaping from a restrictive, Puritan morality by discovering the significance of art Gissing now unfolds, yet once again, in an Italian setting. No one was likely to be upset by such things happening in Italy. And since Miriam Baske's initial puritanism was given an extreme, north of England, Methodistic character, no one was likely to be upset, either, by her final rejection of it. Furthermore, Miriam's 'legitimate' emancipation, achieved by means of a growing awareness of the cultural significance of Italian art, is contrasted with the runaway, 'irresponsible' elopement of the other principal woman character, Cecily Doran. No reader needed to doubt the high seriousness of the contrast.

A situation is contrived in which a gruff, bohemian bachelor, a moderately successful though unfashionable painter called Mallard *seems* unsuited for matrimony either because he has repressed his infatuation for his ward, Cecily Doran, and is therefore resigned to a solitary life or because, in his own estimation, he knew himself to be vastly superior to everyone else (including, of course, people he had never met – such is the advantage of superiority!), superior in culture, education and knowledge of the world, and morally superior, in that his 'humanitarian' ethic was untainted by silliness on the one side, or dogmatic puritanism on the other. His opposite number, soul mate or sexual opponent, Miriam Baske, a widow from Lancashire of Methodist upbringing, whose character was not at the beginning of the novel 'complicated' by any 'strain of modern humanitarianism', *seems* to be so rigid in her views, so committed to dogma, so ignorant and so immature (particularly by comparison with Cecily Doran whom Gissing said maliciously was more emancipated even than a young lady from Girton), that she too was unsuited to matrimony as indeed she was unsuited to anything. This 'situation' is sustained by a plot in which Mallard seems to obstruct the marriage of his young ward, Cecily Doran, to the rakish Reuben Elgar because of self-interest and in which, much later in the novel when Cecily's marriage to Elgar has broken down, is thought to have gone off with Cecily after she has left her home. The reader is never in doubt that Mallard's infatuation for Cecily was of the most superficial kind, that he was a person of complete personal integrity, though without religious belief, and indeed that, to the extent that he became involved in Cecily's affairs at all, he behaved with the utmost propriety. Gissing in fact allowed himself a somewhat low-key, romantic plot, so that Miriam Baske would have time to mature.

Miriam's slow maturing is the result of Italy, of her reading – Cecily once discovers her reading Dante *on a Sunday*! – and of Mallard's gruff instruction on sculpture and painting. Mrs Baske, like Gissing, was made to think about the problem of the fig leaf, then much in evidence. At the beginning of the book it was her 'nature to distrust the beautiful'. In Volume III she can tell Mallard: 'You have given me a new way of looking at a thing; and I have to think'.[6] One could say that Miriam Baske was a character conceived entirely within the terms of Matthew Arnold's *Culture and Anarchy* and *Literature and Dogma*. From Mallard she learns to associate the Italian landscape with classical literature, to see the landscape for its own sake, to read for a new type of instruction and (in the sternest of tests!) to abandon prudery when studying statues. They visit museums and galleries together. She becomes more and more troubled by the fact that she cannot tell her friends of the change within her. She grows physically stronger and proves this to herself by being prepared to walk home from a museum. Mallard shows Miriam that pleasure generally, but particularly pleasure in art, is not itself corrupt – she becomes free to feel, enjoy, think for herself – but nonetheless, so determined is Gissing to arrive at an acceptable, publishable formulation, an essential chapter to appease the right has the rather grim title of 'Learning and Teaching'.

Individual scenes in *The Emancipated* are more relaxed, bland, less bitter, satirical or ironical than many in earlier books, and certainly different from similar scenes in *New Grub Street*. The novel has an overall structure, though, which depends upon a central, controlling irony. This is that Cecily Doran, who appears to be emancipated, who is already knowledgeable and free when the story begins, and who elopes with Reuben Elgar because by upbringing she does not accept the conventions that stand in their way, in fact makes a mistake and only discovers too late her husband's fundamental depravity and unsteadiness, while Miriam Baske who, during the course of the book, succeeds in freeing herself from convention ends by making an entirely 'proper', conventional marriage with Mallard. When Gissing said in his letter to his sister that he was 'able to look at both sides, & to laugh at the weaknesses of both', he meant that he did not associate himself with the way his characters behaved in the predicaments he had created for them. In these years Gissing frequently fretted about the possibility the reader might misunderstand his satire. What he seems to have meant by this was that the novels involved a social critique even after the specifically didactic period of the mid-eighties, though it was a critique less in the didactic intrusions of the narrator than in the very conception and structure of the novel. In *The Emancipated* he walked the fine line between satire that would have destroyed the book by making the characters seem mere manipulations and the satire that was compatible with the structure of the plot. In contrast, for example, to the vivid depiction of the breakdown of Cecily Doran's marriage, a breakdown in which an individual's right of self-determination is emphasized, Gissing has Miriam submit to what, at least nowadays, a century later, seems Mallard's patronizing male attitudes. In the scene in which they become engaged, she accepts his strictures about her character, does some sewing for him, and makes tea. Gissing understood, of course, that real emancipation did not involve actual flight and manifest disruption, but rather occurred within the character in a way that made day by day activity – the activity that was once a bother – irrelevant. So Miriam submits freely, secure in the knowledge that she knows she did not have before. Gissing manages this successfully, leaving the sexual emancipation so remotely implied that no reader could be offended, and the success, from the novel writing point of view, is not reduced even if the reader realizes Gissing must have derived sardonic pleasure from the tactic of allowing this newly-liberated woman, now deliciously independent in her own mind from moral convention, to submit after all to a conventional Victorian marriage, obedient and submissive to her husband, serving him, accepting his opinions, taking instruction from him and making a married life with him entirely within the limits of his ideas and desires. The novel has a Jamesian quality to it, in the play of irony within a balanced structure involving two pairs of characters. In fact it is such a remarkable advance on his earlier work that one regrets it has rarely been widely available.[7]

The even more important novel, *New Grub Street*, was also created securely within the confines of his imaginative world as it existed in the autumn of 1890. Admittedly the ostensible subject, the private life of the literary hack, had not been used before. On the other hand, there was not much in the book that would surprise a reader already familiar with three or four of the earlier novels. With the possible exception of Jasper Milvain, the characters are rather familiar. Yet another light-weight plot is made to depend upon the contrivance of a will which at a certain point – one cannot even say a crucial point – changes their fortunes. Yet again the contrivance of the plot does not matter very much. The balance between the increasing misfortune of some characters (Reardon, Biffin and Mr Yule), and the increasing good fortune of others (Milvain, Milvain's sisters, Whelpdale and, in a sense, Amy Reardon) is reminiscent of those self-compensating devices in earlier novels, as for example the survival of Hubert Eldon in *Demos*, by which Gissing habitually took the sting out of satire and social protest.

Gissing had taught himself to write a three-decker novel at great speed. This one he seems to have written rapidly in the autumn of 1890, after meeting Edith Underwood, who was to become his second wife, but before giving up the lease of his London flat so that he could move to Exeter. In his notebook he recorded that the book was written between 6 October and 6 December. Entries in the diary confirm this. What Gissing actually meant was that the novel, as published, was written during this brief, two-month period, for in a more general sense the book was already in his mind in the spring of 1890 and indeed probably existed as an early draft.[8] For financial reasons, particularly if he were to marry Edith Underwood, Gissing was obliged to write and get published a novel of some kind that winter.

Back in London after the previous year's extended trip abroad (after finishing *The Emancipated* he had gone once again to Italy and then to Greece), he suffered from debilitating fits of loneliness and despair. He had travelled too far intellectually and as an artist and knew too much for him to have any real links with his own family. He knew many more people in London than in his early days a decade earlier but none of them was a close friend. He had written himself out: further novels of the same kind as *Demos* and *The Nether World* would have been boringly repetitive. He was lonely but also restless – lonely because he had lived by himself for seven or eight years, was unmarried and aged thirty-two, an age at which he ought to have been able to relax, he thought, and enjoy his accomplishments, and restless because, having completed the first essential journeys to Italy and Greece, he found it difficult to return, simply, to his old London life. As he told Bertz: '*New Grub Street* is dull and unhappy; the wonder is that I succeeded in writing any book at all during those weeks of uttermost misery'.[9] Though he told Algernon that when correcting proof he was 'astounded' to find how well it read, he continued to associate the novel with the severe depression he had experienced while writing it. 'Writing it, I believed it trash', he told his sister, Ellen, 'for it was wrung page by page, from a sluggish and tormented brain'.[10] To Bertz, in the same month, that is April 1891, he adopted the same tone: 'I wrote it in utter prostration of spirit: no book of mine was regarded so hopelessly in the production'.[11] Between these letters and the writing of *New Grub Street*, Gissing had moved to Exeter, re-married, and started a new, more interesting novel. It is not surprising, therefore, that looking back he should have regarded the second part of 1890 as one of the low points of his life. Nor is it surprising that, when he revised the novel for Gabrielle Fleury's translation into French some years later, he was able to regard it with a far greater detachment.

New Grub Street is better known and more written about than the other novels in this first half of Gissing's career.[12] In it, he depicts a small group of hacks, literary idealists, unsuccessful writers of fiction, littérateurs, and critics, who live partly in the British Museum reading room, partly on the fringes of literary London, whether for mercenary or for idealistic reasons eking out a living as best they can. In one way or another they are all part of the 'literary machine' which, according to Jasper Milvain, had made literature a trade – a fact which he thought should be acknowledged frankly – and which according to John Yule, a business man, was 'ruining the country'. They manage as best they can. Alfred Yule, 'a battered man of letters', whose constitution has been ruined by a sedentary life, late nights, and the bitterness of literary in-fighting, aspires to be the editor of a critical journal. Biffin, connoisseur in bread and dripping, copes by taking pupils at sixpence a time while he writes his novel of 'absolute realism in the sphere of the ignobly decent', risking his life on the roof tops during a house fire to save his manuscript but later committing suicide. Whelpdale, on the other hand, leads – eventually with success – an entrepreneurial life in the world of fringe literature and women's magazines. And there are others – though not too many, for the day by day life of minor literary figures is of limited interest.

Consistent with the naturalist mode he had adopted in books like *The Nether World* is his handling of the literary idealism of one of the main characters, Edwin Reardon. Gissing treats his literary idealist in exactly the same way as he earlier treated religious, social and political idealists. His stance has not altered: he has simply taken a new subject. Gissing's own attitudes, preferences and experiences have little to do with this, since Edwin Reardon suffers the same fate as other romantics, his happening to be a writer being of secondary importance. If a reader identifies with Reardon, it is because he misunderstands the main drift of the novel in which Reardon, having enjoyed an initial success, attempts to earn a living with his pen and fails. His failure is not presented as in itself surprising. Nor is it something which any sensible man would have expected, unless he knew Reardon. His failure happens and Gissing shows how it happens. He does so, however, without encouraging the reader to think that a writer *ought* to be an inspired, Byronic, independent, non-mechanical creature, or that Reardon's failure was the direct result of the circumstances of his life. Reardon does not fail because literature had become a trade or because something outside himself prevented his writing a masterpiece. He fails because of himself. He is just one part of the larger scene that Gissing is describing.

Gissing adopted a fairly sharp tone when he wrote to his sister on this subject:

> As for your comments on the philosophical tone of the book, well, it is too late for me to change my views of the universe. I do not dogmatize, remember; my ideas are negative, & on the whole I confine myself to giving pictures of life as it looks to my observation. The outlook, certainly, is not very cheerful; impossible for me to see the world in a rosy light. At the best it looks to me only not-intolerable. As for human aspirations, I know not their meaning, & can conceive no credible explanation – even as I am unable to understand what is called the instinct of animals. The problem does not trouble me, either; I have reached the stage at which one is content to be ignorant. The world is to me mere phenomenon (which literally means that which *appears*) & I study it as I do a work of art – but without reflecting on its origin.[13]

In other words, as novelist he regarded himself as a neutral observer. At least this was the theory. There is no reason to be surprised, really, that it took Gissing a number of years to develop the art that would allow the theory to be put into practice.

The novel is made to depend upon a straightforward but sharply drawn contrast between Reardon, a type of literary failure, and Jasper Milvain, a type of literary success. Jasper called Reardon 'the old type of unpractical artist' and said, correctly, that 'in favourable circumstances he might write a fairly good book once every two or three years'.[14] Reardon's friend, Biffin, called him 'a rabid idealist'.[15] These three, Reardon, Milvain and Biffin, were old friends, intellectual friends whose meetings were unaffected by feelings of class or status, just like similar groups which appear in the other novels. They pass the Gissing test, as it were, with flying colours: they are brainy but penniless, they eat bread and cheese or bread and dripping during their long evenings, and they are expert in classical metres. What binds them is their intellect, interest in literature, and personal honesty. And they *are* bound: it is Biffin who helps Reardon when the need arises, while despite the sharp contrast drawn between Reardon and Milvain and despite their different attitudes to literature they themselves remain close friends. Few novelists match Gissing in the portrayal of adult, male friendship. It is a standard feature of his novels and here treated well, without being overdone. Reardon and Milvain are not presented as rivals, as people in conflict with each other, because of their different literary attitudes. They are friends who are not immediately concerned with such differences. It is extremely important to notice that, when Reardon begins to go downhill, his state of mind is referred to more in clinical than in moral or tragic terms. He is said to have a 'nervous disease'. Jasper in fact refers to his 'nervous illness'[16] while even Biffin tells him that he is 'depressed and anaemic'.[17] In short, Reardon is an intelligent, educated or 'cultured' man who has a nervous breakdown when he fails to earn his living with the pen, in the process alienating his wife, Amy, who cannot accept either the poverty itself or the agonies of self-justification and recrimination that go with it. It is not suggested by *New Grub Street* that Reardon deserved to earn a living by writing his kind of book, only that it was a sad business when he failed. At last Gissing is avoiding those intrusive judgements that marred earlier novels.

Jasper Milvain, on the other hand, is presented as 'an alarmingly modern young man' who acknowledges frankly – too frankly for the taste of some – that 'to please the vulgar you must, one way or another, incarnate the genius of vulgarity'.[18] Jasper accepts the world as he finds it, knows he is not a genius and tries to do the best that is possible for himself under the circumstances. Though an egoist unfettered by moral or religious principles, and unaware of laws of nature that would incline him to sacrifice himself for the benefit of others, he is not amoral. Rather, he adopts a limited morality appropriate to the world in which he finds himself. In that well-written chapter entitled 'Jasper's Magnanimity' he tells Marian how he feels:

> My aim is to have easy command of all the pleasures desired by the cultivated man. I want to live among beautiful things, and never to be troubled by a thought of vulgar difficulties. I want to travel and enrich my

mind in foreign countries. I want to associate on equal terms with refined and interesting people. I want to be known, to be familiarly referred to, to feel when I enter a room that people regard me with some curiosity.[19]

In England, in the middle of the twentieth century, these remarks have a somewhat familiar ring. In passing, one can say as well that, while it is correct to insist that the literary convention adopted by Gissing precludes the identification of author with character, Gissing himself could much more easily have shared the ideas attributed to Milvain than those expressed by Reardon. Milvain is similarly outspoken (to Whelpdale) on the subject of love and marriage:

I haven't much faith in marrying for love, as you know. What's more, I believe it's the very rarest thing for people to be in love with each other. Reardon and his wife perhaps were an instance; perhaps – I'm not quite sure about *her*. As a rule, marriage is the result of a mild preference, encouraged by circumstances, and deliberately heightened into strong sexual feeling. You, of all men, know well enough that the same kind of feeling could be produced for almost any woman who wasn't repulsive.[20]

These remarks of Milvain's are not part of an argument. They come out in the course of friendly banter with Whelpdale, who is someone habitually, carelessly, but persistently in love. No wonder Gissing's family in Wakefield was outraged yet again.

In most of these early novels Gissing has examined a group of men and women – the unclassed, alienated, dispossessed – putting the relations between them under stress and watching the consequences. The setting is important, but not overwhelmingly so. It has been argued already that the strong political element in *Demos* is not enough to make it a political novel; the educational element in *Thyrza*, though important, is not sufficient to make *Thyrza* a novel *about* education. In the same way, *New Grub Street* is not *about* publishing. In point of fact the reader is given very little information about the state of the publishing 'industry' in 1890. There are not any publishers, newspaper owners, publisher's readers or indeed anyone connected with a publishing house in the novel. Reardon's relations with his publisher or with his publisher's readers are not examined. Nor are publishing houses part of the setting of the novel. Small flats and claustrophobic sitting rooms are the setting for the action, as is consistent with Gissing's realist procedures. The story does not concern in any way, even for purposes of contrast, successful authors, great authors or established authors, and since, within the novel, it is not suggested that the world of Milvain and Reardon is *the* literary world, one is left only with the certainty that Gissing has made a portrait of New Grub Street, that is, the periphery or twilight zone of a literary universe. How people lived in such circumstances is what interested Gissing. What they wanted is another question. The prevailing theme to Gissing's early work is in this novel expressed by Jasper and Amy after their marriage:

> 'Happiness is the nurse of virtue'.
> 'And independence the root of happiness'.
> 'True. "The glorious privilege of being independent" – yes, Burns understood the matter'.[21]

If the novel can be considered from Jasper Milvain's point of view, not Reardon's it can be seen immediately that Gissing has returned to the situation that obsessed him: a triangular situation in which one man is loved by two women. Marian Yule is a more sophisticated, cultured, emancipated Helen Norman. She is the same type of person though described with less emotion, greater clinical attention. She had short hair, which Jasper was good enough to pretend he liked, though without deceiving her. Her 'head and neck were admirably formed'.[22] Jasper, himself, at the beginning of the novel, was characteristically blunt.

> A fright! Not at all. A good example of the modern literary girl. I suppose you have the oldest-fashioned ideas of such people. No, I rather liked the look of her. *Simpatica*, I should think, as that ass Whelpdale would say. A very delicate, pure complexion, though morbid; nice eyes; figure not spoilt yet.[23]

Like Miriam in *The Emancipated*, she gradually learns to think for herself, though unaggressively. (How shattered the Gissing men would have been had they encountered a genuinely aggressive feminine intellect!) The physical description of the other woman in the novel, Amy Reardon, aged twenty-two, is not of the kind that one would expect in a romance. Her 'shoulders seemed rather broad in proportion to her waist and the part of her body below it'; she had the superior, masculine air of a young boy; her mouth and lips were 'not reassuring to anyone who had counted upon her for facile humour'; and though she had a 'magnificently clear-cut bust', her manner was controlled. 'The atmosphere was cold; ruddiness would have been quite out of place on her cheeks, and a flush must have been the rarest thing there'.[24] Thus there is a contrast between the repressed romantic, Marian Yule, who imagines herself marrying Jasper the first day she meets him, and the cool Amy, who without having been unfaithful to her husband, nonetheless finds it convenient to marry again after his death.

Of course, the novel *cannot* be seen merely from the point of view of one of the characters, especially because it is their unheroic coexistence with each other that Gissing depicts. He does this without much pity, perhaps remorselessly. Because Gissing denied his characters, if denied is the right word, any creed, or independent set of values, or political belief, and because his interest, as novelist, was in secular relationships, person to person, it follows – as has been mentioned earlier in this book – firstly that in a secular ethic the characters themselves will place a high premium upon directness, personal honesty, straight dealing and so forth (since they do not believe in anything else) and secondly that these limited, secular values will be most seriously challenged, not by offences against traditional, social morality (they would not necessarily care about that at all) but by acts of bad faith by which the characters in some way let each other down or let themselves down. Thus, in the context of *New Grub Street*, Reardon does not expect Amy to leave him because he is a failure. Indeed, he wants or needs her all the more as he fails and uses his failure, psychologically, as a means by which he can express his desire. But the book itself, if one can put it in this way, does not expect her to stay with him. Similarly, Jasper's proposal to someone else when he is already tacitly engaged to Marian is an act of bad faith of a type that is consistent with the secular ethic that informs *New Grub Street* as a whole. The familiar phrase from Sartre is used deliberately here, not to suggest that Gissing was ahead of his time, (shaky logic at the best of times) but to make clear that Reardon, Milvain, Amy Reardon and Marian Yule are not being 'judged' by the author, any more than by themselves, in the light of a socially accepted and established morality. 'The world is to me mere phenomenon . . . and I study it as I do a work of art'.

The problem that faced Gissing as he wrote a novel like *New Grub Street* can be expressed in very simple theoretical terms. He chose to write about urban subjects without imposing upon them a moral, political, even public structure. His characters rarely do anything that is of public consequence. Nothing of public consequence happens to them. Indeed they are almost by definition outside society. This being the case it is their relationships with each other that are important. Yet a novelist who wishes to examine personal relationships which are not in the realm of public life is brought inevitably to the two crucial and related aspects of such relationships, the psychological and the sexual. Gissing, in these novels, demonstrated that he perfectly understood the matter, although to find ways of writing about the inter-relationship of the sexual and the psychological was naturally difficult. He also understood that the implied critique of normal social relationships, vaguely trusted but desperately needed as they were, would render the creation of acceptable fiction more difficult, because he had to convince his reader that his unusual account of how people behaved was really an accurate account, in fact the only account possible. The art of achieving this was unfamiliar, in fact alien.

In *New Grub Street* convention is flouted. Jasper changes his lodgings so that he will have an extra room in which he can meet Marian. Marian, for her part, is too proud to allow herself to think that living freely, in this case feeling free to meet Jasper, necessarily meant a relaxation of moral standards. So they do meet each other. This, for many of Gissing's readers, was rebellious enough. In order to exploit this situation Gissing had recourse to convenient and perfectly intelligible Victorian euphemisms, partly because there were limits beyond which, as he once complained to Hardy, he did not dare openly go and partly, no doubt, because he literally lacked a non-euphemistic language that would have served him as well. He was for practical purposes pre-Freud. He was not a D. H. Lawrence. Genuine personal emancipation ought to have included sexual emancipation and many Gissing characters knew this. Finding a way to put it on the page was a different matter, as the following example demonstrates. It is taken from the crucial scene between Jasper Milvain and Marian Yule which ends Volume II.

> The emotional current which had passed from her flesh to his whilst their hands were linked made him incapable of standing aloof from her. He saw that her face and neck were warmer hued, and her beauty became more desirable to him than ever yet.
>
> 'You are more to me than anything else in the compass of life!' he exclaimed, again pressing forward. 'I think of nothing but you – you yourself – my beautiful, gentle, thoughtful Marian!'
>
> His arm captured her, and she did not resist. A sob, then a strange little laugh, betrayed the passion that was at length unfolded in her.
>
> 'Do you love me, Marian?'
>
> 'I love you'.
>
> And there followed the antiphony of ardour that finds its first utterance – a subdued music, often interrupted, ever returning upon the same rich note.
>
> Marian closed her eyes and abandoned herself to the luxury of the dream. It was her first complete escape from the world of intellectual routine, her first taste of life. All the pedantry of her daily toil slipped away like a cumbrous garment; she was clad only in her womanhood. Once or twice a shudder of strange self-consciousness went through her, and she felt guilty, immodest; but upon that sensation followed a surge of passionate joy, obliterating memory and forethought.
>
> 'How shall I see you?' Jasper asked at length. 'where can we meet?'[25]

Although it was 'with a sense of relief that Jasper had passed from dithyrambs' (a phrase that Gissing must have borrowed from Meredith), and although they talked cooly about whether or not Jasper should speak to Marian's father, when they embraced again 'her touch had the same effect as before. His blood warmed again, and he pressed her to his side, stroking her hair and kissing her forehead'. Gissing here depicts her release from the daily toil of work for her father, a release which is both psychological and sexual, and at the same time depicts Jasper's rapid callousness, energy, and withdrawal, for when she 'at length attired herself, and they left the house together', Jasper walked quickly away 'in profound meditation'. Jasper's 'affair' with Marian is easier to accept and understand if it is straightforwardly sexual (though not, of course, inhuman because of that) and such an interpretation is in accord with Gissing's earlier treatment of other 'sensual' women. He has freed himself from the Victorian sexual ethic, but he has not freed himself from Victorian, sexual euphemism, and phrases like 'her beauty' and the 'antiphony of ardour' and 'the luxury of the dream' in one sense represent the extent to which he was writing a type of novel for which the public was only partly prepared.

Equally important is Chapter ix, the chapter called 'The Last Resource', in which Amy and Edwin Reardon express the extent to which they have been separated from each other because of Reardon's inability to write and to a lesser extent because of their child. This is actually a strong scene, certainly by comparison with those scenes in earlier novels in which the honesties and dishonesties of direct confrontation are avoided. Here Gissing creates dialogue which expresses the direct, immediate stress of personal crisis, the very thing that he shirked, for example, in *Thryza*. This directness allows him to convey the mixture of feeling the characters experience, particularly in the case of Reardon whose desire for Amy increases as she drifts coldly away from him.

> Amy had abandoned too soon the caresses of their ardent time; she was absorbed in her maternity, and thought it enough to be her husband's friend. Ashamed to make appeal directly for the tenderness she no longer offered, he accused her of utter indifference, of abandoning him and all but betraying him, that in self-defiance she might show what really was in her heart.
> But Amy made no movement towards him.[26]

On the contrary she leaves him to return to her parents' home, where Gissing shows her enjoying the privacy of a locked bedroom and the luxury of clean sheets. The half moral, half psychological word 'ashamed' in this passage is characteristic of Gissing. Reardon has a sexual need that his wife refuses to satisfy. Why should Reardon be 'ashamed'? But despite the retention of the slightly moral word, the rest of the sentence shows that the emphasis is psychological, that we are not here concerned with rights and wrongs, but with the desires and dependencies and disengagements of two individuals.

Gissing did his best to prepare for Amy Reardon's change of heart, by showing that Reardon was aware of the fact she was attracted by 'Milvain's energy and promise of success' and that she in turn was aware of her husband's jealously and fear. Though it must be admitted that he brings the situation to a close in a rather facile way by means of Reardon's death, the emphasis in *New Grub Street* is much less on the mere contrivance which brings people together or holds them apart and much more on the tangle of thoughts and emotions that constitute their relationship. To the extent that Gissing succeeded in creating a personal relationship of genuine psychological depth, *New Grub Street* is a great advance on the novels which preceded it.

All this is seen much more clearly when one considers the way in which he revised the book. If Gissing's revision of *New Grub Street* for Gabrielle Fleury's translation into French had been an isolated phenomenon, it would naturally still have considerable interest, as any revision of his own work by an author must have, but since the revision was made for the sake of publication in France, since it was first published there in a journal and only later in book form, and since Gissing had every reason to humour and help her in her enterprise, one might hesitate to attach too much importance to the changes. Only hesitate, however, since Gissing's revision of *New Grub Street* was quite unlike that sometimes authorized by Meredith, for example, who under pressure was prepared to entrust the serialization of a novel to the publisher's staff. Here, whatever the circumstances, the revisions are definitely Gissing's own. The revision of *New Grub Street* was not, in any case, an isolated event, as readers of this book will realize, since it had been preceded in the early nineties by Gissing's revision of his early three-deckers for publication in one-volume form by Lawrence and Bullen. It has been seen that, when Gissing revised *The Unclassed, The Emancipated, Workers in the Dawn, Thyrza* and *Isabel Clarendon*, he reduced the novels in size by about one-fifth, eliminated episodes that did not contribute to the main action, curtailed the amount of direct authorial 'intervention' and severely shortened the dialogue wherever it was loose or repetitive. Gissing treated *New Grub Street* in exactly the same way, reducing it by the equivalent of 110 pages of the Penguin text which is being used here for reference purposes. It will be remembered that Gissing had not been free, at the earlier date, to revise *New Grub Street* because Smith, Elder had refused to release the copyright that Gissing had sold to them outright.[27] This being so, one is scarcely stretching the argument at all by suggesting that Gissing would have revised it then had he been free to do so and that since, when he did revise it, he followed the same procedure as he had before, there is ample reason for taking the revision seriously. 'There will be no difficulty at all about making cuts', he told Gabrielle Fleury. 'When all is decided, you shall let me have your copy, and I will return it to you with passages marked for revision'.[28]

These 'cuts' deserve a brief examination. Nothing is added, beyond a few connecting sentences that the disruption occasionally made necessary. Essentially there are two types of deletion: those that eliminate superfluous material, and those that change the emphasis of a scene or chapter, or even of the book itself. In the first category, Gissing was really eliminating that type of harmless, distracting, minor episode that so much slowed down the pace of his first few novels. Among the episodes that go or are severely reduced are the initial Wattleborough gossip and the account of the life and hopes of John Yule in Wattleborough (pp. 48–9); the account of Alfred Yule's literary career (p. 127), his relationship with Mrs Yule (p. 128), his literary friends (pp. 133–4), and all the early references to his failing eyesight (e.g. p. 352); the description of Mrs Edmund Yule (pp. 269–70), and her discussion with her husband about Amy, after Amy has left Reardon (pp. 276–8); and the discussion between Jasper Milvain and Whelpdale on how to succeed in the 'trade' of literature (pp. 494–8). In other words, the Alfred Yule part of the novel was quite savagely curtailed. The effect of this curtailment was to shift the focus of the novel away from New Grub Street and on to the domestic drama affecting Amy and Edwin Reardon, Jasper Milvain and Marian Yule. To this extent the revision would confirm the more general remarks made earlier in the chapter. In this first category (the reduced emphasis upon the physical New Grub Street) some parts of the novel disappear completely, including the account of Mrs John Yule as a typical London working girl (p. 116); the hack writer, Ralph Warbury (p. 60); the entire Mrs. Groby episode (pp. 311–17); the entire Sykes episode (pp. 414–16); and that account of how Whelpdale survived in North America that is treasured by critics who argue that Gissing wrote solely to subsume his own experience (pp. 427–31). These changes perhaps reduce the interest of *New Grub Street* when regarded as a document containing 'soft-facts' about nineteenth-century publishing, but they certainly improve it as a novel, giving it firmer direction and a better pace.

The second type of revision, that which significantly alters the balance or effect of what is left, is even more important. Three examples will be given here of the type of change Gissing made. In the first place he deleted not all, but the most obtrusive of the authorial 'interventions'. For instance, he cut out his comment on Alfred Yule's marriage to a girl of 'no beauty' but of 'amiable disposition' whom he had met as 'she was walking with a younger sister in the streets', the comment detracting from a narrative which was slow enough even in its shortened form. The rejected sentences were:

> Many a man with brains but no money has been compelled to take the same step. Educated girls have a pronounced distaste for London garrets; not one in fifty thousands would share poverty with the brightest genius ever born. Seeing that marriage is so often indispensable to that very success which would enable a man of parts to mate equally, there is nothing for it but to look below one's level, and be grateful to the untaught woman who has pity on one's loneliness.[29]

Few would regret the excision of such a mawkish passage. A similar deletion was made at the beginning of Chapter XXXI where Gissing had foolishly expatiated on the extent to which his reader was likely to sympathize with characters like Reardon and Biffin.

> The chances are that you have neither understanding nor sympathy for men such as Edwin Reardon and Harold Biffin. They merely provoke you. They seem to you inert, flabby, weakly envious, foolishly obstinate, impiously mutinous, and many other things. You are made angrily contemptuous by their failure to get on; why don't they bestir themselves, push and bustle, welcome kicks so long as halfpence follow, make a place in the world's eye – in short, take a leaf from the book of Mr Jasper Milvain?
> But try to imagine a personality wholly unfitted for the rough and tumble of the world's labour market . . .[30]

The greater part of the first three paragraphs on p. 462 are deleted, much of the first paragraph on p. 463, and the whole of the last. This is a case where the authorial comment is cut out entirely: retained are only the third person fragments that begin the narrative of Harold Biffin's expedition for bread. If it is accepted, as it must be, that Gissing took every opportunity to revise his early work, it is all the more difficult to identify him with the literary drudges in his own books, including this one, who scarcely have the time or the energy to write a book at all, let alone revise it. This is by the way. Gissing had evidently realized a long time before 1898 that the narrative of a novel can be severely weakened if the author attempts to take the reader by the elbow and instruct him on how he should think. There is nothing surprising, then, about the deletion of such exhortations at the beginning of Chapter XXXI. It was not actually to Gissing's advantage to suggest that, had Reardon and Biffin been 'gifted with independent means', they would in some way have flourished because 'richly endowed with the kindly and the imaginative virtues', or even 'that the sum of their faults was their inability to earn money', not just because the special pleading defuses the character as it were but because an emphasis on the idea that Reardon and Biffin might have been victims of circumstance detracts from the psychological tension that existed between Reardon and his wife. At all events the authorial comments that most critics have regarded as offensive in Gissing were once again cut out.

Secondly, Gissing deleted a number of passages which, if anything, muddled the reader's impression of a principal character. Often this muddling results from the attribution to the character a degree of cynicism that is incompatible with what the reader already knows or must believe, if the main part of the action is to be taken seriously. Gissing shortened, for example, the soul-baring episode in which Jasper Milvain explained to Marian his selfishness towards his mother and sisters. Deleted are sentences like: 'I shall do many a base thing in life, just to get money and reputation; I tell you this that you mayn't be surprised if anything of that kind comes to your ears. I can't afford to live as I should like to.[31] The whole of this page is in fact deleted and the effect is not to cancel the reader's knowledge of Jasper Milvain's egocentricity but simply to reduce the emphasis upon it. It is part of a balancing exercise by which, within the novel, the various parts are arranged in a slightly modified relation to each other. Another instance of this type of improvement is the removal of a subversive passage in which Gissing commented on Marian's thoughts when she returned home after talking with Jasper. The deleted part ends with the following two paragraphs:

> Marian often went thus far in her speculation. Her candour was allied with clear insight into the possibilities of falsehood; she was not readily the victim of illusion; thinking much and speaking little, she had not come to her twenty-third year without perceiving what a distance lay between a girl's dream of life as it might be and life as it is. Had she invariably disclosed her thoughts, she would have earned the repute of a very sceptical and slightly cynical person.
>
> But with what rapturous tumult of the heart she could abandon herself to a belief in human vitures when their suggestion seemed to promise her a future of happiness![32]

One calls this subversive because Marian does not in fact have a 'clear insight into the possibilities of falsehood' – she is thoroughly misled by Milvain, because to refer to 'a girl's dream of life' undercuts the scene in which she becomes engaged to Milvain – the scene that was discussed earlier, and because to say that she could 'abandon herself to a belief in human values' suggests that to do so would be incompatible with her being a 'very sceptical and slightly cynical person', which is the opposite of what Gissing means. Instances of this kind, when Gissing seems at first to have let the pen run away with him, also occur fairly frequently in the writing of *Born in Exile*, as will be seen. Gissing appears in the first writing to have indulged himself by attributing to the character thoughts which he probably had himself but which were in the end inappropriate to the character. A rereading would make this obvious and the matter was, therefore, remedied.

Thirdly, it must be mentioned that in at least one case Gissing probably went too far. He deleted the paragraphs about the way in which there was a 'noticeable maturing of intellect' in Amy Reardon after she left her husband. This certainly is an important change. Whether it was an improvement or not is perhaps debatable. The maturing of Amy Reardon after her husband's death was consistent with the overall portrait of a marriage that failed: perhaps Gissing was unwilling to have his translator suppose that intellectual growth came more easily out of wedlock.

Above and beyond all the revisions and deletions mentioned so far is one of far greater significance. Gissing evidently realized that something was wrong with his portrait of Reardon and, given the opportunity to revise, tried to put it to rights.

What was wrong was residual. When *New Grub Street* was first published in 1891, the character of Reardon was made up of the residue, as it were, the imaginative residue of earlier books. Like Arthur Golding, or Waymark, he was egocentric, regarding himself in his own terms without reference to other people. He was imagined from within. A degree of mawkishness was the result; it is difficult to sympathize completely with someone who generates so much self-pity. More precisely, Reardon's neurotic self-analysis and self-concern, his introspective brooding and his general but overwhelming worry about his own ability as a writer to write further books, a worry which might have existed whatever the circumstances, was not wholly compatible with the dramatic and psychological interest in the novel or the breakdown of an unequal marriage. Not much of a novel will result from the contention that nineteenth-century publishing practices were so bad that the domestic life of authors was under greater strain than that of professional people. Critics interested in the publishing parts of *New Grub Street* have, as a matter of fact, been obliged to discount the interest of the personal part. If the novel were about the male characters' fate in a hostile publishing world, their relations with their wives would be of subsidiary importance. So the book has been regarded. The revision, however, would seem to indicate pretty plainly that Gissing did not intend the matrimonial part of the story to be just an illustration or consequence of publishing world events.

The deletions to that part of the narrative which concerned Reardon were comprehensive. Gissing either deleted entirely or severely shortened a large number of episodes: the conversation between Amy and Reardon in Chapter IV; Reardon's history as given in Chapter V; the account of his travels which occurs in Chapter VI; his anticipations of suicide (pp. 152–3), a passage that would make the reader suppose he carried the seeds of his own destruction, irrespective of what happened to his marriage; the long argument between Reardon and Amy about money and about their child (pp. 157–60); his conversation with Milvain about literary success (pp. 194–5); the longish account of the sale of Reardon's books and furniture (pp. 266–8); and a rather vast set of recollections by Reardon about his own books and the reception of his novel *Margaret Horne* (pp. 233–40). Embedded in the first edition text were conversations and reflective passages whose relation to the structure of the novel were arbitrary. Arbitrary at least in the sense that Reardon could have gone on talking for ever about his own problems, as he regarded them, and that for the sake of the three-volume length Gissing let him. Arbitrary, too, because the way he thought about himself in these maundering, pathetic passages had more to do with his personal, interior past than with his present emergency. Gissing had started his novel-writing career with a distinct interest in the spiritual or intellectual development of the single character. It was mentioned earlier that his admiration for Charlotte Brontë and George Eliot was part of this interest. In many of his early novels, he gave himself free rein, so that the character's growth of mind or sensibility could be studied. This growth, as suggested already, was a type of emancipation, one of the most important types. But strictly in terms of writing a realist novel, the emphasis upon a single character would necessarily detract from the detached depiction of a group or a society. This being the case, it is not really surprising that Gissing should prune the Reardon episodes rather drastically. Reardon had to be cut down to the scale of the other characters if the non-heroic features of the book as a whole were to be seen clearly.

A few examples will illustrate the type of passage that Gissing deleted from the Reardon episodes. The account of Reardon's work habits is reduced and one of the passages deleted is the often quoted one about 'the ordering of the day'.[33] Secondly, a certain amount of melodrama is taken out, as, for example, the following passage:

> He had but one thing to do: to seize her by the arm, drag her up from the chair, dash her back again with all his force – there, the transformation would be complete, they would stand towards each other on the natural footing. With an added curse perhaps –
> Instead of that, he choked, struggled for breath, and shed tears.
> Amy turned scornfully away from him. Blows and a curse would have over-awed her, at all events for the moment; she would have felt: 'Yes, he is a man, and I have put my destiny into his hands'. His tears moved her to a feeling cruelly exultant; they were the signs of her superiority. It was she who should have wept, and never in her life had she been further from such display of weakness.[34]

This passage was melodramatic, even if ironical, in context. Perhaps it contains the germ for a different type of novel, a novel of a more pronounced psychological type. As it was, the degree of calculation or cynicism implied by Reardon's thoughts detracted from the tension of a crucial encounter between husband and wife.

Something of the same kind might be said about the deletion of a conversation that Reardon and Biffin had much later in the book about marriage in general. In the course of the conversation, Gissing has Reardon say:

> I ought to have looked about for some simple, kind-hearted work-girl; that was the kind of wife indicated for me by circumstances. If I had earned a hundred a year she would have thought we were well-to-do. I should have been an authority to her on everything under the sun – and above it. No ambition would have unsettled her. We should have lived in a couple of poor rooms somewhere, and – we should have loved each other.[35]

Of this kind of passage it might be said perhaps that Gissing deleted it because too glaringly autobiographical, because the transference of Gissing's own experiences to Reardon disrupted the surface of the novel and weakened it, and because, when Gissing revised the book for Gabrielle Fleury, for whom he had left his wife, it was natural that he should apply the scalpel to those parts of the novel that were most directly reminiscent of the time at which the book had first been written. At any rate, he did delete it, for whatever reason. In doing so, he continued the balancing process by which the Reardon episodes were reduced so that the Jasper Milvain part of the story could be seen more clearly. This balancing process also involved thoroughgoing re-arrangements in Chapters X and XVII which had to be rendered consistent with the detailed revisions which preceded them.[36]

As suggested earlier, the changes Gissing made to *New Grub Street*, changes which certainly improve the novel, represent the author's assessment of his own early work as he looked back at it. What he saw when he looked back was a psychological novel set in a fictional environment conceived in the naturalist's mode. He had not, after the first publication of *New Grub Street*, lost his ability to depict the contemporary environment; on the contrary, he had become more skilful at it, if being spare, economical in detail, and direct in vision is to be more skilful. He had, on the other hand, developed greater skill in the analysis and depiction of personal relationships, so that when he looked back at *New Grub Street* he saw that he had been attempting then what he later managed to achieve more powerfully. The revision of *New Grub Street* is in fact an illustration of Gissing's awareness of his own artistic problems, which of course were also the problems of his reader. If, in the early 1890s, he wanted his reader to accept his particular amalgam of realistically conceived environment with a certain penetration of the psychology of the individual set aside from his or her environment, he had to find ways of improving upon *New Grub Street*. Alien though this was in the 1890s to the main tradition of the English novel, he on the whole succeeded.

6
Born in Exile

A logical outcome of Victorian anxiety was that same nihilism which spread rapidly through Europe during the second part of the nineteenth century. Doubt the validity of institutions, question the ancient sanctities, became cynical about people's motives in a predominantly capitalist world, give credence more and more to a habitually sceptical temper and be, in consequence, almost unavoidably attracted by a nihilism that frankly accepts, as its principal tenet, the basic idea that a thinking individual can never, except for good or bad reasons of expedience, be part of the world in which he lives. Whether it is correct to call these attitudes nihilistic or not – but surely it is – they prevailed in France, Germany and Russia during the 1880s and 1890s, and indeed were adopted wherever there occurred a sharp, apparently irreconcilable conflict between bourgeois institutions and the freedom of mind that derived from recently acquired knowledge. Gissing had throughout the 1880s thought so deeply about English life, English institutions, English urban life and English morality that it was natural for him to associate the disintegration of received opinions and values that he already knew with the continental nihilist movement represented by writers like Huysmans and Laforgue, Ibsen and Turgenev. To Gissing it seemed reasonable to think about the kind of novel that might incorporate nihilist characters, that is characters who could not believe their lives could ever be fundamentally meaningful. From Gissing's point of view, an almost inevitable consequence of this type of intellectual nihilism (the internal conviction that nothing mattered) was the alienation of the individual from other individuals and from society as a whole (i.e. his behaviour in the external world of normal life was crucially affected by his conviction). Characters who believed life to be meaningless must necessarily have special, and for the novelist, new types of relationships with each other. So Gissing thought. This is not to say that the alienated characters in Gissing's early work could not also have a social conscience – of a kind. Without it what would have become of the Gilbert Grails of the world? Now Gissing pushed the matter one stage further, in a development we can see in retrospect was absolutely logical and necessary for him, by accepting the possibility that a person might have to live his life in the knowledge that 'society' was an abstraction and that a personal reconciliation with the larger purposes of others was most unlikely. What is the fate of the man who is *merely* alienated? A man who subscribes to no faith, whose experience has not involved in any way the acceptance of traditional moral standards?

Godwin Peak in *Born in Exile*, Gissing's eleventh published novel, is such a man; to this point in his career Gissing's most daringly conceived character and a natural cousin, as it were, of many similar characters in Chekhov and Ibsen, though perhaps because social hypocrisy was an inherently Victorian subject, as well as being inherently a phenomenon of western-European bourgeois life, it would make more sense to see the book as a major human document of the time than just notice literary parallels. That the insights that informed the novel were alien to the type of person who might buy the book Gissing perfectly well understood: it was this very understanding that made *Born in Exile* so difficult to write. At all events, Godwin Peak is presented to the reader as 'the born rebel, the scorner of average mankind, the consummate egotist', a man who was 'essentially a negativist, guided by the mere relations of phenomena'. By having this rebel perpetrate an act of bad faith, practise a deception which temporarily placed him securely but falsely in the good company of an English home (which the narrator calls sardonically 'the best result of civilization in an age devoted to material progress')[1], Gissing contrived a situation that exposed the uneasy relationships of those who believed and those who did not believe in the orthodox norms of work, behaviour and doctrine.

Born in Exile is Gissing's geological book. Just as he paid great attention to physical detail when he wrote books like *Thyrza* and *The Nether World*, so now he took care that his character's intellectual life was sketched in credibly, and in a detailed way. Their environment did not consist of city streets, but of ideas. Their ideas they associated with their layman's grasp of geology as it had developed as a science through the century, a science that is represented in *Born in Exile* by the books they read and the geologists' names they mention.[2] Taken together the book titles and personal names constitute a pretty fair summary of the process by which the Victorian had become aware that his physical universe could be studied systematically, that the evidence of fossils ran counter to traditional religious belief based on the Bible, and that stratigraphical geology entailed the need for a sense of time different from that imagined by Christians, because more vast. But in *Born in Exile* those details are not concentrated in one place: they are scattered throughout the novel as part of the everyday pattern of thought of the principal characters. Thus Godwin Peak stops by a quarry on his way back from college; Mr Warricombe reads scientific papers; Marcella Moxey can ironically trade references with Peak, having read Darwin; most of the characters understand what is meant if a book like Buckland's *Bridgewater Treatise* is mentioned. The reader soon becomes aware, more from the characters themselves than from the narrator, that the fragility of belief, the uncertainty of social values, and the hesitant attitudes of the individual are all, in *Born in Exile*, a function of the impact on Victorian society of new geological knowledge. Whatever the source of his information, Gissing manages this well, making the overall intellectual context they share the environment in which they try to make sense of their lives individually. In other words, modern geology plays the same part in *Born in Exile* as Italian art played in *The Emancipated* and the London publishing world in *New Grub Street*, not as background, which would imply that what happened to the characters could be separated from their environment, but as an integral part of their observed world, the very world in which they searched for a consistency of belief and action.

What makes the book special is that Gissing sees this in a human context. The book is not an academic study of the impact of a thoroughgoing, late nineteenth-century agnosticism on Victorian religious and moral beliefs. It is about characters imagined as trapped in a world where, in any absolute sense, nothing makes sense for them. What are such people to do? The realization that her love for Peak existed despite or in defiance of her upbringing, of all she had been brought up to believe in, brought Sidwell Warricombe to the edge of breakdown, to 'a paroxysm of tearful misery'. For her, for several characters, the nihilism of the age was not a lightly held intellectual concept: it became a fact of life so profoundly upsetting that it pervaded and influenced love and friendship and companionship of every kind. For Gissing this insight was a victory of the imagination because he perceived that his proper subject, the subject of his age, was very simply the impact of what people thought upon what people did.

Published in three volumes by A. & C. Black in 1892, *Born in Exile* is a penetrating study of social hypocrisy. Gissing invents a set of characters all of whom are sceptical about both the conventions of the society in which they live and the ideas on which these conventions were based. Their attitudes to society, to the world at large, range from the mild, intellectual worries of Mr Warricombe, who will go so far as to accept that Lyell, Darwin and Huxley *may* have to be taken seriously, to the utter cynicism of Godwin Peak and his immediate group of friends, all of whom think that they are set apart, almost excluded, from society by an unshakable belief that the convictions on which most other people base their lives are untenable.

To succeed in devising a strategy for personal survival, a strategy which allows a man to earn his living and keep his radical opinions to himself is a type of hypocrisy: this idea is part of the essential texture of *Born in Exile*. John Earwaker does not blazon abroad his deep-rooted scepticism about conventional morality, convention and behaviour patterns. He is a newspaper editor, needs to earn a living, in a limited way enjoys his life, and keeps his opinions to himself. Janet Moorhouse understands that what the educated minority and the uneducated majority believe cannot be reconciled, but in order to live and work in the same world as the majority, she finds it easier to keep her thoughts to herself. Buckland Warricombe knows that he is more of a 'free-thinker' than his father, Martin Warricombe, realizes, but then why should he give his father the pain of argument and confrontation? And so on. The compromise entailed in keeping one's 'advanced' ideas to oneself, in order to avoid confrontatins with the orthodox opinion of the less enlightened, is in all instances a type, though perhaps a harmless type, of hypocrisy. This being the case, why not be a total hypocrite? Gissing puts this to the test by having Godwin Peak, the greatest sceptic of the whole group, pretend that he is preparing to become a minister of the Church of England so that, disguised and illicitly on the same social footing as the Warricombes, he can aspire to marry Sidwell Warricombe who is presented at first as one of the daughters in a thoroughly conventional, middle-class, country household.

As usual, Gissing only allows his main characters prominence in a social milieu in which other characters might equally well have been the main ones. Here the coterie of friends and acquaintances is a large one, as it has to be if Peak's extreme behaviour is to be given a context in which it can be understood. The group includes Bruno Chilvers, who carves out a career for himself in the Church by cultivating modishly advanced religious views which disguise his almost total lack of faith; John Earwaker and Buckland Warricombe, who meet up with each other in London after being, like Chilvers, contemporaries of Peak's at Whitelaw College; Warricombe's comfortably well-off family and, in particular, Martin Warricombe, who will talk geology and biblical criticism with Peak as long as there is no real threat to the traditional sanctities – 'his life indeed was one of debate postponed'³ – and Buckland's two sisters, Sidwell and Fanny; Christian Moxey, the nephew of a man who at one stage assisted Peak in his scientific career, Christian's sister, Marcella, and their cousin Janet; a friend of Earwaker's called Malkin; Sylvia Moorhouse; and a west-country family called the Walworths. None of these characters believes, precisely, in the existing social order. Even Sidwell Warricombe, the mildest of them all, 'shows the direction of her thoughts' by asking Sylvia Moorhouse whether she had ever known a woman agnostic. When Sylvia had been at school in London, she had known such a person, she said. That was Marcella Moxey, who hated injustice and who helped Sylvia 'to picture the Russian girls who propagate Nihilism'. In this way, by establishing vague but credible connections between characters, Gissing created a group of liberated intellects, people united by disbelief.

Non-believers, social misfits, sceptics, nihilists, all – whatever the degree of social alienation – must live. Only in the extreme case (like that of Biffin in *New Grub Street*) will such a person be led to suicide simply by logic. But supposing that this mild hypocrite, the one who keeps his convictions to himself for the sake of avoiding confrontation with the orthodox, actually succeeds in devising a personal strategy for survival, he is faced with two immense problems. On what basis will he get on with people whom he likes and with whom he wishes to be honest, and, much more serious, how will men and women get on with each other, given the obvious fact that the institution of marriage is a part of the social order that for the nihilist or 'advanced radical' has been discredited?

Buckland Warricombe says in the course of the book that 'the task of the modern civilizer is to sweep away sham idealisms' but in this book, as elsewhere, the task is a difficult one. It's all very well to be alienated from society. Do you have also to be alienated from women? Must you deny yourself companionship and sex for the sake of a consistent nihilism? And if the answer is a negative, are there emancipated women who have minds and characters of their own, but are not *too* emancipated? Earwaker resigns himself to the complete negative and towards the end of the book, 'without these preposterous spectacles', establishes himself in a bachelor flat 'in perpetuity'. His friend Malkin, however, decides his 'only chance of getting a suitable wife is to train some very young girl for the purpose', hits upon the fifteen year old Bella Jacox as the one who might benefit from his discreet attentions, and eventually becomes so infatuated with the idea of her he has created that, in a moment of Petrarchan passion, he bites off the end of his pipe. There seems at first no answer to the marriage problem. To sweep away 'sham idealisms' involves a distrust of marriage but if an intelligent man cannot marry a woman of his own class because she would be opinionated and expensive, will he for that reason be denied the companionship of women altogether? Most of the men in *Born in Exile* regard the denial as inevitable.

So do the women. What makes *Born in Exile* particularly interesting is that Gissing gives the women characters an independence of mind that allows them to share the ideas of their male friends, even though social convention makes it impossible for them to share their lives. Furthermore, whereas Miriam Baske in *The Emancipated* gained her enlightenment, her emancipation, almost exclusively from Mallard, without whom she would never have managed, in *Born in Exile* the women read, think, talk, argue independently, coming to conclusions about current ideas by themselves and basing their lives on the conclusions they arrive at, though not, perhaps, in a particularly ostentatious way. Part of the essential irony of *Born in Exile* is that the women are more 'advanced', more liberated than the men, though the men do not realize it. Sidwell Warricombe, superficially protected by her bourgeois home-life from *avant-garde* ideas, reads and listens and thinks. She wants to understand what she sees her friends already understand. One of her friends, Janet Moxey, practises medicine at Kingsmill, having previously studied at the Women's Medical School. Marcella Moxey, having already thought her way through the problem of the position of women in Victorian society, has private means which allow her to avoid a conventional role. She is 'going in for comparative philology', because as far as she can see her life is without prupose. Sylvia Moorhouse, in her 'ant' letter to Sidwell Warricombe (the one in which she uses the flying ant as a metaphor for human sexuality), says that she is coming to the conlusion that emancipation and sexuality are mutually exclusive, 'that some human beings are never winged at all' and that in the future 'there will be an increasing number of female creatures who from their birth are content with *walking*'. As a matter of fact the only women in the novel who uphold the old values of church and home are the mothers of Godwin Peak and Sidwell Warricombe, neither of whom plays an important part in the development of the story. The women of Godwin Peak's generation are all, to one degree or another, emancipated, which does not mean, however, that they know how to live with other emancipated people, least of all men. In the Gissing world the personal emancipation tends always to alienate, rarely to unite.

Early in the novel, as Godwin Peak and John Earwaker walk to the railway station after an evening at the Moxeys, Peak gives vent to a feeling which is at the heart of the novel. 'I hate emancipated women', he says, thinking of Marcella Moxey. 'Women ought neither to be enlightened nor dogmatic. They ought to be sexual'. Then, when he explains that Marcella grows more 'antipathetic' to him each time they meet because she 'has not a single feminine charm', Earwaker agrees, saying that though she has a good mind she is 'certainly an incomplete woman'.[4] Peak and Earwaker mean that Marcella is plain, intellectual, reserved, that she makes no attempt to be sexually attractive, and that there would be no point in desiring to live with a woman who, because educated, would necessarily also be independent.

In this way, Gissing establishes one of the principal conundrums of the novel. To be intellectually emancipated means to be free oneself from the superstitions and conventions of one's contemporaries: it does not mean that the problems of living with other people have been solved. Far from it. The novel contains a gallery of people who fail to cope, who fail to solve the conundrum. Christian Moxey harbours a romantic passion for a Mrs Palmer for eleven years only to find that when her husband dies she regards his infatuation as ridiculous, having previously been ignorant of it. Thomas Malkin chooses his future wife when she is fifteen and, unbeknown to her, surreptitiously guides her education, only to find that he has to flee to Australia to escape from the girl's mother, who has fallen in love with him. These characters, for better or worse, are at the disposal of the novelist in the sense that what happens to them eventually is only in some larger sense than they perceive the logical outcome of what they think and do on their own initiative. They are seen as part of a situation so hopeless for the individual that a 'happy' resolution of it is quite possible. Thus, just as Peak's rival, Bruno Chilvers, marries a socialite, one Bertha Jute, so Christian Moxey is allowed to recover from his 'own absurd romanticism' and be forgiven by his cousin, Janet, who had 'begun to inspire him with a hopeful activity, and to foster the elements of true manliness which he was conscious of possessing', while Malkin also recovered and after all married Bella, who had managed to grow up despite his absence. Even Buckland Warricombe, the friend who exposed Peak to his family and to their mutual friends, in the end marries a Mrs Renshaw who 'is something more than good-looking, has had an admirable education, is five-and-twenty, and for a couple of years has been actively engaged in humanitarian work in the East End. She has published a book on social questions, and is a very good public speaker. Finally, she owns property representing between three and four thousand a year'. In short, whatever their ideas, their pretensions, their hopes, Peak's friends in the end suppress, for reasons of convenience, their radical and non-conformist attitudes, making compromise accommodations with the society from which they have always felt alienated. This is the sense in which *they* fail to cope. Only Peak himself declines to make that kind of compromise. *He* fails to cope in the other sense of not being able to compromise.

Obviously Gissing set himself a difficult task when he adopted the idea of hypocrisy as the informing principle of a fiction that would permit both social and psychological analysis. The strategy gave him Godwin Peak, the almost perfect anti-hero, but it also presented him with a whole set of novelistic problems having to do with Peak's relationships with other people. It was a difficult novel to write for this reason, as is partly demonstrated by the fact that the writing was spread over many years, during which time the character of Peak and the design of the novel as a whole gradually evolved. Once again a crucial question is raised by the very fact of Gissing's rapid development as an artist. Was he a weak novelist who had the desire but not the technical skill to be an English Turgenev? Or was he a strong novelist whose drafts and revisions, experiments and new attempts, show that not only did he want to practise an art somewhat alien to the English state of mind but also that he would have to learn how to make plausible fictions – novels that worked – from apparently intractable material? The answer on this occasion must be a positive one. *Born in Exile* clearly shows us how Gissing in various stages succeeded in writing a book that had previously been beyond his range. A first draft of Volume I had probably been written by the mid-1880s, a supposition that will not surprise anyone who has noticed the considerable difference between the naïve, almost juvenile writing of Volume I[5] and the denser, more controlled writing of Volumes II and III. Several novels later, and after the extremely important experiments of *The Emancipated* and *New Grub Street*, Gissing took up the novel again, wrote the second two volumes, revised the whole book at least once, and even made changes at the eleventh hour just before publication. So *Born in Exile* shows us Gissing at work and lets us judge the effect of his awareness of what he was doing. This being the case, a brief review of the evidence seems in order.

In summary, then, the documents that bear upon any discussion of *Born in Exile* are, first, the printed book itself as published in 1892, reissued in 1893 and then left unrevised by the author;[6] secondly, the extensively corrected autograph manuscript of the novel now in the Huntington Library; thirdly, Gissing's diary, being edited for publication by Pierre Coustillas from the original in the New York Public Library – a diary that Gissing used to record his day-by-day progress with the books he wrote; and, fourthly, a large collection of published and unpublished letters.[7] Taken together these reveal both the process by which the novel was written and its final structure which in an extremely interesting way only achieved its present balance during the process of revision. To notice this is to become aware of the way in which Gissing worked, for when he took the book up again it was on the basis of a fuller understanding of the problems of writing nihilist fiction than he had had when he first thought of writing the book in the early 1880s. The evidence shows that at some time before 1885 he wrote a version of Volume I; that in 1888 he rewrote Volume I; that the novel was put aside until 1891 when he quickly wrote or rewrote all three volumes; that having submitted the book to various publishers he saw the need for a fairly extensive revision, which he made during the spring of 1892; and that after A. & C. Black had accepted the novel for publication, he decided to add an entirely new chapter, the penultimate one. This time span is important, because in the 1880s, when Gissing began *Born in Exile*, he was preoccupied with a social realism that is represented by *Demos, Thyrza* and *The Nether World*, novels in which there is a focus on working-class districts of London and an insistence upon determinist motivation, whereas in 1891 and 1892, after his travels in France, Italy and Greece and his renewed study of French fiction, he had turned away from descriptive social realism and was more interested in the psychological relations of people who believed in little at all and certainly not in society. It turns out that the weak parts of the novel are fossils from the early version, whereas the strong parts are the result of last minute revision.

Born in Exile was not at first about relationships; it was about Godwin Peak, the main character. That was in 1888, when Gissing returned to an early draft and converted it into the seventy-five manuscript pages of the first volume of a new novel. The main evidence to support this is a diary entry at the beginning of 1888, which reads as follows:

    4 January   Resumed writing. From 3 to 9:30 did six pages, bringing me

	into Chap VI of Vol I.
5 January	Wrote from 3 to 9:30, & did my six pages, bringing me into Chap VII. I am almost satisfied with Vol I so far. The construction, I think, is neater than anything I have done yet.
6 January	Wrote from 3 to 9 but with no result; it must all be cancelled. Never mind; have recast the chapter in my thought, & will go at it again tomorrow. My patience is inexhaustible.
7 January	Finished, thank heaven, the Chapter of Peake's antecedents.
12 January	Began to write at 4:30, & went on to 9:30, with effort. Did nearly five pages, however, bringing me to 75 of Vol I.
16 January	Finished Vol I.
7 February	Will it be credited, that I must begin a new novel?
8 February	Did actually begin a new story, to be called, I think, *Marian Dane*.
29 February	Think a good deal of my novel – the *old* one once more, upon which I have no doubt I shall re-settle when I get back to 7K.[8]

What all this amounts to is that Gissing had on his hands during the mid and perhaps the early 1880s a partial, semi-autobiographical manuscript about a young man, Godwin Peak, who acts hypocritically for the sake of social advantage; that he wrote or rewrote what is now Volume I in January 1888; and that three years then passed before he completed the novel. The progress of this second stage of composition is summarized in Gissing's correspondence with Bertz and more tersely in the diary:

6 May	finishing Vol I
15 June	finishing Vol II
17 July	finished *Godwin Peak*

That was July 1891, when Gissing in his personal life was at a low ebb, not just because of loneliness, but also because his actual achievements ought, he felt, to have secured him a better reputation and a greater reward for his unceasing labour. Nonetheless, the three years that had elapsed between his writing Volume I in 1888 and the completion of the first draft of the novel in July 1891 had been extremely important ones for him, as a brief review will show.

His first wife had died in February 1888, an event which obliged him to return to London from Eastbourne and simultaneously put an end to his work on *Born in Exile*. In February 1891 he had remarried, having moved out of London in anticipation of a new life with a woman much younger than he was. The three year period between the death of his first wife and his second marriage had seen the publication of *The Nether World* and *The Emancipated*, in many ways the most important books he had written to date. He had also written *New*

Grub Street late in 1890, apparently in a burst of creative energy that followed his first meetings with Edith Underwood. Though he himself did not like *New Grub Street*, it was – with *The Emancipated* – both a notable milestone in Gissing's move away from naturalism and – with *Born in Exile* – an early exploration of the possibilities of psychological realism. By 1891 Gissing had it in his mind to write a novel quite different from books like *Demos* and *Thyrza*. This change of direction had been confirmed by his travels. He once said he forgot about London social conditions when he got on the Paris train at Victoria Station and he had done that twice, first travelling in France and Italy and going as far south as Naples and then, a year later, extending a similar journey to southern Italy and Greece. These journeys literally took him away from his subject, allowed him to assess the position he had reached as a writer, gave him a new cosmopolitan perspective that affected his ideas about environment, and made him see that amongst his earlier subjects there were some – such as the inhibiting effect of puritanism – that were characteristically, narrowly English. Whatever he precisely thought, he returned from his second journey with the desire to write a new kind of book.

These feelings were strongly reinforced during the same period by his reading. He had always read widely. He had always, since his early days in the libraries of Manchester and Boston, read contemporary fiction in both English and French. Now he read books that seemed to have had a direct impact upon his development, turning him away from working-class subjects (to which he never returned) and making him more interested in the nihilistic or purely intellectual attitudes of his characters than in those of them who had a Walter Egremont type of social conscience. Thus he re-read Bourget,[9] on Bertz's recommendation looked at J. P. Jacobsen's *Niels Lyhne* and *Marie Grübe*, reread Turgenev's *Fathers and Sons* (for the seventh time), reread Dostoevski, whom he recommended to his brother but disliked himself, once again mulled over Hardy's *The Woodlanders* and *The Mayor of Casterbridge* (he later said that *Jude* was poor stuff by comparison with these) and began to ponder Ibsen, starting with *Hedda Gabler*.[10] The point is not that any one of these books had an influence on him, in the direct sense that *Born in Exile* would have been different had he not known it, rather that when he told people his peers were not English but Continental writers he had quite specifically in mind an interest in what he took to be the 'modern condition', where this vague phrase meant a fully felt, everyday awareness of the futility or impossibility of absolute beliefs. At the same time, he to a certain extent abandoned his early masters,

Charlotte Brontë and George Eliot, in order to concentrate, not on the slow growth of moral awareness in a sensitive soul, but on the brittle relations between people who could take very little on trust and on the psychological rather than the moral conflicts, or dilemmas, or situations in which his principal characters became involved. *Born in Exile* actually started out as a story told exclusively from the point of view of Godwin Peak, becoming more complex, and much more interesting, as Gissing learned how to place the action in a larger context.

By 1891, Gissing had created in Godwin Peak a fascinatingly conceived character, who would not have been out of place in a play by Ibsen or Chekhov or a novel by Turgenev or Dostoevski, someone who had moved to London from the provinces optimistically thinking himself 'on a voyage of discovery, to end perchance in some unknown land among his spiritual kith and kin', but who in London and at work in Rotherhithe, soon found himself constrained so rigidly by limits of personality and by limits of circumstance, that he had to accept and learn to live with what seemed the unalterable discrepancy between what he desired and what he saw was possible. Part of Peak's awareness of this discrepancy came from his habit of 'double consciousness': his interior life continued, and he allowed it to continue because he felt he could not do otherwise, even when his being with other people required, socially, some response to what they were doing and saying. Intelligent men are bound, he thinks, to be socially gauche and 'only the cultivation of a double consciousness puts them finally at ease. Impossible to converse with suavity, and to heed the forms of ordinary good breeding, when the brain is absorbed in all manner of new problems: one must learn to act a part, to control the facial mechanism, to observe and anticipate, even whilst the intellect is spending its sincere energy on subjects unavowed'.[11] This is partly a strategy for survival, partly an insight – by Gissing – into the psychology of alienation.

From Gissing's point of view, as narrator, and from Godwin Peak's as he reflects incessantly on his encounters with the outside world (the real world in which others seem to have a less perplexing time than he has), this double consciousness or fragmented personality takes the form of snobbery, where snobbery is seen as an inevitable feature of social alienation. On one level, Godwin Peak is a simple snob. He leaves college because he cannot bear the thought of his uncle opening a shop opposite the college gates. It would have been demeaning to see the family name on a shop! And to have his friends hear his uncle's accent! On another level, Godwin Peak is a complex snob at least in as far as he understood that the egotistical sense of superiority in snobbishness was suspect and hampering. For example, he says – through the narrator – that 'so strangely had circumstances moulded him' that 'he was preoccupied with the qualities which characterize a class', meaning that although he ought to have been as emancipated in his attitudes to other people as he was in every other respect, he in fact hankered for the satisfaction of making the grade in a middle-class social sense, the sense that 'would excite the democrat to disdain or fury'.[12] The fatalist in Peak tended to rationalize this predicament. In childhood, what he called the 'elaborate hypocrisy' of pretending to have normal feelings (for example of gratitude) while he in fact felt ashamed of his family Godwin Peak saw as personal injustice: 'he laid the blame on fortune, which had decreed his birth in a social sphere where he must ever be an alien'.[13] Later, though his feelings remained the same, he realized he had more responsibility for the situations he created and, indeed, that a good relationship with another human being was impossible unless he accepted responsibility for his own part in it.

This did not mean that he was capable of 'democratic', that is to say equal, relationships. When he pretended that he was preparing to become a clergyman for the sake of the social standing that would allow him to continue to know people like the Warricombes, 'what he proposed to himself was a life of deliberate baseness . . . Injury to himself he foresaw and accepted; he could never be the man nature designed him'.[14] In Godwin Peak's case, this deliberate baseness was not for the sake of worldly advancement, as it was in the case of Bruno Chilvers. It was a more basic sexual desire but one which could never be satisfied because Godwin Peak's intellectual emancipation was, sexually, always the slave of his sense of class. In youth he said 'the spectacle of female beauty sometimes overcame him with a despair which he could not analyse'. Later on, he expresses this in class terms when he talks with Earwaker about the ideal wife: 'Please remember that I have in mind a woman of the highest type our civilization can produce'. He means by this someone who has 'always lived among people of breeding and high education'.[15]

He also means a woman who is sexually complacent. In the course of the novel, he dismisses out of hand the woman who both loved him and was in every sense his equal. Peak's failed relationship with Marcella Moxey is one of the most interesting things in the book. Instead Peak wanted a well-bred companion who would be civilized enough to put his needs before hers. 'Godwin had absolute power of dominating the woman whom he should inspire with tenderness.'[16]

In the important scene in Chapter II of Volume II when Peak reviews the situation he has created by deceiving the Warricombes, this basic question is broached directly.

> But in the meantime he was leaving aside the most powerful of all his motives, and one which demanded closest scrutiny. Not ambition, in the ordinary sense; not desire of material luxury; no incentive recognized by unprincipled schemes first suggested his dishonour. This edifice of subtle untruth, had for its foundation a mere ideal of sexual love. For the winning of some chosen women, men have wrought vehemently, have ruined themselves and others, have achieved triumphs noble and degrading. But Godwin Peak had for years contemplated the possibility of baseness at the impulse of a craving for love capable only of a social (one might say, of a political) definition. The woman throned in his imagination was no individual, but the type of an order . . . The sense of social distinctions was so burnt into him, that he could not be affected by any pictured charm of mind or person in a woman who had not the stamp of gentle birth and breeding.[17]

Godwin's ideal of sexual love was a false ideal and in the 1891 version was doomed to an exposure at the hands of Buckland Warricombe which would show that to be 'born in exile' meant to remain in exile for ever. Social stability and intellectual emancipation could not be reconciled without hypocrisy.

Gissing as narrator allowed himself to explore and enjoy the multiple ironies created by his character's act of bad faith. Here, for example, is the way he describes in Volume I Peak's reaction to the predicament he had created for himself.

> The murmur of amiable voices softened him to the reception of all that was good in his present surroundings, and justified in the light of sentiment his own dishonour. This English home, was it not surely the best result of civilisation in an age devoted to material progress? Here was peace, here was scope for the kindliest emotions. Upon him – the born rebel, the scorner of average mankind, the consummate egoist – this atmosphere exercised an influence more tranquillising, more beneficent, than even the mood of disinterested study. In the world to which sincerity would condemn him, only the worst elements of his character found nourishment and range; here he was humanised, made receptive of all gentle sympathies. Heroism might point him to an unending struggle with adverse conditions, but how was heroism possible without faith? Absolute faith he had none; he was essentially a negativist, guided by the mere relations of phenomena. Nothing easier than to contemn [sic] the mode of life represented by this wealthy middle class; but compare it with other existences conceivable by a thinking man, and it was emphatically good. It aimed at placidity, at benevolence, at supreme cleanliness – things which more than compensated for the absence of higher spirituality. We can be but what we are; these people accepted themselves, and in so doing became estimable mortals. No imbecile pretensions exposed them to the

rebuke of a social satirist; no vulgarity tainted their familiar intercourse. Their allegiance to a worn-out creed was felt as an added grace; thus only could their souls aspire, and the imperfect poetry of their natures be developed.[18]

This passage from the unrevised novel was all very amusing in a way, but it left Gissing with a book of social criticism or commentary on his hands, hardly a modern European novel. Late in 1891, something happened that made him see that the book had to be revised once more. When the novel was turned down by Smith, Elder, or at least withdrawn because the publisher refused to offer more than had been paid for the copyright of *New Grub Street*, Gissing placed it in the hands of a literary agent, A. P. Watt, who then tried a number of other publishers before placing it with A. & C. Black. While the book was in Watt's hands, Gissing realized, or perhaps was brought to realize, that the novel would be improved if he rewrote those parts that concerned the relations Peak had with other characters, particularly the two women, Sidwell Warricombe and Marcella Moxey.

Consequently, when Gissing wrote to Bertz on 15 January 1892 to tell him that 'Godwin Peak' had been accepted for publication by A. & C. Black, he also mentioned that he would have to revise it.[19] This is confirmed by an earlier entry in the diary. On 8 January 1892 his entry had been: 'Wrote to A. & C. Black, saying I must revise *Godwin Peak*'. The revision took about a month and the diary entries turn out to be important.

12 January	Recd MS of *Godwin Peak* from A. & C. Black.
22 January	Think of calling *Godwin Peak – Born in Exile*.
24 January	Worked at *Born in Exile* morning & evening, rewriting several pages of Vol I.
25 January	Finished revision of MS, but find I must re-write a good deal of it; the end is especially feeble. Got a few ideas for improvements.
27 January	Finished revisal of Vol II.

The importance of this clue in the diary about the eleventh hour revision of *Born in Exile* is that the changes made at this stage can be traced with relative ease in the Huntington manuscript, a fair copy which was used by the compositors when the book was set and which has the same physical features, generally speaking, as the manuscript of *Workers in the Dawn* as described earlier in the book. Because it has the same physical features, it can be analysed in exactly the same way, the difference being that whereas in *Workers in the Dawn* it was the deleted material that proved to be important, here in *Born in Exile* it is the additional material incorporated during the rewriting of crucial scenes.

This is not to say that every single change made to the manuscript of *Born in Exile* is of great significance. A few of the corrections were editorial and prove little. For example, where Gissing had said in the unrevised copy that 'the elder of his [Peak's father's] sisters had walked the streets of the East end', the first edition reads 'the elder of his sisters had married poorly'. At another point, the names 'Tyndall, Huxley, Darwin' are deleted. There is not much of this type of correction, however; it represents perhaps five per cent of the total.

Leaving aside the perfectly normal editorial disturbance that would have occurred no doubt whatever Gissing may have thought about the book as a whole, we can return to the rewriting that is traceable to manuscript pages added after the fair copy had been paginated and presumably after the book had first been submitted to a publisher. The rewriting was immensely important, because in a single spell of work Gissing radically altered *Born in Exile* by converting it from a book narrated principally from the point of view of the main character, Godwin Peak, into a book in which a number of characters co-exist, the action now being presented to the reader from a multiple point of view. Gissing achieved this by completely rewriting the parts of the novel in which Sidwell and Buckland Warricombe and Christian and Marcella Moxey appear. In each and every case, he rewrote their scenes so that they were independent in thought and action from the third person narrative that concerned Peak. Thus, in the revised novel the reader gets to know about these characters independently, not through Peak – obviously a highly significant change as far as the art of the novel is concerned.

In the course of this rewriting, Buckland Warricombe becomes a man who, aware of the complexities of Peak's position yet obliged, he thinks, to unmask him, is himself involved in a desperate liaison with the idea of love, so that the reader, seeing how desperate it is, finds himself forced into a comparison of the hypocrisy of Peak and the fantasising of Buckland. Both are creatures trapped within their own sexual manoeuvring, as indeed is Christian Moxey. At the same time, and as a result of the same rewriting, Marcella Moxey becomes a character whose unspoken love for Peak the reader sees to be a reality which affects the whole structure of the book, in as far as in a crucial scene – the one in which she visits Peak's home town – she now acts independently, of her own volition, and thus must be assessed separately by the reader, who without the revision would have known about her only at second hand. In the same spirit, Gissing rewrote all the sections of the novel in which Sidwell Warricombe appeared. He was no longer satisfied with a novelistic situation in which the reader gets to know about the women characters through the eyes of the male ones. The parts of the action which concern Sidwell Warricombe are now seen from her point of view; she is seen to be a character deeply affected by her understanding of Peak's actions and of his predicament generally; which means, in effect that she has been re-imagined by the novelist as a modern, fallible, yet independent character, for whom a relationship with a man like Peak matters a lot and is not just a question of stereotype. Indeed the overall effect of the rewriting, re-imagining, restructuring of *Born in Exile*, as this can be observed in the autograph fair copy, is to transfer the interest away from Peak as a single character to a much more penetrating study of the relationship between characters, something which could only be achieved if the other characters were strengthened. This transforms the book. In the first version, Marcella Moxey, Sidwell Warricombe and Buckland Warricombe were seen by the narrator from the point of view of Peak, and the cynicism of Gissing's treatment was unrelieved. In the revised version, Peak is seen from the point of view of the other main characters, who themselves are made much more interesting simply by virtue of changes in the plot which let their actions result from what they understand rather than what they cannot understand. Specifically, they understand that, in the world of an agnostic, an immoral action does not damn a man for ever but rather that, since they all live in a world of hypocrisy, disbelief and fallibility, the fact of social alienation provides a basis upon which fellow feeling, even love, might survive.

The deliberately revised structure of *Born in Exile* shows that Gissing had an insight into the relationship of the individual to society which many readers and critics may more easily associate with the twentieth century, though it would be wrong to say that Gissing was ahead of his time just because he wrote a novel which explored the psychological implications of an act of bad faith. Meredith had already done so in *Diana of the Crossways*; Chekhov handled a similar situation in *The Seagull*. Gissing was not ahead of his time. Rather he had written a novel that was consistent with the mainstream of Continental European literature, although it was not consistent with the moral tradition of the Victorians. In this sense his was an alien art. Had Gissing revised the novel thoroughly, by attending to the residual weaknesses of the first volume as well as by altering it at more significant points as he did, the brilliance of *Born in Exile*, the brilliance of conception that is, might have been recognized even more widely. By not bothering or by not having time to revise the bulk of Volume I, he left the door open to the type of biographical criticism that has tended to destroy his reputation and conceal his real skill, and more important left the novel in an unbalanced state, the first fifty pages or so remaining weak by comparison with the rest.

Interestingly, Gissing continued to think about the nature of the relationship between Godwin Peak and Sidwell Warricombe, for at the proof stage he added the penultimate chapter (i.e. III, pp. 235–54). In the previous chapter occurred the exchange of letters which resulted in Sidwell Warricombe's final refusal of Peak because she lacked the courage to leave her 'little world'. In the newly written chapter, the reader sees that Sidwell's dilemma was deeply felt, that she desired Peak but did not dare to offend her family, that the family without exerting itself actually prevailed over her wish to be free, and that her caring for him included an understanding of what he had said in his letter, that is that he had been 'betrayed' into a mad action, but that there was no 'soil' upon his spirit. In other words, the possibility of love, friendship and affection based upon the weakness rather than the strengths of human beings is affirmed, although the situation of Godwin Peak and Sidwell Warricombe is such that she believes she has to deny what she has come to understand.

Born in Exile shows Gissing addressing, as ever somewhat experimentally, a very basic novelistic problem. In the Gissing world characters are held apart from each other by educational and class barriers and by their inability to believe in those things which others take for granted, notably sexuality and marriage. The problem is to know how to write a novel about alienation which is not merely negative and cynical. The answer seems to be that such a novel can be written, but that it is stronger if not written naïvely from the point of view of a single character. Gissing experimented with this, not always successfully. In *Thyrza*, for example, in contriving a plot which denied the character, Thyrza, the love she briefly experienced and obliged her to settle for much less, a marriage in which the determining limits set on ordinary existence were accepted and acknowledged, Gissing only managed by not letting his main characters talk with each other at all. In *The Nether World* he had created a passionately self-assertive amoral, distinctively 'modern' woman in Clara Hewett only to make her, also, by the contrivance of plot return to the confines of place and circumstance. For as long as Gissing wanted to show the pressure of environment on personality he could do this. But when his attention was diverted away from this type of determinism, he had to allow his alienated characters to talk to each other. That happens to a very limited extent in *The Emancipated* and to a greater extent in *New Grub Street*, where Jasper Milvain and Amy Reardon's marriage is based upon what they have been seen to go through. In other words, Gissing moved his fictional interest away from characters whose actions were based upon a very limited understanding of the sense in which they were at the mercy of environment and towards characters whose alienation was explored psychologically in sets of situations where they must talk about their motives, talk about this relationship with each other. That *Born in Exile* is part of this movement is clear enough if one compares it with Gissing's next novel, *The Odd Women*. It is as though Rhoda Nunn and Everard Barfoot in that book pick up the problems of Sidwell Warricombe and Godwin Peak exactly where *Born in Exile* left them. By this time the basic problem involved had been solved, for Gissing now knew that a psychological study of alienation would be more credible, more impressive, in a novel with a multiple point of view.

7
The Art of Social Alienation

GISSING's later novels, and particularly the four strong novels that here are of immediate concern, *The Odd Women* 1893, *In the Year of Jubilee* 1894, *The Whirlpool* 1897, and *The Crown of Life* 1899, could be seen as the documentary art of a period of social and political change. As usual, Gissing thought about what he was doing, found himself a new subject, studied it, and from what he knew, from what he had learnt, attempted to create fictional worlds in which the interplay and conflict of character would have contemporary relevance.

That there had been social changes in many parts of England which resulted in new, as yet undescribed and unexplained patterns of behaviour Gissing knew well from long experience. That existing political institutions had little to do with how many people lived was also obvious. Indeed, it is a feature of English political life that the lack of connection between those in power and those being governed leads, and in Gissing's time led, to there being sizeable segments of society with no political voice whatsoever. The social change that Gissing studied was the emergence of such people; in more immediate terms he took as his subject people living in the suburbs or in 'conurbations', people with urban occupations and urban expectations. In this limited sense, his novels of the 1890s had a documentary basis.

By comparison with earlier books like *The Emancipated* and *Born in Exile*, where the emphasis as well as the narrative strategy had been mainly psychological and where the characters were literally, that is to say geographically dislocated, the novels of the 1890s seem more directly connected to contemporary London life, descriptively and by insistence upon new middle-class urban occupations. In *The Whirlpool*, Cecil Morphew runs a photography shop and Hugh Carnaby helps to manage a bicycle factory in the Midlands. In *The Odd Women*, Rhoda Nunn teaches shorthand, book-keeping, and commercial correspondence to those 'superfluous' women who cannot or do not expect to marry. In *The Crown of Life*, Miss Bonnicastle and her friend Kite are commercial artists, who perpetrate for advertising purposes what the narrator called 'clever brutalities' such as the pictorial association of Ariadne with Higginson's Hair Wash. In *In the Year of Jubilee*, Barnaby is in life insurance, Morgan is a debt collector, and that 'keen man of affairs', Luckworth Crewe, is an advertising agent and entrepreneur with a tiny office in Farringdon Street. In the same novel, Beatrice Peachey is the woman who manages for herself in a bachelor flat while masterminding the South London Fashionable Dress Supply Association. In the so-called pot-boilers Gissing also wrote in the 1890s, there are similar characters, like Patty Ringrose in *Eve's Ransom* who works in a music shop in Camden Town and the Mumfords in *The Paying Guest* who can contrive to sustain the genteel existence of their 'Runnymede' in suburban London only if they take in a lodger. These people, and the many people like them – for the complete list would be a long one – constitute Gissing's new cast, his new set of London characters, his new set of rootless, necessarily egotistical 'persons' who once again, for Gissing, are fictions drawn from an observed world.

Of course these novels are not only peopled by lower middle-class characters – to use the later phraseology. There are also those who barely manage to survive at all, like Monica Madden's sisters in *The Odd Women*. Alice has to live on £16 p.a. as a governess; Virginia, the alcoholic, on £12 as a lady's companion; Gertrude is a stage assistant who gets only room and board. Similarly there are those at the other end of the social scale who are wealthy enough to be careless about their social position and their lack of a political role – people like the Derwents in *The Crown of Life* and Lionel Tarrant in *In the Year of Jubilee*. By and large, however, Gissing made groups of characters whose occupations very much placed them socially even though that place was not in any real sense a social position. The occupations are important. So is the lack of social role. People are defined, and define themselves, by what they do and by what they think; they are not defined in terms of purpose or by social standards by which they could reasonably be judged. The modernity of these novels, for the 1890s, lay exactly in Gissing's perception that for large groups of people such standards lacked relevance. He therefore set about the task of imagining and creating relationships between them without reference to social norms. Thus one finds a novelistic situation in which the characters are drawn from life and have documentary interest, while the relationships between them – always the subject of a Gissing novel – are more profoundly imagined.

This insistence upon characters whose lives are not at all imagined within the context of stable, traditional social patterns is one of the more radical elements of these later novels. To behave in a socially acceptable manner did not imply belief in traditional values. It was merely a strategy for survival in an extremely unfriendly world.

> 'Well, what do you aim at?' Hilliard asked disinterestedly [in *Eve's Ransom*].
> 'Safety', was the prompt reply.
> 'Safety? From what?'
> 'From years of struggle to keep myself alive'.

In this struggle, some are by nature energetic. Luckworth Crewe and Beatrice Peachey in *In the Year of Jubilee* are self-possessed, determined, active: they accept the circumstances in which they find themselves and try to make the best of them. Others are less energetic. Kite, in *The Crown of Life*, more or less drifts through his career, squandering his talent with the help of a 'too seductive' cheap claret. Others still, like Hugh Carnaby in *The Whirlpool*, are energetic in the struggle for economic survival only of necessity. But, although these characters are very different from each other, there is one thing they have in common. All are pragmatic in their attitude to life. None is a moralist.

Gissing places them in a world in which moral values, or social values, scarcely exist. They could not use, do not believe in, do not try to find comprehensive sets of standards which would be the measure of the meaningfulness of their lives. Morality is for all practical purposes irrelevant. But this does not mean that they behave badly. They behave as they find they are obliged to behave. This struggle for existence in an essentially amoral environment has a number of interesting features. In the first place, Gissing characters rarely compete with each other. In their relations with each other they do not *wish* to be in conflict with each other. To avoid trouble they tend to interrogate each other in order to detect possible conflicts of interest. If there are no conflicts of interest, there ought not to be a conflict of character either, because what one person does is of no concern, really, to anyone else. For example, Beatrice Peachey is only interested in Nancy Lord because she suspects Luckworth Crewe of being the father of Nancy's child. Once she is satisfied that he is not, her whole attitude changes. In fact she actually helps Nancy by giving her a job. In the same way Monica's friend, in *The Odd Women*, is only interested in Monica's affairs for as long as she fears she may be a competitor. Of course no one's life runs smoothly. Trouble does occur. Yet when it does, the conflict between characters is not seen in terms of deviation from a generally accepted moral norm but is made to result from an act of bad faith, from an action which is unreasonable because in the rationalist's vision any reasonable man or woman would have avoided it. Tarrant's brothers did not have to misrepresent him, for example. When they did so, Gissing characteristically depicted the situation in environmental, but not in moral terms. Another person's act of bad faith is part of the environment in which one has to struggle to survive and is only important because of its bearing on this. There are few criminals in Gissing's novels. Why is this? Since he took as his subject contemporary London, where the struggle for existence often gave rise to acts of a dubious and often criminal nature, why did he not treat the subject of criminality in his novels? The answer seems to be that to have done so would have involved him in the type of moral consideration which, throughout his writing career, he had preferred to avoid.[1]

In *The Emancipated, Born in Exile, New Grub Street* and perhaps even in *Denzil Quarrier* there are lingering elements of youthful idealism in characters who, despite the world, want to make something of life. This element is not strong but it is there. By the time Gissing wrote *The Odd Women* the lines were more tightly drawn. Human beings were primarily concerned with the struggle for psychological and physical survival; they were for the most part unclassed, separated from society, dislocated; society had no interest in them and certainly no interest in their desire for identity and emancipation; the normal relationship between them, if they thought about their existence at all, was that of alienation. More strongly drawn than in earlier novels is the huge rift between those who understand and are troubled by the human predicament and those who accept life as they find it, unthinkingly. The Maddens are in this latter category in *The Odd Women*. Mrs Madden, 'having given birth to six daughters, had fulfilled her function in this wonderful world', while Dr Madden's 'hopes for the race were inseparable from a maintenance of morals and conventions such as the average man assumes in his estimate of woman'. Looking back over the long period in which novelists have exposed the crass, middle-class acceptance of the social order they inherit, as if for those who accept it on its own terms it had a meaning which these novelists feel it obviously lacks, a reader in the final quarter of the twentieth century might well sigh wearily about it all. Why bother to be satirical about middle-class *mores* unless you have something better, something more meaningful to propose? And why extoll the condition of intellectual alienation, when it turns out that thinking men and women alienated from society are more often miserable with themselves than exuberantly emancipated? For Gissing in the 1890s, these questions were simply part of a social situation which in London, at least, he understood to exist. There existed an important, huge gap between the morals and conventions of the Maddens and the lives of the many human beings in modern life for whom these same morals and conventions seemed to have no relevance. Gissing therefore continued to write about it.

In *The Odd Women*[2] he wrote about it by imagining two parallel masculine – feminine encounters; the one the meeting of the independent gentleman, Everard Barfoot, with Rhoda Nunn, the educated and emancipated woman; the other the meeting of Edmund Widdowson, a miserably lonely, middle-aged city clerk, with Monica Madden, the youngest of the Madden girls who at the beginning of the novel is an assistant in a draper's shop in Walworth Street. Apart from the first few chapters which Gissing rather bungled when he rewrote and shortened them at the request of the publisher,[3] *The Odd Women* is one of the most fully realized of Gissing's later novels. Perhaps it is the best of them in fact. When he described the efforts Rhoda and Mary make to teach interested and willing girls the shorthand, book-keeping, commercial correspondence that will allow them to live, that will allow them to escape the slavery of other types of employment, Gissing as usual shows that he has taken the trouble to know what he is writing about. When he describes the working conditions in the shop in Walworth Street, and the way in which the shop girls live after hours, the same applies. In this respect, the novel is extremely well sustained. Included within this picture of London life, in one of its aspects, are two sexual encounters. Rhoda Nunn teaches in the house to which Monica Madden eventually comes for help. Their lives are disrupted by the intrusion of the two men, Everard Barfoot and Edmund Widdowson. This intrusion gives rise to what in the novel is called 'the Othello business', that is to a situation in which sexual need and sexual jealousy disrupt the lives of all four characters in ways which in the long run really do them no good whatsoever. The conventions and *mores* of Dr Madden require that in normal circumstances men and women should marry one another. Why? What brings this about? And why are the results so frequently bad? To show how, if not why, Gissing arranges two parallel relationships in which the rationalities of social survival become confused with the irrationalities of sexual attraction and need.

Edmund Widdowson became infatuated with the sight of Monica

Madden when she was a shop assistant, fed his 'affection' with the idea that she deserved something better than a twelve hour day for low wages, without ever knowing her as a person went through the motions of a conventional wooing by taking her on expeditions and by introducing her to his family, and then, once they were married, expected her to be a prisoner to her new condition, willingly confined within the duties and responsibilities of a Victorian marriage. Widdowson's possessiveness was his only expression of affection, was all he had to reassure himself of his very real affection for the person he had been so determined to marry. To satisfy him, Monica had to be 'sweet, lovable and docile'; fulfilment of her domestic duties was the way in which she was expected to prove her affection. 'Never had it occurred to Widdowson that a wife remains an individual, with rights and obligations independent of her wifely condition'. As the marriage deteriorates, the narrative is punctuated by laconic or satiric remarks at Widdowson's expense: 'A woman ought never to be so happy as when she is looking after her home'; and (on being reconciled to one's station) that it is the law which 'points out a woman's place, and commands her to follow her husband's guidance'; and again, women have 'no right to be miserable. They are doing their duty and that ought to keep them cheerful'. And so on. Gissing in this book mercilessly exposes the common enough Victorian double standard by which the woman was jealously desired, sexually, before marriage and after marriage jealously, possessively guarded as a chattel, being dishonoured throughout countless years of domestic slavery by the same man as had made such a fuss of her at the outset.

Jacob Korg said that Widdowson's tyranny in marriage drove Monica to be unfaithful.[4] This is true only to a point. Because hardly anything would have been worse for Monica than domestic imprisonment, because it was galling to live with a man who had six hundred a year and never have a penny to spend, she was vulnerable to Bevis' shallow love-making, anxious for adventure, willing to go away with him, willing certainly to desert her husband. But she does not commit adultery, as Korg later in the same paragraph claimed. Had she done so Widdowson would have been in the right. Actually it is because she is pregnant with Widdowson's child that she returns to him, for the child's sake, at the same time resolving that part of the plot in which Everard Barfoot was suspected by Rhoda Nunn and others of having an affair with Monica. Widdowson suspected Monica of having a lover and was jealous. Rhoda Nunn suspected Barfoot of having a mistress and was jealous. In this parallel, Gissing can carry the plot no further than to resolve matters by showing them both to be mistaken, which is close to saying that sexual jealousy is both the cause and consequence of relationships between men and women except for those sensible marriages, like that of Micklethwaite, in this novel, where the expectations are extremely modest from the very beginning.

The rather emotive term 'sexual jealousy' here means the desire to possess. None of the four main characters in *The Odd Women* knows much about love, though they use the word. Rhoda Nunn is presented bluntly as a woman who 'could no longer be without a male companion'. Though she has exactly what she believes she desires – an occupation, self-respect, a trained sensibility, enough money to live on, freedom – she is frustrated sexually. In this condition, while in her early thirties, she meets Everard Barfoot, who is a cousin of the woman with whom she works. Gissing, the remorseless social analyst, gives her little chance.

> At first view the countenance seemed masculine, its expression somewhat aggressive – eyes shrewdly observant and lips consciously impregnable. But the connoisseur delayed his verdict. It was a face that invited, that compelled, study. Self-confidence, intellectual keenness, a bright humour, frank courage, were traits legible enough; and when the lips parted to show their warmth, their fulness, when the eyelids dropped a little in meditation, one became aware of a suggestiveness directed not solely at the intellect, of something like an unfamiliar sexual type, remote indeed from the voluptuous, but hinting a possibility of subtle feminine forces that might be released by circumstance.[5]

In such terms is the reader invited to think about her. Rhoda Nunn may be an 'unfamiliar sexual type', though socially and educationally emancipated, but she is for all that a sexual type. As such does Everard Barfoot respond to her.

> He scrutinized her, at discreet intervals, from head to foot. To Everard, nothing female was alien; woman, merely as woman, interested him profoundly. And this example of her sex had excited his curiosity in no common degree. His concern with her was purely intellectual; she had no sensual attraction for him, but he longed to see further into her mind, to probe the sincerity of the motives she professed, to understand her mechanism, her process of growth. Hitherto he had enjoyed no opportunity of studying this type.[6]

When Everard Barfoot thought about Rhoda Nunn later on he wondered whether it would not be a 'joke' to ask her to marry him. After all she was a fine creature: 'yes, physically as well'. Although his ideal to this point in his career had been a very different one, he knew at least that he had no desire to 'tie' himself to a 'tame domestic female'. On the contrary, 'Rhoda might well represent the desire of a mature man, strengthened by modern culture and with his senses fairly subordinate to his reason'. Because he was sure that Rhoda, like him, would regard heartbreak as a 'very old-fashioned disorder, associated with poverty of brain' and because she was sure to be studying him in the same cynical spirit as he was studying her, the 'amusement', as he put it, was only just beginning and it seemed legitimate to wonder whether she would be most challenged by the offer of marriage or of a 'free union'. Sex, in short, is seen as conflict, as desire to dominate, as the urge to possess, not as a response to another individual involving mutual understanding and willingness to search out the accommodations that permit relationships to prosper. Just as Widdowson, who thought he wanted the companionship of marriage, was really just sexually lonely, so Rhoda Nunn and Everard Barfoot, who regard themselves as interesting people because emancipated, are sexually motivated in their desire to dominate each other. So fierce and irrational is this feeling that Widdowson hires detectives to follow Monica because he suspects her of infidelity, while Rhoda Nunn – caught up in the 'Othello business' – first suspects (on the basis of gossipy rumours) that Everard had disgraced himself earlier in life by molesting a woman in a railway carriage and then, because of the coincidence of Bevis and Everard Barfoot having flats in the same building, lapses into suspecting him of being Monica's lover and the father of her child. As in *Othello*, a paltry coincidence was enough to expose the feelings that had all the time existed, though Rhoda Nunn, and indeed probably Barfoot too, were incapable of a genuinely 'modern' honesty. 'The man's presence', says the narrator, 'affected her with a perturbation which she had no difficulty concealing at the time, though afterwards it distressed and shamed her'. With this sort of phrase does Gissing expose the ambivalence of sexual desire and social emancipation. Rhoda Nunn and Everard Barfoot sport with each other, enjoy the thrust and parry, enjoy the orthodoxies of wooing while affecting to argue, and go so far as to adventure in the Lake District, defying each other to capitulate into a conventional gesture of the kind that Barfoot's eventual proposal of marriage in fact is. And although Everard does capitulate, showing the woman in this instance to be dominant, for Rhoda Nunn it was a Pyrrhic victory: Everard makes a conventional marriage with another woman and Rhoda returns to the secure solitude of emancipation.

Where Gissing has been quite brilliant in this book is in the depiction of the psychological effects of sexuality as these effects are expressed in the way each character responds to particular situations. Characters, who are in some sense rational, become irrational as a result of the relationship with someone of the opposite sex, the characters noticing how perverse they have become without wishing to rectify the matter. For example, Monica knows that Widdowson's suspicion is itself the catalyst which inclines her to provide his suspicion with a cause. Rhoda Nunn incites Barfoot to propose to her for the very reason that she suspects his motives. So throughout the novel. Love and sexuality cannot be reconciled, so the point seems to be. Love in *The Odd Women* does not involve shared thoughts and experiences: people do not search out common ground and build companionship on the basis of common interests. Nor does love involve mutual respect, except the respect of adversaries, and people have no wish to see anything from the other person's point of view. For the species to perpetuate itself human beings must frequently abandon themselves to their sexual desires, but these desires in no sense relate to the business of living with others. Better to curb your desires, therefore, if you wish to preserve your self-respect. Give way to them and the likelihood of an Othello-type tragedy is high.

Despite the psychological probing of *Born in Exile* and *The Odd Women*, Gissing's vision of the world remained fundamentally pessimistic. Whatever his characters' aspirations in these and later novels, they are obliged for the most part to remain preoccupied with the brute struggle for survival in a society indifferent to them. In this struggle, their normal condition is one of alienation. They are motivated for the most part by the private need to be selfish, self-assertive, and realistic in their day-by-day assessment of the utility or futility of friendship. If they come to know each other at all well, their relationships are more likely than not also seen in terms of self-assertion and alienation. Gissing's anti-heroic stance did not allow him to attach much importance to whatever might happen to individuals or grow between them and, since the alienation of most people much of the time occurred on the surface of existence, it is the surface of existence that in these later novels he for the most part treated. *In the Year of Jubilee*, *The Whirlpool* and *The Crown of Life* are the most interesting novels in the last group and each of them demonstrates a characteristic irresolution of this kind.

Of the three, *In the Year of Jubilee*[7] is the weakest, probably because Gissing failed to convince Lawrence & Bullen of the integrity of the novel as he originally conceived it. The novel as we have it is a merciless, even clinical depiction of materialism at work. The characters for the most part are without standards of any kind. They simply survive. They are also for the most part without background;

like Nancy Lord, 'they wanted to live in the present', and to do this it was often easier to conceal their origins. Lionel Tarrant, for example, conceals the fact that his financial independence comes from the fortune his grandfather made in the black lead business. In any case, their origins are obscure or unsatisfactory. Luckworth Crewe was abandoned when an infant and never knew his parents. Nancy Lord's parents were divorced and, though her mother returns during the course of the novel, as mother she has no effect upon Nancy's life. Lionel Tarrant's parentage is also obscure, to say the least.[8] They are what they are because of their parents but the parental contribution has been biological, not moral. How indeed could it be moral for people who find themselves swept by the tide of existence and must simply sink or swim? In a capitalist society, they must earn money, struggle to improve their lot, grasp such pleasures as they can and above all look out for themselves.

This, to the best of their abilities, they do. Arthur Peachey works in the disinfectant business; Mr Morgan is a debt collector. Luckworth Crewe, that 'keen man of affairs', becomes an advertising agent and a business entrepreneur with an office in Farringdon Street. Beatrice Peachey founds the South London Fashion Club, a retail clothing outlet designed to exploit the need for cheap clothes, however tasteless. Jessica Morgan, 'a dolorous image of frustrated sex', works herself to the bone in pursuit of the London University BA that she imagines will make her independent. Samuel Barnaby, more successful than the others, is made to characterize the meaninglessness of *petit-bourgeois* existence when it is devoted solely to money making and creature comfort. And so on. They feel themselves to be engaged in the 'battle of life' and have little time for speculation about the meaning of their existence. Why speculate, when one is forced to live entirely in the present?

The love affair of Nancy Lord and Lionel Tarrant, which results eventually in a loveless marriage of convenience, is seen as part of the fabric of a materialist society – a universe, in fact, where convenience rules. Even in the published version of the novel, the sexuality which attracts them to each other in the first place is represented as an aberration, both in the sense that Nancy Lord would have been more sensible had she not encouraged Tarrant to 'seduce' her,[9] and in the sense that sex was an inconvenience for anyone whose main energies had to be devoted to survival. Nancy Lord's 'ambitious desire' for Tarrant was a response to his attitude of superiority, as she thought it, and when she allowed him to dominate 'a languor crept upon her, a soft and delicious subdual of the will to dreamy luxury'. Gissing understood, and here portrayed, the mutual sexuality of man and woman, although not as a profound force that deepened their awareness of each other. Instead he bent the plot to a modern solution in which Nancy Lord and Lionel Tarrant accepted that they had little in common, were in fact alienated and loveless, even though, rationally, Tarrant comes to recognize and acknowledge his responsibility for their child. So much for hasty, seaside marriages, the satirist in Gissing seems to say, while leaving the psychological potential of this central relationship undeveloped. In a passage deleted from the manuscript at the last moment, Beatrice Peachey was made to say: 'It's a stupid sort of thing, getting married . . . You're either a man's slavey, or you have to live a cat & dog life with him; best & worst, rich or poor, it comes to the same thing after a month or two'.[10] Gissing saw the institution of marriage as part of his vision of a fractured society. Lionel Tarrant's limited acceptance of responsibility for his child (an acceptance anticipated in *The Odd Women* when Rhoda Nunn asks Barfoot what he would do in like circumstances) and his assertion of the need for individual independence, as opposed to acceptance of a conventional domestic role, is a version of how a person might cope. To hope for better than this would be a wild dream.

For most readers, *In the Year of Jubilee* is too disjointed, too episodic, and they are not helped at all by the understanding that Gissing's anti-Romantic purposes made this almost inevitable. It is worth noting in passing, however, that once again Gissing had to soften the impact of the novel at the last moment by deleting the derogatory remarks about marriage, or many of them, by deleting the passages concerning Nancy Lord's possible breach of promise action, by deleting some of the more satirical remarks about conventional attitudes (for example, Mrs Romane's ignorance of the Bible) and by deleting all but the most oblique references to Tarrant's illegitimacy. Whether the novel as a whole was strengthened or weakened by the removal of passages that might have been deemed offensive, this last change clearly altered the balance of the novel by removing from it what might have been seen as the cause of Tarrant's 'instability'. Obviously in the novel as first conceived, Tarrant's illegitimacy was on a par with the broken marriages, divorces, matrimonial alienations and so on that characterize the whole world of *In the Year of Jubilee*. It may have been the publisher who objected to the implication that, because illegitimate, Tarrant was likely to 'take advantage' of Nancy Lord, but if so it remains the case that Gissing failed to replace it with anything very convincing. In the unrevised novel Nancy Lord forced Tarrant to marry her and then found out that he was illegitimate. In the published novel, the reader is not told what passed between them beyond the fact that their first sexual encounter immediately led to marriage. In the unrevised novel, called at first 'Miss Lord' and then 'Miss Lord of Camberwell', this was seen as partly Nancy Lord's doing, was in fact a consequence of the woman's as well as of the man's sexuality. In the published novel, Gissing reverted to the conventional notion that it had to be the man who 'seduced' the woman. It seems amazing that a well-established novelist would have to adapt to Victorian taste in this way, as late as 1894, but it was so. The novel was damaged beyond repair and Gissing never revised it.

He did, however, after an interval devoted to pot-boilers and the writing of short stories,[11] return to his study of capitalism as made manifest in the business world of London. *The Whirlpool*,[12] in this respect, is much more successful than *In the Year of Jubilee*, chiefly because it is a more tightly organized book. The organization inevitably resulted in melodrama, but that was the price Gissing had to pay in order to avoid the merely superficial, the merely episodic.

Readers have criticised Gissing for having given Harvey Rolfe in *The Whirlpool* a private income,[13] as though he were not after all writing about the actualities of existence but only about those who hold aloof from it. This is once again to make the mistake of identifying with a single character as though he were a character in a romance. Harvey Rolfe is himself on the edge of the whirlpool, is not independent of its motion. He says as much in his letter to Hugh Carnaby after the suicide of Bennet Frothingham: 'I feel as if we were all being swept into a ghastly whirlpool which roars over the bottomless pit'.[14]

It is the whirlpool of materialism, in which the individual, however frugal, however adventurous with money, struggles for financial independence in a world whose capitalist mechanisms make independence from the system virtually impossible. Preoccupied throughout his lifetime by the problems of individual liberty, Gissing saw that the arrangements of modern society inevitably denied it. Thus the calamities of modern life were not primarily the fault of the individuals concerned. It was not a moral matter. Rather the individual, unless he was extraordinarily lucky, was sucked into the processes of society where he was at the mercy of economic and social forces for the most part beyond his comprehension.

Partly these forces were hereditary. 'So does a man repeat the experience of the race, and with each step onward live into the meaning of some old word that he has but idly echoed'.[15] Not for nothing did Mary Abbot refer Harvey Rolfe to Ribot's *L'Hérédité psychologique*, a book which Rolfe dismisses as uninteresting but which Gissing had recently read. 'Heredity is that biological law', it begins, 'by which all things endowed with life tend to repeat themselves in their descendents: it is for the species what personal identity is for the individual'.[16] Editor of the principal French journal of psychology and eminent practitioner in the school of Charcot, Théodule Ribot was only one of the psychologists whose work in the 1890s was receiving popular and professional attention. As mentioned in chapter I, most Victorians who had been convinced by their reading of Spencer and Darwin, or who had been impressed by talk about their ideas, understood that they had psychological implications in as far as the whole basis for thinking about human motivation had altered. At the same time, the theorists who would provide workable, conceptual frameworks within which these ideas might be worked out had not yet appeared on the scene. Consequently, there occurred a generation of writers,[17] and Gissing was one of them, for whom the notions of heredity and evolution had great weight (particularly because responsibility for human actions was no longer vested in the individual) but for whom, nonetheless, heredity and evolution functioned much more as forces that were known but not understood than as clearly definable aspects of motivation. The difficulty was to connect the overall causes of human behaviour with the motives of individuals, but this was only possible on a superficial level. Thus, in a book like *The Whirlpool*, Gissing keeps his sense of characters acting out a role over which they have little control, resigned to a relatively passive acceptance of the circumstances of life as they found them. But there is also the lurking idea of degeneracy. A society is in decay and this, too, is an inevitable part of the evolutionary process.

Social disintegration is powerfully expressed in *The Whirlpool*, albeit without stridency. Jacob Korg was perhaps misled by this lack of stridency when he said that, in this novel, 'trivial causes produce grotesquely disproportionate effects'.[18] Not so. The causes of social decay are far from trivial in Gissing's world but their manifestations obviously occur on the surface of life where they can be experienced. The characters in *The Whirlpool* are allowed to participate in an action where what they do matters to them, but for them, as for the narrator, lacks fundamental meaning, or at least lacks meaning that can be related to the specific things that occur. To say that the action lacks fundamental meaning, philosophically, is not to claim that it lacks importance for the characters. On the contrary, they find themselves struggling for survival – for both personal and economic survival – in the competitive world of a commercial centre, London, a world that depends not upon sets of values that could be stated unambiguously but upon compromise. To survive at all involved compromise, of one kind or another. Bennet Frothingham embezzles his clients' funds, is found out, and commits suicide. Alma Rolfe compromises herself for the sake of a career as an artist by indiscretions with Felix Dymes and Cyrus Redgrave, is alienated from her husband, takes to drugs, and kills herself with an overdose. The Carnabys lose all their possessions to a professional thief who masquerades as a housekeeper and who, when she turns up later in the novel as the housekeeper of Cyrus Redgrave, is perfectly willing to use her knowledge of the women who visit the house for purposes of blackmail. These women include Sybil Carnaby and, on one occasion, Alma Rolfe. The forces of social disintegration that cause disruption in the professional life of the city, leading to bankruptcies, embezzlements, frauds, financial disasters, also cause the disruption of personal life, because marriage has become unstable, even undesirable, while sexual emancipation (or indifference to taboo) has resulted in complicated, modern (but in the Gissing universe, or at least in the universe of this book, never satisfactory) relationships between people. Why should the housekeeper not steal from the employer whose wealth itself derives from a type of theft? Why should Felix Dyce not want to sleep with Harvey Rolfe's wife, particularly since the Rolfe's marriage was visibly unsuccessful? No one in this 'universe' is positively good; no one is positively bad. They are all part of an alien world in which they must cope as best they can. It is only natural that many of them fail.

That Gissing saw social disintegration in contemporary, evolutionary terms is quite clear. For example, when Harvey Rolfe tries to puzzle out for himself Cyrus Redgrave's motive for helping Hugh Carnaby financially, not knowing at that time that there was anything between Cyrus Redgrave and Sybil Carnaby, for indeed she concealed 'the gross necessities of life' by being a woman who could 'look and smile at one without conveying the faintest suggestion of her actual thoughts', he felt himself threatened by the anarchic life of speculation and mere adventure that others were leading.

> He had always thought with uttermost contempt of the man who allows himself to be gripped, worried, dragged down, by artificial necessities. Was he himself to become a victim of this social disease? Was he, resistless, to be drawn into the muddy whirlpool, to spin round and round among

gibbering phantoms, abandoning himself with a grin of inane conceit, or clutching in desperation at futile hopes?[19]

If a man does not over-extend himself financially, if his personal life is governed by commonsense, if he observes the ancient social proprieties, Harvey Rolfe thinks that it is possible to stay out of trouble — certainly out of the trouble that almost engulfed his friend Cecil Morphew when he put £500 (shadily garnered on the stock market) into a 'proprietory club' whose business terminated in a police raid. The metaphor of 'social disease', always current during Gissing's writing career,[20] consolidated itself in the 1890s as part of the language that allowed discussion of urban anarchy, of moral anarchy, that is. As part of all this, Gissing in his normal sardonic fashion, allows his main character, Harvey Rolfe, to deceive himself. The retention of the old values involved absurdities like not telling Alma their financial position: 'this was a matter which did not immediately concern Mrs Rolfe'. For his wife, on the other hand, it implied a mismatch: 'how much better for him and for her if they had never met! Their thoughts and purposes so unalike; he with his heart set on grave, quiet, restful things, hating the world's tumult, ever hoping to retire beyond its echo; she, her senses crying for the delight of an existence that loses itself in whirl and glare'.[21] This is late in the novel, but earlier Rolfe himself in a moment of irritation had said: 'What has it to do with *you*, the kind of life that suits *me*'.[22] They themselves in short are a prime example of social disintegration manifesting itself in an unequal, unsatisfactory marriage, and Harvey Rolfe's habit of keeping up appearances and deceiving himself is a necessary part of Gissing's overall view. He is not nostalgic for the ancient verities: people who *are* nostalgic are simply part of the fragmented mosaic of modern life.

It is difficult to avoid the thought that in writing *The Whirlpool* Gissing had pushed his alien art, if not to its limit, at least to his. His special subject had come to be the negation of desire. In his novels, love was rarely consummated; love affairs were scarcely ever allowed to begin, let alone last; marriages rarely developed; rarely did people find understanding and wisdom in shared suffering; time itself, it is almost true to say, was denied. Whereas at the outset of his career, one saw Gissing 'studying' the contemporary as an integral part of the Continental European art he wished to emulate, towards the end of it he seemed to retain a pre-occupation with the contemporary because of an ignorance of or indifference to all else. This is not strictly true, of course; he retained his own love of traditional culture while noticing its disappearance from contemporary England and in the balance he placed sane, post-Romantic characters like Mary Barfoot in *The Odd Women* (nothing negative in her speech on the role of women in modern society) and Micklethwaite, the level-headed, pure mathematician in the same novel with his *avant-garde* interest in theories of relativity. In the main, however, Gissing was a consistent nihilist, who denied meaning to desire and aspiration, isolated the present from both past and future, and consistently saw a much greater likelihood of misunderstanding and disagreement between human beings than the opposite. For a nihilist to create fictions at all had been a triumph, but how could he have continued? There is a limit to the exposure of other people's social predicaments and the art of alienation leads eventually to the literature of the absurd. Whether Gissing felt this is difficult to determine. In *The Crown of Life*[23] he maintained the stance of social commentator and satirist, but for once – perhaps because of his own affair with Gabrielle Fleury – allowed a love affair to prosper. Some readers will see this as a finale to a career that could not have continued for long on the same lines. Others will see it as a significant change of direction.

For twenty years Gissing's fiction had involved social commentary and as he mastered the technique of narration, and limited the power of the narrator who in the early novels had so coloured the writing by his moralizing, so the documentary element was subsumed by an art whose essential features derived from the late nineteenth-century nihilist conciousness. Social commentary and narrative art were thus held in balance, the one with the other, the nihilist vision always dominant. In *The Crown of Life* the documentary element is strong, for as in *In the Year of Jubilee* and *The Whirlpool* the lives of individuals – Olga Hannaford, Piers Otway, Irene Derwent, Miss Bonnicastle, Mr Kite, Mr Fiorio, and others – are seen in a social context in which most of their energies are devoted merely to the business of trying to cope. Again London, the business capital, is imagined as a place which negates humanity:

> Piers Otway saw it all in a lurid light. These towering edifices with inscriptions numberless, announcing every imaginable form of trade with every corner of the world; here a vast building, consecrate in all its commercial magnificence, great windows and haughty doorways, the gleam of gilding and brass, the lustre of polished woods, to a single company or firm; here a huge structure which housed on its many floors a crowd of enterprises, names by the score signalled at the foot of the gaping staircase; arrogant suggestions of triumph side by side with desperate beginnings; titles of world-wide significance meeting the eye at every turn, vulgar names with more weight than those of princes, words in small

lettering which noted the fate of millions of men; – no nightmare was ever so crushing to one in Otway's mood. The brute force of money; the negation of the individual – these, the evils of our time, found their supreme expression in the City of London. Here was opulence at home and superb; here must poverty lurk and shrink, feeling itself alive only on sufferance; the din of highway and byway was a voice of blustering conquest, bidding the weaker stand aside or be crushed. Here no man was a human being, but each merely a portion of an inconceivably complicated mechanism.[24]

Passages of this kind speak for themselves. The individual is involved in the struggle for existence: he must stand aside or be crushed if he does not wish to participate in the struggle. He is at the mercy of what we call the big corporation: there is no connection between his basic humanity and the corporate machine. This is London seen through the eyes of Piers Otway and it is the effect of the nightmare on him with which the narrator is concerned. Hardly subtle, one might say, this link between character and environment, but it is much better than anything Gissing would have done in the 1880s. Meanwhile Gissing has developed a very sure documentary touch, despite the retention of words like 'vulgar' and 'brute'.

Piers Otway's hatred of London was reinforced later in the novel when he visited a hospital to see a friend who had been run over by a cab.

In these gaunt streets along which he passed at night, how many a sad heart suffered, by the dim glimmer that showed at upper windows, a hopeless solitude amid the unnumerable throng! Human cattle, the herd that feed and breed, with them it was well; but the few born to a desire for ever unattainable, the gentle spirits who from their prisoning circumstance looked up and afar, how the heart ached to think of them! Some girl, of delicate instinct, of purpose sweet and pure, wasting her unloved life in toil and want and indignity; some man, whose youth and courage strove against a mean environment, whose eyes grew haggard in the vain search for a companion promised in their dreams; they lived, these two, parted perchance only by the wall of neighbour houses, yet all huge London was between them, and their hands would never touch. Beside this hunger of love, what was the stomach-famine of a multitude that knew no other?[25]

Gissing, if not Piers Otway, was familiar enough with 'stomach famine' for this remark not to be taken lightly: only a decade earlier he had given a haunting depiction of destitution and hunger in *The Nether World*. He now, in *The Crown of Life*, contrived a novel which is similar in almost every respect but one to those he wrote earlier in the decade. The concern is still with dislocated urban characters. The scandals and problems that disrupt their lives are again seen as a function of 'civilization'. Again the fabric of society is made more complex by a vision of degeneracy, whether it be Otway's illegitimacy or Irene Derwent's breach of promise. The characters are as much fallible people in an imperfect capitalist and ultimately destructive world as they were in *In the Year of Jubilee* and *The Whirlpool*. The only difference is that Gissing allows the love of Piers Otway and Irene Derwent to prosper and endure. What would have happened had Rhoda Nunn and Everard Barfoot met after an interval of years? The question is pointless. In 1893 Gissing saw love from a negative point of view. When he wrote *The Crown of Life* he permitted his characters a greater optimism, gave them more of a chance. The difference was not in the plot: he was as interested as ever in the interplay of character and environment: he simply allowed his two main characters, this once, to overcome the obstacles that usually in modern life held people apart.

It seems fairly obvious that the novels Gissing wrote in the 1890s, at least his principal novels, constitute a logical extension of his writing career and that he succeeded in perfecting a means by which his social and psychological interests could be integrated in convincing, but also enigmatic fictions. He had made himself into a successful novelist, overcoming some of the difficulties enumerated in earlier chapters and achieving a synthesis which the novel reading public could and did accept, despite his nihilism. This development, and this success, show by themselves the extent to which Gissing for two decades had been concerned with the art of the novel. His experiments had produced results and his questions about the art appropriate to the end of the nineteenth century had been answered in his own books.

8
Conclusion

IN *The Whirlpool*, Harvey Rolfe's 'heart went forth to protect and cherish' his son, Hughie, whom he loved deeply. 'He liked to feel the soft little hand clasping his own fingers, so big and coarse in comparison and happily so strong. For the child's weakness he felt an infinite pathos; a being so entirely helpless, so utterly dependent upon other's love, standing there amid a world of cruelties, smiling and trustful'.[1] One of the warmest, most natural relationships in the whole of Gissing's work is that between Rolfe and his son, as it is felt by both of them, for example, when on a different occasion they travel down to Kent together by train. 'Harvey could not see too much of the little boy, indoors or out, and it rejoiced him to know that his love was returned in full measure; for Hughie would at any time abandon other amusements to be with his father'.[2] It is the father, most positively not the mother, who willingly becomes responsible for his son's upbringing and Gissing describes the way they talk to each other and their reading at bedtime, when the strong bond of affection was reinforced.

This affection grows naturally in a house where the love between husband and wife has died and it is interesting to notice the context the novelist creates for it. The intelligent and, as Gissing said elsewhere, over-civilized couple have become alienated. Alma Rolfe has lost her second child, has become seriously ill, is addicted to morphine. 'Happy she was not, and probably nothing in his power to do could make her so'.[3] In this important chapter (Chapter VI), innocence and experience are contrasted. The love of father and son depends upon the son's innocence; the lack of love between husband and wife results from the lifetime of experiences that has rendered them unable to think about each other except negatively. Rolfe 'found solace in remembering that after no great lapse of time he and those he loved would have vanished from the earth, would be as though they had not been at all; every pang and woe awaiting them suffered and forgotten; the best and the worst gone by forever; the brief flicker of troubled light quenched in eternal oblivion'.[4] Here is the old nihilist who has inhabited Gissing's pages from the outset.

A characteristically cool, seemingly dispassionate Gissing paragraph follows the simple statements about Rolfe's affection for his son.

> Nothing else seemed of moment beside this one duty, which was also the purest joy. The word 'father', however sweet to his ear, had at times given him a thrill of awe; spoken by childish lips, did it mean less than 'God'? He was the giver of life, and for that dread gift must hold himself responsible. A man in his agony may call upon some unseen power, but the heavens are mute; can a father turn away in heedlessness if the eyes of his child reproach him? All pleasures, aims, hopes that concerned himself alone, shrank to the idlest trifling when he realised the immense debt due from him to his son; no possible sacrifice could discharge it. He marvelled how people could insist upon the duty of children to parents. But did not the habit of thought ally itself naturally enough with that strange religion which, under direst penalties, exacts from groaning and travailing humanity a tribute of fear and love to the imagined Author of its being?[5]

It was typical of Gissing to insist, humanely, on the responsibility of the father, even though it was a responsibility mixed with fear. His entire *opus*, after all, constitutes a strong humanist statement, in which a negative social and philosophical attitude to life as a whole, and Victorian society in particular, is balanced by a positive preference for an ethic based upon understanding, honesty and self-control. But what of Rolfe's perception that his relationship with Hughie was akin to the supposed relationship between a human being and Christian God? Of course the sardonic turn of thought is at the expense of Christianity: given the strength of feeling between father and son, Gissing or Harvey Rolfe is saying, the association of the feeling with those of a religion should cause little surprise, an idea which renders both sides of the equation suspect. Although the love between Harvey and Hughie Rolfe is presented as genuine, spontaneous, natural, and needing no explanation, Gissing was incapable of leaving it at that. The world created in these novels, though conceived by an agnostic humanist, was essentially loveless. Only very rarely are there moments filled with the pure pleasure of affection. Only very rarely does Gissing allow his characters spontaneity and relaxed pleasure of any kind. When he does, the occasion is notable.

Indeed, as one thinks back over his whole work, it is with the realization that his sustained attack upon false or Romantic love has left little room in his imaginative universe for any other kind of love. This seems in fact one of the principal controlling elements of all his fiction. Waymark and Ida Starr enjoyed an easy and relaxed companionship in *The Unclassed*; Gissing has *The Crown of Life* end with an affirmation of love between Irene Derwent and Piers Otway. 'All at once, he thought amid his triumph of those unhappy ones whom the glory of love could never bless; those, men and women, born to a vain longing such as he had known, doomed to the dread solitude from which he by miracle had been saved. His heart swelled, and his eyes were hot with tears'. As Piers Otway returned from this night-time meeting with Irene near the castle, 'he whispered the beloved name, and it gave him peace; such peace as follows upon the hallowing of a profound passion, justified of reason, and proof under the hand of time'.[6] Between *The Unclassed*, one of Gissing's earliest books, and *The Crown of Life*, one of his last, few characters had known a passion that was 'justified of reason, and proof under the hand of time'. Most lived in a world where passion had to be denied, either because it was false or because circumstance held out no chance of fulfilment. Often it was circumstance that taught a Gissing character the necessity of resignation; Gissing's resolutely, anti-Romantic bent involved a denial of the possibility that strong feeling, strong attachment, might allow people to triumph over circumstance. Thus Thyrza and Walter Egremont, Godwin Peak and Sidwell Warricombe, Rhoda Nunn and Everard Barfoot give up, though they love each other, and abandon themselves to what they take to be the limitations of existence. If people come together, it is necessarily not under the pressure of passion but with the extremely modest expectations that they consider to be rational, as in the conclusions to *The Emancipated* and *New Grub Street*. Gissing saw that mutual respect and calm, rational understanding might stand a married couple in better stead than violent passion, but this was only part of a more general analysis of human relationships where happiness was more or less a matter of luck and not really to be expected from life.

It was Gissing's achievement to have explored, in a series of remarkably interesting novels, sets of 'modern' relationships between people in the class-structured but nonetheless essentially fragmented and dislocated urban societies of late nineteenth-century England. He was in fact the English master of dislocation, alienation, estrangement; fiction's foremost nihilist and the poet, one might almost say, of the rootless, displaced intellect. An important part of this was his perception that sexuality as often held people apart as united them (with which, of course, we need neither agree nor disagree here), that sexual desires and needs undercut the type of rational behaviour associated 'with being civilized', and that sexual jealousy was a powerful determinant of human behaviour. He understood that, in a godless world and in an urban society where the forces of an inhuman materialism always tended to overwhelm, or at least dwarf the individual, patterns of behaviour were bound to suffer, with the traditional giving way to the chaotic and unexpected. Evidently, in these circumstances, it was important for a novelist to know how people related to each other, just as it was important for a person who was not a novelist. This must be the very stuff of fiction. But while Gissing became adept at creating the breakdown of relationships, indeed was more adept at it than anyone else in England, the almost total denial of love in novel after novel gave his work as a whole a devastatingly negative quality. Nothing really withstands examination. Nothing is ultimately meaningful.

Of course, other writers, particularly existentialist writers at the beginning of the twentieth century, have been as negative. Where they differed from Gissing is chiefly in allowing their characters to suffer and agonize merely as a result of their failure to discover the Absolute. This *angst* Gissing would have regarded as a Romantic indulgence. If there is not a God, why agonize? If the forces of heredity and environment are always stronger than the individual will, why cry out? If sexual loneliness is a function of the need to perpetuate the species, why attach importance to marriage? If merely to think about the world leads to the conclusion that none of one's fundamental questions about its meaning will ever be satisfied, why suppose that two thinking people will ever find a basis for living with each other for the whole of their lives? What distinguishes Gissing from existentialist novelists, who allow their characters to agonize, is his ruthless or logically unremitting reluctance to resort to a panacea of any kind. Even limited and modest stratagems for living are regarded with the greatest scepticism, are always on the edge of the whirlpool, are invariably depicted within a larger environment characterized by breakdown and social dislocation.

It has been seen that Gissing's novels were part of the process by which established ideas about the author and society were challenged during the last two decades of the nineteenth century. In them the techniques of a more deliberately critical social realism that ever strained in the direction of an imported naturalism became, briefly, one of the means by which the novelist asserted his independence, his seriousness, his right to incorporate within his fiction the brainstuff of which Meredith talked and, in the case of Gissing, contained his most deeply felt insights, perceptions, and thoughts. Straight-forward advocacy of principles of social realism lasted only for a short period before the tide of public opinion turned against it. The Vizetelly case had brought the issues into the public domain. Zola by 1890 was familiar to English readers. Novelists like Hardy and Meredith had also begun to be more assertive, more free, and a new generation of novelists was already on the scene. The story of this process of liberation is familiar and a good number of critics have dated it precisely. G. T. Becker, for example, in the Introduction to *Documents of Modern Literary Realism*, wrote:

> The initial impact of realism had spent itself in France before the end of the century. 'The Manifesto of Five against Zola' in 1887 and Jules Hûret's *Enquête* in 1891 indicate the turn of the tide. Huysmans broke away from the Médan group; Bourget's *Le Disciple* (1889) attacked the moral premises and influences of realism. Actually 1893 is often taken as a terminal date: Maupassant and Taine died in that year; the Rougon-Macquart was completed; and Zola's arch-enemy Brunetière defeated him in a contest for a place in the French Academy.[7]

This sort of comment raises, of course, as many issues as it resolves. The 'initial impact of realism had spent itself' but the impact of the movement continued to be felt, in as far as the novel was regarded as a serious not an escapist mode, was taken more and more to be a legitimate artistic activity, not a second-rate citizen in the world of letters, was accepted as the vehicle for social commentary in fictions where the reader could understand the commentary was the characters' not necessarily the author's and was, in a more general sense, taken to be worthy of attention because no longer in its very nature committed to euphemism, evasion and the creation of fantasy worlds so utterly different from those in which the readers lived that no connection could be made between the two. Contemporary reviews, of the kind gathered together in the *Critical Heritage* volume,[8] show that Gissing was understood to have played a major role in this process of liberation. But then so, of course, did the reader play a major role, by becoming more sophisticated, more capable of distinguishing between character and author, more appreciative of novels written from a variety of points of view, and more open minded about the doctrinal implications of books that did not directly satisfy his own moral sense. The reader had in part been put in this position by writers like Gissing, who in progressive stages tested what the reader would accept as they discovered what they themselves could do. It is important, historically, to see the extent to which Gissing developed as a craftsman – and at the centre of this book is the assertion that he did develop – because we happen to have here a writer whose career proceeds in step with public taste, as measured by what the public is prepared to accept, which is not to say that the novelist is the cause, certainly not the single cause, of the change. In England, the change was brought about by a combination of factors: the pragmatic judgements of publishers who realized, with their fingers on the public's pulse, that mid-Victorian restrictiveness was no longer wanted; the manufacturing processes that allowed the publication of cheaper, one-volume novels and so contributed to the demise of the circulating library; the changes in the American copyright law which made American agents travel to England to secure rights, thus introducing an element of competition which made the English novelist less dependent upon the judgement, or whim, of the English publisher;[9] and the extension of the reading public itself, where rapid population growth, popular education and accelerated urbanization combined to produce new social circumstances and, literally, more people who wanted fiction to read. Gissing, as much as any other late nineteenth-century writer, was for two decades at the centre of all this. He perceived an opportunity, which he met by devising a type of social realism different in important respects from anything that had previously been published in England.

What Gissing might have done had he lived twenty more years is a matter of conjecture. His own work had brought him to the point at which he needed the breakthrough that was in fact achieved by D. H. Lawrence, the break-through involved in the perception that sexuality was not to be dismissed in Spenglerian terms as part of the 'decay' of civilization, nor condemned as a destructive force in the whirlpool of modern life. Despite obvious differences, Gissing and Lawrence have much in common, not least their ability to make relationships between characters develop by means of vivid, tersely written dialogue. If social realism, as it veered towards naturalism, were seen as a brief period of transition between high-Victorian fiction and the modern novel, then Gissing's work would fall completely within that period, so one would need to note that he was not only the principal, but perhaps the only major English novelist who did not span a different period at either end of his career. He never inhabited the world of George Eliot; he had only glimpses of the world of D. H. Lawrence. This being so, his fiction in all its strengths and weaknesses is inextricably mixed up with the process by which both the novel itself and the social role of the novelist altered radically.

He himself wrote an essay called 'The Place of Realism in Fiction' (1895), a calm summing up of his ideas and feelings about the art of which he had been one of the earliest English practitioners. Amongst other things he said:

Realism, then, signifies nothing more than artistic sincerity in the portrayal of contemporary life; it merely contrasts with the habit of mind which assumes that a novel is written 'to please people', that disagreeable facts must always be kept out of sight, that human nature must by systematically flattered, that the book must have a 'plot', that the story should end on a cheerful note, and all the rest of it. Naturally, the question arises: What limits does the independent novelist impose on himself? Does he feel free to select *any* theme, from the sweetest to the most nauseating? Is it enough to declare that he has looked upon this or that aspect of life, has mirrored it in his imagination, and shows it forth candidly, vividly? For my own part, I believe he must recognize limits in every direction; that he will constantly reject material as unsuitable to the purposes of art; and that many features of life are so completely beyond his province that he cannot dream of representing them. At the same time I joyfully compare the novelist's freedom in England of to-day with his bondage of only ten or twelve years ago. No doubt the new wine of liberty tempts to excess. Moreover, novels nowadays are not always written for the novel's sake, and fiction cries aloud as the mouthpiece of social reform. The great thing is, that public opinion no longer constrains a novelist to be false to himself. The world lies open before him, and it is purely a matter for his private decision whether he will write as the old law dictates or show life its image as he beholds it.[10]

In the novels which followed *Born in Exile,* Gissing rapidly succeeded in using this new freedom. Other novelists – Proust, Mann, D. H. Lawrence, Kafka, Virginia Woolf – succeeded in different ways. Once the battle for increased artistic freedom was over there was no point, anymore, in writing as Gissing had done in the 1880s. The novelist's problems in the face of his subject had altered. It followed that his technique and indeed his whole attitude to his craft would have to alter also.

Looking back over Gissing's career as a novelist, one can see the strenuous, determined way in which he had explored his 'province', sought out his freedom and developed his craft, from the times in those early novels when the passionately concerned, moralistic narrator had to be Gissing himself, so unsubtle was the narrative technique, to the later novels which show, relatively speaking, his mastery of change of pace, change of perspective, change of narrative point of view. The new generation of novelists at the beginning of the twentieth century simply abandoned the conventions of the Victorian novel and started afresh; it was Gissing's special place to have been a profoundly committed novelist during the period of transition.

It is hoped that the particular studies contained in this book will contribute in a small way to the reassessment of a writer who wrote at least a handful of good books and made an important contribution to the way in which the English novel developed. To sustain the notion that an author whose work was so varied and extensive failed to develop as a craftsman because preoccupied with his own early experiences is simply a mistake, as well as an injustice. Of course there is, there must be, a relation between a writer's life and his work and of course this relation can be studied in the case of Gissing just as well as in any other case. *The Unclassed* is a novel of his first marriage; *Demos, Thyrza* and *The Nether World* books written when he lived by himself in London; *New Grub Street* and *Born in Exile* reassessments of his own early work and his own turbulent existence written at the time of his second marriage; *In the Year of Jubilee* and *The Whirlpool* the novels of his stoutly professional years when he was an established writer; *The Crown of Life* a novel written during the full flood of Gissing's friendship with Gabrielle Fleury. And so on. Furthermore, when closer critical work has been done on Gissing's fiction, it will no doubt emerge that many characters in the novels are in fact portraits of people like Edith Sichel, Morley Roberts, Clara Collett and people Gissing knew in London and Wakefield. It will probably also emerge, not that the moralistic and pessimistic tone of the early books reflected his own early traumas, but that the repression of those traumas affected, maybe resulted in, his depiction of urban alienation later in his career. Whatever the merits of such lines of speculation, it would seem best, as a prudent first step, to extricate ourselves from the muddle of critical–cum–biographical talk about Gissing and avoid making simplistic connections between the man and his work. Gissing, the writer, quite obviously thought a great deal about how to write a modern novel. He experimented a lot. He revised his early work. He adopted new techniques at various stages of his career. He wrote a range of books that few others could emulate. It is on this level, as a writer, that it seems best to try to meet him.

As a powerful, resourceful and widely recognized contemporary writer, he clearly had limitations and some of them, like the avoidance of metaphor, were self-imposed. Realism denies metaphor. If the physical world in all its detail, down to its last detail, is to be described dispassionately just as the novelist sees it, novelist and character seeing it in a virtually identical way, it follows that the same details cannot participate, as it were, in metaphorical constructions which would tend to invalidate 'phenomena' as *the* reality. A serious step for any writer to take. Throughout the manuscripts Gissing deleted passages that had the resonance of metaphor, which were in some way – perhaps unintentionally – symbolic. In doing so he was being entirely consistent. He was accepting one of his own 'limits', to keep his own word (which does not mean 'limitation'). Thus, in *In the Year of Jubilee*, Gissing deleted Tarrant's dream in which he had sighted Nancy Lord peering over a thick hedge luxuriant with flowers, had pursued her into the woods, feeling that if he could only reach her everything would be all right again, and had found, not her, but a baby lying by itself in a glade. There is no firm evidence of the reason for this particular deletion but one can see easily enough that its inclusion would have given the story a different dimension.[11] This is only another way of saying that the unmetaphorical surface of a Gissing novel, which has the texture not of image but of brittle dialogue, was part, an essential and logically necessary part, of its overall design. A reader may crave for excitement, for metaphorical disturbances, for enigmas compatible with a sense of mystery and uncertainty, but there is no room in a realist novel for such indulgences. Gissing wrote a pure, disciplined English with great directness and economy, throughout his life admiring the same qualities in some Latin authors and avoiding rhetoric. His style was an efficient instrument that he adapted to his particular needs, learning in the end to balance crisply, economically written third-person narrative with vividly realized dialogue, in which characters realize themselves through their own words in dramatic situations that are so well conceived the intrusion of the novelist is no longer necessary. The merits of this style are, it must be repeated, more apparent in the revised texts.

Gissing, man and novelist, may elude us for many a year yet. When he makes remarks like 'the new wine of liberty tempts to excess', many readers may feel that he might well have allowed himself to be tempted. But that was not Gissing's way. He knew the difference between old wine and new, just as he knew the meaning of the word 'province'. He had lived through the period of bondage, had indeed become preoccupied with many versions of emancipation, but in the end succeeded as an artist, his distinctive, personal, private preoccupations becoming absorbed within his fiction as his skill increased and his wide knowledge of contemporary European literature being utilized efficiently for contemporary local purposes. As far as the art of fiction is concerned, this was a considerable achievement.

Notes

Abbreviations to the notes

Beinecke	The Beinecke Rare Book Room and Manuscript Library, Yale University, New Haven, Connecticut.
Berg	The Berg Collection of the New York Public Library.
Bertz	*The Letters of George Gissing to Eduard Bertz, 1887-1903*, A. C. Young (ed.), Rutgers University Press and Constable, 1961.
Commonplace Book	*George Gissing's Commonplace Book*, Jacob Korg (ed.), New York Public Library, 1962.
Diary	*London and the Life of Literature in Late Victorian England: the Diary of George Gissing, Novelist*, Pierre Coustillas (ed.), Harvester Press, autumn 1978. Here the references are to the original in the Berg Collection of the New York Public Library.
Essays and Fiction	*George Gissing: Essays and Fiction*, Pierre Coustillas (ed.), the John Hopkins Press, 1970.
Fleury	*The Letters of George Gissing to Gabrielle Fleury*, Pierre Coustillas (ed.), New York Public Library, 1964.
Gettman	R. A. Gettman, *A Victorian Publisher*, Cambridge University Press, 1960.
Huntington	The Henry E. Huntington Library, San Marino, California.
Korg	Jacob Korg, *George Gissing: A Critical Biography*, Washington University Press, 1963, and Methuen, 1965.
Letters	*The Letters of George Gissing to Members of his Family*, collected and arranged by Algernon and Ellen Gissing, Constable, 1927.
NBL	Coustillas and Spiers (eds.), *The Rediscovery of George Gissing*, National Book League, 1971.
Pforzheimer	The Carl H. and Lily Pforzheimer Library, New York.
Ryecroft	George Gissing, *The Private Papers of Henry Ryecroft*, Constable, 1903.
Wells	*George Gissing and H. G. Wells*, R. A. Gettman (ed.), Hart Davis, 1961.

Chapter 1 *The Struggle for Acceptance*

1 One can only speculate. *Isabel Clarendon* (see chapter 3) seems to have been an attempt to write a polite novel that would be more acceptable than 'Mrs Grundy's Enemies' and *The Unclassed*. It will be seen, incidentally, that Gissing was not in the least like Dickens, though from time to time a critic will see a similarity because of their shared social concerns. Gissing's anti-Romantic, unmetaphorical treatment of urban subjects ensured that his books would be utterly different from those of Dickens, as he himself often pointed out.
2 Now available is Joseph Wolff's convenient guide to criticism and discussion of Gissing's work, *George Gissing an Annotated Bibliography of Writings about him*, Northern Illinois University Press, De Kalb, 1974.
3 As C. D. Stewart put it in the *University of Toronto Quarterly* (Summer 1977), p. 430: the discerning readers of Gissing 'have been vastly out-numbered by those who would agree with James Joyce's description of his work as *pastefazoi* (noodles and beans)'. In the latter camp would appear to be Walter Allen in his Pelican History of the Novel (*The English Novel*, pp. 287ff.) and Arnold Kettle, who relegates Gissing to the second rank in his Open University publications. In general, readers will veer away from Gissing if they seek what they consider to be an 'English' moral treatment of character (as in George Eliot) rather than the amoral disinterested (even scientific) treatment associated with Zola and other Continental writers.
4 Jacob Korg has drawn attention to the encouragement Eduard Bertz gave the young Gissing, especially while he was writing *Workers in the Dawn*. Other friends may also have encouraged him. Clara Collett, for example, admired *Born in Exile*: it is distinctly possible that she encouraged him to keep going during the nineties. On the other hand, apart from his brother, Algernon, to whom he once or twice wrote for practical information, the people with whom he lived – his sisters, his two wives, Gabrielle Fleury – had little influence upon his writing, except in a negative sense; that is, he frequently had to defend, explain and justify his work to them. The two most likely contenders for the role of a literary friend are Morley Roberts at the beginning of Gissing's career and H. G. Wells at the end, but very little survives to suggest that these men had conversations with Gissing similar to those of Howells and Henry James, or Pound and T. S. Eliot, or George Eliot and George Lewes. And, specifically, there is no record of Gissing showing a novel to a friend, while he was writing it – except, again, *Workers in the Dawn*.
5 The next few paragraphs are closely related to my *George Gissing: a Bibliography*, Dawson and the University of Toronto Press, 1976. Also useful are *The Rediscovery of George Gissing*, a reader's guide by Pierre Coustillas and John Spiers, National Book League, 1971, and the Introduction to Coustillas' *George Gissing Essays and Fiction*, the Johns Hopkins Press, 1970.
6 Unpublished letter, Pforzheimer Library, 24 June 1884. Few will doubt that Gissing's work involves a thorough-going critique of English society that has as much in common with Zola as with Dickens, but whether his problems with his publishers were of his own making or not is debatable.

He got on well with Smith of Smith, Elder & Co., and with Bullen of Lawrence & Bullen, which makes one think that his difficulties were not personal but had more to do with the publishing situation at the time he began to write.

7 For Gissing's relationship with Hardy, see R. L. Purdy, 'George Gissing at Max Gate', *Yale University Library Gazette*, XVII (January 1943) pp. 51–2, and my *George Gissing: a Biography*, Dawson, 1977.
8 See Wolff for the best listing of studies of Gissing's relationship with single authors like Turgenev and Schopenhauer. See R. A. Gettman, *Turgenev in England and America*, University of Illinois Press, 1941, pp. 144–8, and Gilbert Phelps 'Gissing, Turgenev and Dostoevsky', in Coustillas (ed.), *Collected Articles on George Gissing*, Frank Cass, 1968, pp. 99–105.
9 Although Gissing was himself aware that he had lowered his standards, modern readers may nonetheless decide that these novels are not without interest. See, for example, Pierre Coustillas' introduction to *Sleeping fires*, reprinted by Harvester Press in 1977.
10 *Essays and Fiction*, p. 70.
11 *Korg*, pp. 197–8.
12 *The House of Cobwebs and Other Stories*, Constable, 1906, p. xlix.
13 This was for the most part during the period of his second marriage and especially during the mid-1890s when new journals began to flourish and new editors, like Clement Shorter, tried to meet their constant need for new 'material' by approaching established authors directly. In Gissing's case this process was facilitated by the agents – especially W. M. Colles and J. B. Pinker – whose services he found he needed when he was away from London.
14 For Gissing's various writings on Dickens see *George Gissing: a Bibliography*, pp. 83–6 and Pierre Coustillas' *Gissing's Writings on Dickens*, Enitharmon Press, 1969.
15 Although this travel book, coming late in his career, only relates obliquely to a discussion of the art of fiction, it does of course confirm his cosmopolitan outlook.
16 Again, this work, *The Private Papers of Henry Ryecroft*, which took its present form while Gissing was living in France and which was first published in the *Fortnightly Review* in 1902–3, appeared too late in Gissing's life for it to have much bearing on his development as a novelist. A person bent on proving Gissing's Englishness would have it in mind, but would have to balance its expressions of patriotism with distinctly unpatriotic sentiments voiced in earlier books.
17 *Commonplace Book*, p. 33.
18 *Charles Dickens*, Blackie & Son, 1898, p. 1.
19 *Ibid.*, p. 282.
20 A superbly fascinating example of this type of misreading is Gillian Tindall's *The Born Exile*, mentioned below. Particularly stupefying is the circular argument which first states that some episodes in Gissing's novels are autobiographical (for example that Reardon in *New Grub Street* is a self-portrait) and secondly states that the autobiography reveals a weakness in Gissing, despite the lack of other evidence, that made him incapable of writing other than autobiographical novels. Notice that Reardon is not in the least like Gissing and the argument falls to the ground.

Another example of this damaging type of Gissing criticism is Patrick Yarker's 'Meredith, Hardy and Gissing' in *The Sphere History of Literature in the English Language*, Arthur Pollard (ed.), Sphere Books, 1969, pp. 231–62. This account is riddled with factual error: apparently Gissing, in Yarker's opinion, is an author about whom one can write without checking the evidence. Relevant here, though, is what Yarker says about *New Grub Street* (the unrevised *New Grub Street*, incidentally). 'No single character represents Gissing' he says, implying that Gissing is in some sense represented. But Reardon 'is a projection of Gissing's own worst fears' while Milvain is 'an ironic comment on the temporizing shrewdness necessary for survival, which Gissing, being incapable of it, sometimes almost envied' (p. 256). So with the other novels. The critic is content to let pseudo-biography replace genuine criticism and does not bother to come to terms with the novels themselves.

21 Repeated here in a slightly expanded form are the opinions earlier expressed in 'How George Gissing Disappeared', *English Studies in Canada*, Vol. 1 (Winter 1975), No. 4, pp. 434–49. 'Not available' means not readily available in good texts. The AMS reprints are not textually adequate editions. Nor in most cases are the Harvester Press photographic reproductions, insofar as the errors of the original are reproduced, while the choice of text is itself sometimes wrong and often debatable. One needs, not a photographic reprint series, but the republication of the novels based upon the establishment of the correct copy text. Ten novels are available from Harvester Press at the time of writing: *The Whirlpool, The Nether World, The Emancipated, Sleeping Fires, The Unclassed, In the Year of Jubilee, Thyrza, Our Friend the Charlatan, Demos* and *Isabel Clarendon*, with a further four due to be published later in 1978 (*The Odd Women, Born in Exile, Denzil Quarrier* and *The Crown of Life*).

22 Jacob Korg, *George Gissing: A Critical Biography*, University of Washington Press, Seattle, 1963, and Methuen, 1963. An important and extremely influential book in that it represented the first real attempt to see the overall shape of Gissing's writing life and to utilize unpublished material, Professor Korg's 'biography' nonetheless fails to distinguish satisfactorily between types of biographical evidence. The biographical 'meaning' of the novels is assumed; Gissing's letters are taken at face value.

23 In particular, the Enitharmon Press Gissing Series: *Gissing's Writings on Dickens*, 1970; *Henry Hick's Recollections of George Gissing*, 1973; *Gissing at Alderley Edge*, 1970; *Gissing East and West*, 1970; '*My First Rehearsal*' and '*My Clerical Rival*', 1970; *Letters to Edward Clodd*, 1973; as well as the bilingual edition of *The Private Papers of Henry Ryecroft* (*George Gissing: Les Carnets d'Henry Ryecroft*, Editions Montaigne, Paris, 1966); and his introductions to Harvester Press reprints of Gissing's novels. Although there is a parish magazine element to these publications, as there is to the *Gissing Newsletter* which fails regularly to distinguish between the important and the trivial (for nothing that relates to Gissing is unimportant to Mr Coustillas), the present resurgence of Gissing studies obviously owes a lot to his tireless enquiries and his painstaking attention to detail. These enquiries certainly compensate for the naïvité of his critical opinions as expressed, for example, in *George Gissing Essays and Fiction*.

24 Gillian Tindall, *The Born Exile, George Gissing*, London, 1974; Adrian Poole, *Gissing in Context*, London, 1976.
25 In the Introduction to my *George Gissing: a Bibliography*, Dawson, 1976.
26 See, for example, Walter Allen in *The English Novel*, p. 287: 'Gissing is not a great novelist but he is considerably more than a minor one. He is one of those imperfect artists whose work inevitably leads one back to the writer in person. His fiction is not, except in perhaps three instances, sufficiently detached from its creator; it is too personal, the powerful expression, one cannot help feeling, of a grudge'.
27 The work of Mrs Gaskell is available, for example, in a Penguin edition and is fairly well known because of various television productions, yet she is in no sense a better writer than Gissing, nor for that matter was her response to the contemporary scene more accurate or sensitive than his.
28 'Books on Hardy are legion', says Norman Page at the beginning of his excellent new book on Hardy (Routledge, 1977). Hardy, like Gissing, has easily distinguishable limitations of range, and like Gissing is an unequal writer: a lot has been written on Hardy, much less on Gissing; this by itself seems to account for the difference of reputation.
29 Like, for example, the rearrangement by which modern literature starts with the death of Dickens, or with the publication of *Les Fleurs du Mal*. A fairly recent example of this type of rewriting of literary history is provided by Raymond Williams in *The English Novel*, Paladin, 1974. 'I've argued before that in the late 1870s, the early 1880s, the Victorian period ended' (p. 98). Such statements merely represent the author's desire to ignore part of the evidence, the part that does not interest him.
30 'Bowdlerized' is perhaps too strong. In many instances, only part of the letter was printed; the omissions were not indicated; the dating is incorrect; and the order was disturbed. The editor's note reads: 'Portions have necessarily been omitted from many of the letters. Except in those cases where a definite theme has been broken into these omissions have not been indicated by dots'.
31 In the Beinecke Library at Yale, the Pforzheimer Library in New York, and the Berg Collection of the New York Public Library.
32 The best account of this is given in A. C. Young's Introduction to *The Letters of George Gissing to Eduard Bertz*, pp. xiv–xv.
33 See Coustillas' note on 'The Text' in *The Letters of George Gissing to Gabrielle Fleury*, pp. 21–2.
34 Gissing's diary, to be published by Harvester Press later in 1978, consists of brief daily entries, rarely more than three or four lines in length and mostly concerned with his reading, the progress of his work, and his health. It is an almost exclusively personal record, the factual content of which has been extensively used in recent books on Gissing. Though it will be useful to have it in print, no revelations should be anticipated. Gissing rarely commented on contemporary figures or events and not by any stretch of the imagination could it be thought that the diaries shed light on 'The Life of Literature in Victorian England' which is a misleadingly pretentious title.
35 Gissing's letters to publishers and agents are utilized extensively, but not reproduced, in my own *George Gissing: a Bibliography*, Dawsons and the University of Toronto Press, 1976.

Chapter 2 *'Tableaux Vivants'*: *the Composition and Revision of* Workers in the Dawn

1 For further details see Robert Shafer's introduction to this two-volume edition.
2 *Le Roman expérimental*, Garnier-Flammarion, 1971, (first published as a book by Charpentier in Paris in 1880).
3 One must part company with the editors of the error-laden *The Rediscovery of George Gissing*, National Book League, 1971, who claim that Gissing's 'chief motivations were all social, even though he rejected programmes and action in organized groups'. (p. 30) Following Jacob Korg (as usual) they say that in *Workers in the Dawn* Gissing 'offered a solution to the conflict of claims between art and social reform', which is a somewhat dangerous half-truth, considering that the main character commits suicide because his problems remain unresolved, having previously abandoned social action and talk of social issues because of his relationship with Carrie Mitchell. Coustillas and Spiers on the same page say that Gissing was wrong to insist that his books were not 'tracts, documents, or propaganda novels'. The reader of Gissing's novels will decide on this issue for himself. Certainly there is a lot in Gissing to interest a social historian, even though a person of any sensibility may be chilled by the Coustillas-Spiers description of the novels as 'a rich source of "soft facts".' On the other hand, one can take seriously Gissing's sense of the novel as art and therefore look at his development as a writer, without in any way diminishing the importance of his social concerns, which would indeed be more powerfully felt by a reader in a novel than in a tract. This course of action is pursued both in this and later chapters.
4 *Workers in the Dawn*, Doubleday Doran, 1935, pp. 381–2.
5 *Letters of George Gissing to Members of his Family*, London, Constable, 1927, pp. 73–4, referred to subsequently as *Letters*.
6 *Letters*, p. 65.
7 *Ibid.*, p. 61.
8 For example, at Volume II, p. 87.
9 Unpublished, *Pforzheimer* No. 355.
10 MS. of *Workers in the Dawn*, p. 60.
11 *Ibid.*, p. 87.
12 *Ibid.*, p. 130.
13 *Ibid.*, p. 298.
14 *Ibid.*, Volume II, p. 273.
15 *Workers in the Dawn*, Remington, 1880, Volume III, p. 101.
16 MS. Volume III, p. 101.
17 *Workers in the Dawn*, Doubleday Doran, 1935, Vol. I, pp. 6–8.
18 *Letters*, p. 46.
19 *Ibid.*, p. 47.
20 *Ibid.*, p. 49.
21 The MS. is numbered to 728. But 20 pp. were extracted from it: pp. 158–69, 366–7, 397–9, 543, 594–5. A detailed account of the physical changes to the manuscript of *Workers in the Dawn* is given in Daphne Pan Yuen's as yet unpublished doctoral dissertation, 'George Gissing: a Textual and Critical Study', York University, 1973. See also Collie, 'The Lost Realist', *English Studies Today*, Fifth Series, Istanbul, 1973, pp.

359–85, and *George Gissing: a Bibliography*, pp. 25–9.
22 *Workers in the Dawn, ibid.*, pp. 54–5.
23 *Ibid.*, Volume II, pp. 58–9.
24 *Ibid.*, p. 64.
25 *Ibid.*, p. 89.
26 *Ibid.*, p. 363.
27 *Bertz*, p. 73.
28 See Michael Collie *George Gissing: a Biography*, pp. 46. ff.

Chapter 3 *1880–5, 'By Indirection Find Direction Out': Gissing's Apprenticeship*

1 False starts and rejected titles are recorded in the letters and diary, but Gissing only kept finished manuscripts, which he often sent to his sister, destroying – as far as it is known – his work papers and rough drafts.
2 *Letters*, p. 132.
3 *Ibid.*, p. 111.
4 *Ibid.*, p. 136.
5 *Ibid.*, p. 154.
6 *Ibid.*, p. 127.
7 One such standard opinion was purveyed in *The Rediscovery of George Gissing*, Pierre Coustillas and John Spiers (eds.), National Book League, 1971, p. 25: 'there was a gap between his expectations and the reality of his life. He had to cope with his guilt, poor health, loneliness and domestic squalor – even without the exasperations of first steps as a professional writer. His temperament hardly suited a literary career, and his fiercely masochistic self-criticism made writing an anguished occupation'. Like many of Coustillas' opinions about Gissing's life, this one is unsubstantiated by factual evidence. Spiers and Coustillas were merely repeating without acknowledgement an opinion previously expressed by Jacob Korg. The extent to which Gissing felt guilty about his early experiences has yet to be demonstrated, while the masochism interpretation of Gissing's life, as popularized by Korg, is reducible to the proposition that Gissing did things which his later critics would not have done.
8 See *George Gissing: A Biography*, pp. 155–73. Gabrielle Fleury, whom Gissing lived with in France during the last years of his life, knew that she was accepted by some of his friends in England, though only in France could she get away with calling herself Mrs George Gissing, since Edith, Gissing's second wife, was still alive.
9 *Wells*, pp. 231–2.
10 *Korg*, p. 72. As a matter of fact he did not receive anything for the book.
11 *Letters*, p. 121. The letter to Algernon written on 26 December 1882 reads: 'One line to acquaint you with the fact that *Bentley* offers £50 (!!) for the novel. Hurrah!'
12 *Ibid.*, p. 119.
13 R. A. Gettman, *A Victorian Publisher. A Study of the Bentley Papers*, Cambridge University Press, 1960, pp. 196–7.
14 *Ibid.*, p. 217.
15 *Ibid.*, p. 121.
16 *Letters.*, p. 122.
17 *Gettman*, p. 220.

18 *Letters*, pp. 122–3.
19 *Ibid.*, p. 140.
20 As related by Frederic Harrison to H. G. Wells, *Wells*, pp. 231–2.
21 The disclaimers and reservations of early reviewers are sufficient evidence, though the average reader's sense of values was also made clear by his purchasing preferences and by religious observance.
22 The relationship of Gissing and Schopenhauer has not yet been fully discussed. One must start with Gissing's own essay 'The Hope of Pessimism' which was published for the first time in *George Gissing Essays and Fiction*, edited by Coustillas, pp. 76–97, though this of course gives no indication of the later fictional transmutations of Schopenhaurean concepts. No more does C. J. Francis in his 'Gissing and Schopenhauer', *Collected Articles on George Gissing*, Coustillas (ed.), Frank Cass, 1968, pp. 106–16.
23 *Letters*, pp. 138–9. In *The Unclassed* Waymark said that the novel he was writing would be for 'men and women who like to look below the surface, and who understand that only as artistic material has human life any significance. Yes, that is the conclusion I am working round to. The artist is the only sane man. Life for its own sake? – no; I would drink a pint of laudanum tonight. But life as a source of splendid pictures, inexhaustible material for effects – *that* can reconcile me to existence, and that only'. (p. 117).
24 *Ibid.*, pp. 128–9.
25 *The Unclassed*, Lawrence & Bullen, 1894, pp. 170–1.
26 *Gettman*, p. 220.
27 *The Unclassed*, p. 121.
28 Gissing was well acquainted with contemporary controversies about the meaning of heredity. He had read not only Darwin and Huxley, but also Ribot and Maudsley. Because the biological process was not understood, popular writers on heredity were able to discuss the direct transmission of physical characteristics from one generation to the next.
29 *The Unclassed*, p. 224.
30 *Ibid.*, p. 227.
31 *Letters*, p. 141.
32 *Gettman*, p. 220.
33 *Letters*, p. 141.
34 *Ibid.*, p. 220.
35 The Gladstone Papers in the British Library. Gladstone read *The Unclassed* with interest and noted two extracts from it which are perhaps indicative of the contemporary response to Gissing. From Volume III he noted: 'This overpowering consciousness of sin is an anachronism in our time'. A little later: 'Sin, above all, has been a word without significance to me. As a boy, it was so; it is so still, now that I am self-conscious'. In other words, Gladstone found compatible Gissing's neutral treatment of human fallibility.
36 This review was reprinted in *Gissing: the Critical Heritage*, ed. Pierre Coustillas and Colin Partridge, Routledge, 1972, pp. 66–9.
37 *Letters*, p. 142.
38 In an unpublished letter to Algernon, June 1884 (*Berg*).
39 *Letters*, p. 148.

40 *Ibid.*, p. 164.
41 *Isabel Clarendon* by George Gissing, edited with a critical introduction by Pierre Coustillas, in two volumes, the Harvester Press, 1969.
42 *Ibid.*, Volume II, p. 148.
43 *Ibid.*, pp. 277–8.
44 *Ibid.*, pp. 319–20.
45 *Letters*, p. 168.
46 See Roberts' 'George Gissing', *The New Review*, May 1892, No. 2, Vol. 1, pp. 97–103. For Roberts on Gissing see also *Literature*, 20 July 1901, p. 52 and *W. H. Hudson. A Portrait*, Dutton, 1924, pp. 37–52.
47 See *Korg*, p. 81, for an interesting speculation, based on Morley Roberts, about Gissing's revision of the ending of *A Life's Morning*.
48 That is, the copyright of *A Life's Morning* belonged to Smith, Elder but Gissing might in any case not have bothered to revise what he saw to be inferior work.
49 Unpublished letter to Hardy dated 30 June 1886 (*Pforzheimer*, No. 355).
50 *Bertz*, p. 73.
51 This is from the same letter, dated 30 June 1886.
52 See J. J. Wolff, 'Gissing's Revision of *The Unclassed*', *Nineteenth Century Fiction*, VIII (June 1953), pp. 42–52. The second edition of *The Unclassed* is available in both reprint series, i.e. AMS and the Harvester Press.
53 *Bertz*, p. 207.
54 The preface is reprinted in Coustillas and Partridge (eds.), *Gissing: the Critical Heritage*, Routledge, 1972, pp. 74–5.
55 *The Collected Letters of Thomas Hardy*, ed. R. L. Purdy and Michael Millgate, OUP, 1978, Vol. I, p. 149.
56 This would perhaps be worth further study since *Lord Ormont and His Aminta*, though published in 1895, had been written and rewritten during a fairly long period of years.

Chapter 4 *Experiments in Naturalism*

1 Gissing's own participation in politics had been limited to his attendance at public meetings in the early 1880s. Disillusioned, he soon rejected the possibility of reform by means of political action and adopted instead the Victorian idea that only by education could the lot of working people very slowly be improved. But Gissing was scarcely a democrat, so he had doubts even about the efficacy of education. See *Notes on Social Democracy*, Enitharmon Press, 1968. Extremely relevant to any assessment of Gissing's politics would be the character, Dalmaine, in *The Emancipated*, but in contrast to this would have to be placed the anarchic vision expressed by *The Whirlpool*.
2 *The Emancipated*, Volume III, p. 272.
3 *Korg*, 106–7.
4 Gissing possibly had in mind Robert Owen's *Report to the County of Lanark*, 1821.
5 Of course there are sympathetic readers who manage without either part of this formulation. In *The Rediscovery of George Gissing* (p. 50) Coustillas and Spiers said *Demos* had 'a triple importance: as a mirror of a phase in the history of British socialism and the social consciousness of

that movement, as a document in Gissing's thought, and as a literary expression', an opinion that is repeated verbatim in the Harvester Press reprint, edited by Pierre Coustillas. The phrase, 'a document in Gissing's thought' is the sort of non-literary comment habitually used by those, like Coustillas, whose main critical approach to Gissing is biographical. We wait patiently for Coustillas to explain what for him is the difference between a document in thought and a literary expression. Until he does so, this writer at least will remain convinced that he and his disciples regard Gissing *only* as a documentary writer.

6 *Demos*, Volume I, pp. 78–80.
7 P. J. Keating, *The Working Classes in Victorian Fiction*, Routledge and Kegan Paul, 1971, p. 77.
8 *Ibid.*, p. 70.
9 *Ibid.*, p. 71.
10 *Letters*, p. 172.
11 *Ibid.*, p. 174.
12 *Ibid.*, p. 173.
13 *Realism*, by Linda Nochlin, Penguin 1971.
14 *Le Roman expérimental*, Garnier-Flammarion, 1971, p. 80 (first published as a book by Charpentier in Paris in 1880). Interestingly, Zola first published the papers that later made up *Le Roman expérimental* in *Le Messager de l'Europe*, the St Petersburg review to which Gissing was contributing at the same time.
15 *Thyrza*, Smith, Elder & Co., 3 vols., 1887.
16 *Thyrza*, Second Edition, 1 vol., 1891, p. 14. Gissing revised *Thyrza* for a second edition which was published in 1891, and the notes in this chapter are to the second edition except in the two instances stated. On 31 January 1891 Gissing noted in the *Diary* that he had received a copy from Smith, Elder and on 5 March he told Bertz that he had finished the revision. '*Thyrza* I have corrected and greatly abbreviated: I hope the thing is improved' (*Bertz*, p. 118). Essentially Gissing revised the novel by removing the padding by which he had made it into a three-volume novel. Most notable is the almost complete elimination of a character, Harold Emerson, and a severe condensing of all the Emerson episodes. Superfluous dialogue was eliminated and a number of loose ends tidied up. Gissing had indeed greatly improved the book. (The difference between the first and second edition of *Thyrza* is described in detail in Daphne Pan Yuen's doctoral dissertation, 'George Gissing: a Textual and Critical Study', York University, Canada, 1973.)
17 *Ibid.*, p. 16.
18 See, for example, Chapter IV in Jacob Korg's *George Gissing A Critical Biography*, pp. 99–107. 'Although it is Gissing's most sympathetic work about the poor, *Thyrza* is simply a reiteration, in softer terms, of the anti-democratic sentiments of *Demos*'. *NBL* characteristically repeat this: compare Korg, pp. 99–107 with *NBL* pp. 59–60. Frank Swinnerton had earlier noted the novel's strengths in his *George Gissing A Critical Study*, Chapter II. See also C. J. Francis note on 'The Revision of *Thyrza*', *The Gissing Newsletter*, Vol. VII, No. 4, Oct. 71, pp. 7–9.
19 *Thyrza*, p. 16.
20 *Ibid.*, p. 23.

21 *Ibid.*, p. 24.
22 *Ibid.*, p. 28.
23 *Ibid.*, p. 30.
24 *Ibid.*, p. 85.
25 In *The Woodlanders*, a novel contemporary with *Demos* and *Thyrza*, Hardy is explicit about the constraints of environment on character irrespective of country or period. See in particular, chapter 2 of *The Woodlanders*.
26 Compare, for example, the sisters in Arnold Bennett's *The Old Wives Tale*.
27 *Thyrza*, pp. 31–2.
28 Some of Gissing's notes on Ribot's *L'Hérédité psychologique* are reproduced in the *Commonplace Book*, pp. 59–61.
29 See, for example, Maudsley's *Body and Mind*, the Gulstonian lectures for 1870, published by Macmillan in that year.
30 *Thyrza*, Volume I (first edition), p. 59.
31 *Thyrza*, 1891, pp. 34–5.
32 *Korg*, p. 101.
33 *Donnelly*, p. 115.
34 *Thyrza*, p. 83.
35 *Ibid.*, p. 83.
36 *Ibid.*, pp. 83–4.
37 *Korg*, p. 105.
38 *NBL*, p. 59.
39 *Korg*, p. 105.
40 *Thyrza*, p. 132.
41 The Gladstone Papers in the British Library.
42 *The Gissing Newsletter*, Volume VII, No. 4, October 1971, pp. 7–9.
43 *Thyrza*, p. 294.
44 *Ibid.*, p. 297.
45 *Thyrza*, p. 489.
46 *Ibid.*, p. 490.
47 *The Nether World*, Smith, Elder & Co., 3 volumes, 1889. The one volume edition, to which reference is here made, appeared in 1890.
48 *The Nether World*, p. 280.
49 *Ibid.*, p. 262.
50 *Ibid.*, p. 105.
51 *Ibid.*, p. 106.
52 *Ibid.*, p. 107.
53 *Ibid.*, p. 111.
54 See, for example, the interesting essay by John Lucas, 'Conservatism and Revolution in the 1880s' in *Literature and Politics in the Nineteenth Century*, Methuen, 1971. See also John Goode's 'George Gissing's *The Nether World*' in *Tradition and Tolerance in Nineteenth Century Fiction* by D. Howard. J. Lucas and John Goode, Routledge & Kegan Paul, pp. 207–41.
55 *Ibid.*, p. 86.
56 *Ibid.*, p. 294.
57 *Ibid.*, p. 295.

Chapter 5 The Emancipated *and* New Grub Street

1 See Collie, *George Gissing: a Biography*, Dawson and Archon Books, 1977,

pp. 102ff.; *London and the Life of Literature in Late Victorian England: the Diary of George Gissing, Novelist*, ed. Pierre Coustillas, Harvester Press, 1977; and *Bertz*, pp. 8–102.
2 Unpublished letter to Ellen Gissing dated 31 December 1888, *Pforzheimer* No. 170.
3 1 April, 1890, *Boston Public Library*, pp. 335–6.
4 *Bertz*, p. 52; *Letters*, p. 278.
5 *Bertz*, p. 74.
6 *The Emancipated*, Richard Bentley & Son, 1890, Volume III, p. 36.
7 The second, revised edition of *The Emancipated* is now available in the 'Society and the Victorians' series of the Harvester Press, edited with introduction, notes and bibliography by Pierre Coustillas, 1977.
8 See Diary entry for 7 May. 'Made a new beginning, putting my first scene in Brit. Museum reading room'. Early progress on *New Grub Street* was interrupted by other work, notably the first volume of a novel called 'Hilda Woolf'.
9 *Bertz*, p. 115.
10 *Letters*, p. 318.
11 *Bertz*, p. 121.
12 This is well put by Spiers and Coustillas in *The Rediscovery of George Gissing*. '*New Grub Street* is Gissing's most enduring and significant novel, both as literature and as a "way-in" to major cultural problems and the social forces which shaped them. It has been acknowledged as a "unique study of the 'business of literature' " and of "a whole society's response to literary culture", as a "crucial sociological document", as "one of the most candidly autobiographical novels ever written" and as the authentic masterpiece of a man peculiarly equipped to create it. The novel was written at a critical juncture in Gissing's personal and intellectual life and set by him in the years 1882–86 when he was poor and unknown. It was also one of the few of his books which he did not later dismiss as futile. With it, Gissing's work gained a cultural importance and greatly advanced his limited rather modest reputation. In 1891, it was immediately recognised by critics, readers and authors as an extremely significant novel about the life of writing. One reviewer described it as "Almost terrible in its realism . . . a picture cruelly precise in every detail, of this commercial age". Q. D. Leavis – no friend to many of Gissing's books – has attempted to establish a place for it among the great works, insisting that it is "His one permanent contribution to the English novel". ("Gissing and the English Novel", p. 76). In the past ten years it has received attention from many other critics, each of whom has reviewed it as a crucial work in the cultural discussion one associates with Raymond Williams'.
13 *Letters*, p. 318.
14 *New Grub Street*, Penguin Books, 1968, p. 36. *New Grub Street* was first published by Smith, Elder, 1891. For convenience the references are to the Penguin edition throughout.
15 *Ibid.*, p. 174.
16 *Ibid.*, p. 301.
17 *Ibid.*, p. 405.
18 *Ibid.*, p. 43.

19 *Ibid.*, p. 363.
20 *Ibid.*, p. 339.
21 *Ibid.*, p. 550.
22 *Ibid.*, p. 56.
23 *Ibid.*, p. 46.
24 *Ibid.*, p. 79.
25 *Ibid.*, pp. 365–6.
26 *Ibid.*, p. 226.
27 See letter of 7 January 1891: 'They think *New Grub Street* clever and original, but fear it is too gloomy. Offer £150. I wrote at once accepting (ahem!) & asking them to add the £10 they offered for *Thyrza*.' After a second edition in three volumes, Smith, Elder kept the novel in print in various one-volume reissues until well after Gissing's death. The firm must have done quite well from it.
28 *Fleury*, pp. 24–5.
29 *New Grub Street*, p. 124.
30 *Ibid.*, p. 462.
31 *Ibid.*, p. 149.
32 *Ibid.*, p. 219.
33 *Ibid.*, p. 154.
34 *Ibid.*, pp. 261–2.
35 *Ibid.*, p. 404.
36 From Chapter X Gissing deleted the whole of the visit of Mrs Edith Carter (pp. 164–70) and the references to Reardon's sale of books. A few hints suggest the Carter episode was written early. For example, Gissing addresses the reader directly: 'You remember that . . .' Furthermore, Gissing probably preferred to eradicate a character whose first name was Edith. The significant changes to Chapter XVII concern the relationship of Reardon to his wife, notably the lurid paragraph on p. 257 which begins 'A dark fear began to shadow him' and the paragraph about violence which starts on p. 261 with the words 'He had but to do one thing . . .' It is difficult to summarise the overall effect of such changes without consideration of the detail. Clearly, however, Gissing made the parting of Reardon and his wife less sensational, less physical and less autobiographical in the course of revision. For a more detailed discussion see Collie 'Gissing's Revision of *New Grub Street*', *The Year Book of English Studies*, Vol. 4 (1974), pp. 212–24.

Chapter 6 Born in Exile

1 *Born in Exile*, A. & C. Black, Edinburgh, 1892, Volume II, p. 271. This is the first edition and all references are to it.
2 I explore the geological references more extensively in my edition of *Born in Exile* prepared for the *Victorian Text Series*, the University of Queensland Press.
3 *Born in Exile*, Volume II, p. 81.
4 *Ibid.*, Volume I, p. 190.
5 This naïveté shows up in many of the words used, e.g. 'susurration' (p. 28) and 'vicinage' (p. 75). An easy colloquial style eludes the young Gissing and he resorts to pedantically accurate words remote from normal usage.

6 *Born in Exile* was, of course, very much in print when Gissing met Harry Lawrence, so that there was no question of his reconsidering it for publication by Lawrence & Bullen. At some point the copyright was assigned to Clara Collet, who was therefore involved in the discussion of posthumous republication.
7 It is important to have in mind that only about 50 per cent of the surviving letters have been published and that *Letters of George Gissing to Members of his Family* contains many letters from which important parts have been excised. For example, part of the argument about Gissing's writing Volume I of *Born in Exile* early in 1888 involves an assessment of what he was writing in 1887. Jacob Korg's account appears to be based on the published letters, though of course he had looked at the unpublished ones. This led him to think that Gissing worked on *Dust and Dew* in 1887 and on 'The Insurgents' in 1888 (both false starts). The full evidence, however, seems to show that 'The Insurgents' was the title of a novel he had been working at since July 1887 – a novel which he did not complete or work on in 1888.
8 The interpretation of the Diary is not straightforward, particularly because Gissing often discarded working titles, so that relating a published work to an earlier working title must in some cases remain a matter of judgement. In 1887 Gissing had started a number of novels, none of them completed. Before turning to 'Dust and Dew', he spent much of the early part of the year on 'Clement Dorricott', a novel which seems not to have survived in any form.
9 There are about ten mentions of Paul Bourget in Gissing's Diary, beginning with the note that he was reading *Mensonges* on 24 March 1888 to his rereading of *Cosmopolis* in November 1895. Highly relevant to this chapter is his reading of *Études et portraits* and *Essais psychologiques* in 1889.
10 Gosse's translation of *Hedda Gabler* was published in January 1891 and the play was first performed in London in May of the same year. Gissing noted the 'great vogue' for Ibsen in his letter to Bertz dated 5 March 1891 (*Bertz*, 118).
11 *Born in Exile*, I, pp. 113–14. The continuation of this paragraph is interesting. 'The perfectly graceful man will always be he who has no strong apprehension either of his own personality or of that of others, who lives on the surface of things, who can be interested without emotion, and surprised without contemplative impulse'. Avoidance of metaphysical anxiety involves surfacing and Gissing's attention to people who live 'on the surface of things' was in his later novels an inevitable, or at least a logical development.
12 *Born in Exile*, Volume II, pp. 64–5.
13 *Ibid.*, Volume I, p. 84.
14 *Ibid.*, Volume II, p. 61.
15 *Ibid.*, Volume I, p. 224.
16 *Ibid.*, Volume II, p. 66.
17 *Ibid.*, Volume II, pp. 63–4.
18 *Ibid.*, Volume I, pp. 271–2.
19 *Bertz.*, p. 142.

Chapter 7 *The Art of Social Alienation*

1 Gissing chose not to write about his own early experiences, in his novels. In the town-and-gown life of Owens College he had become well acquainted with the town. He had been arrested for theft and had spent a month in prison. His travels in North America were not genteel. Discussion of this must await the biographer, however; guilt is played down throughout and one simply has to accept that Gissing's emphasis was selective.
2 *The Odd Women*, 3 volumes, Lawrence & Bullen, 1893. The novel was published in one volume in 1894 in both Britain and the United States.
3 See Collie, *George Gissing: a Bibliography* for more detailed information about publication. Most readers will realise for themselves that the first two chapters are unsatisfactory and have been tampered with.
4 *Korg*, p. 188.
5 *The Odd Women*, 3 volumes, Lawrence & Bullen, 1894, Vol. I, pp. 55–6.
6 *Ibid.*, pp. 284–5.
7 *In the Year of Jubilee*, Lawrence & Bullen, 1894, was written after many false starts between 1 January and 30 April 1894.
8 Lionel Tarrant is one of those characters in Gissing (another is Clara Hewett in *The Nether World*) who do not conform exactly to the author's environmentalist vision. Here, not only is the biology evaded, but in addition the motivation of the character is only half-stated. Significant dreams, for example, described in the manuscript are omitted from the first-edition text.
9 The word 'seduce', discussed later, is appropriate to Gissing's accommodation to his publisher's sensibility.
10 Page 7 of the MS. in the Huntington Library, San Marino, California.
11 The pot-boilers were *Eve's Ransom*, 1895; *The Paying Guest*, 1895; *Sleeping Fires*, 1895. For a description of these light novels see my *George Gissing: a Bibliography*.
12 *The Whirlpool*, Lawrence & Bullen, 1897, was published simultaneously in the United States by Stokes and issued in Australia by Petherick. It was an instant success being reissued four times in England in 1897 alone.
13 George Orwell, 'George Gissing', *London Magazine*, June 1960, pp. 36–43; reprinted in Coustillas (ed.), *Collected Articles on George Gissing*, Frank Cass, 1968, p. 50.
14 *The Whirlpool*, p. 48.
15 T. Ribot, *L'Hérédité psychologique*, translated as *Heredity*, p. 1.
16 *Ibid.*, p. 1.
17 E.g. Fontane, George Moore, Ibsen, Strindberg, Samuel Butler, Hardy.
18 *Korg*, p. 208.
19 *The Whirlpool*.
20 Gissing used the term 'social disease' in the contemporary medical sense made familiar in the popular writings of Henry Maudsley.
21 *The Whirlpool*, pp. 418–19.
22 *Ibid.*, p. 166.
23 *The Crown of Life*, Methuen & Co., 1899. Gissing wrote this novel during the winter of 1898–9, between Gabrielle Fleury's return to Paris in October 1898 and 17 January 1899 when he told his friend, Bertz, that it

was finished. The manuscript is in the Huntington Library.
24 *Ibid*., pp. 163–4.
25 *Ibid*., p. 268.

Chapter 8 *Conclusion*

1 *The Whirlpool*, Lawrence & Bullen, 1897, p. 384.
2 *Ibid*., p. 383.
3 *Ibid*., p. 382.
4 *Ibid*., pp. 383–4.
5 *Ibid*., p. 384.
6 These are the concluding words of *The Crown of Life*, Methuen, 1899, p. 329.
7 Becker, G. J., *Documents of Modern Literary Realism*, p. 9.
8 *Gissing The Critical Heritage*, Pierre Coustillas and Colin Partridge (eds.), Routledge & Kegan Paul, 1971. This volume reconfirmed what had been briefly forgotten, i.e. that Gissing was recognized as a major writer during the 1890s and that his later novels were, on the whole, well received.
9 Scribner's agent in England, E. L. Burlingame, is an example of the enterprise that coincided with new copyright regulations. It was Burlingame who encouraged Meredith to complete his later novels and publish them in the States, where incidentally they were much more successful than in England.
10 *Selections Autobiographical and Imaginative from the Works of George Gissing*, Jonathan Cape, London, 1929, pp. 220–1.
11 'For a night or two, Tarrant dreamt horribly. The shock of that moment when he learnt that he was penniless returned upon him in his sleep, & formed strange visions. He was wandering, a ragged outcast, in the square of Staple Inn, glancing with vain hope at the window of his old room, where he had lounged away so many a luxurious hour; & presently there looked from the windows a familiar face, which looked but did not recognize him, nor had he any means of making himself known to Nancy; for Nancy it was who looked down at him, but years seemed to have gone by since they last saw each other, and he had no longer any part in her life.

Or again, no less an outcast & poverty-stricken, he was escaping from some vague terror through deep, shadowed lanes, running, panting, all but exhausted. And of a sudden, on a high bank amid thick foliage, appeared Nancy's face, laughing in mockery. Could he get over the high bank into the wood, he was safe. With an inspired effort, he succeeded, but Nancy was not there. He plunged on through fern & bramble, & came to a spot of smooth turf; & there, beneath a bush which somehow he recognised, lay a naked, crying child. And by an instant transference of identity, that naked, crying child became *himself*, & he was conscious only of self-pity, for his parents had forsaken him, & he cried in vain for help'.

Appendix
A Chronological Listing of Gissing's Works

Workers in the Dawn, Remington and Co., London 1880.
The Unclassed, Chapman & Hall, London 1884.
Isabel Clarendon, Chapman & Hall, London 1886.
Demos, Smith, Elder & Co., London 1886.
Thyrza, Smith, Elder & Co., London 1887.
A Life's Morning, Smith, Elder & Co., London 1888.
The Nether World, Smith, Elder & Co., London 1889.
The Emancipated, Richard Bentley & Son, London 1890.
New Grub Street, Smith, Elder & Co., London 1891.
Denzil Quarrier, Lawrence & Bullen, London 1892.
Born in Exile, Adam & Charles Black, London 1892.
The Odd Women, Lawrence & Bullen, London 1893.
In the Year of Jubilee, Lawrence & Bullen, London 1894.
Eve's Ransom, Lawrence & Bullen, London 1895.
The Paying Guest, Cassell & Co., London 1895.
Sleeping Fires, T. Fisher Unwin, London 1895.
The Whirlpool, Lawrence & Bullen, London 1897.
Human Odds and Ends, Lawrence & Bullen, London 1898.
Charles Dickens, Blackie & Son, London 1898.
The Town Traveller, Methuen & Co., London 1898.
The Crown of Life, Methuen & Co., London 1899.
Our Friend the Charlatan, Chapman & Hall, London 1901.
By the Ionian Sea, Chapman & Hall, London 1901.
The Private Papers of Henry Ryecroft, Archibald Constable & Co., London 1903.
Will Warburton, Archibald Constable & Co., London 1905.
Veranilda, Archibald Constable & Co., London 1904.
The House of Cobwebs, Archibald Constable & Co., London 1906.
The Immortal Dickens, Cecil Palmer, London 1924.
Sins of the Fathers, Pascal Covici, Chicago 1924.
A Victim of Circumstances, Archibald Constable & Co., London 1927.
Brownie, Columbia University Press, New York 1931.
Notes on Social Democracy, Enitharmon Press, London 1968.

Select Bibliography

Letters and Diaries

Letters of George Gissing to Members of his Family, Algernon and Ellen Gissing (eds.), Constable, London 1927.
George Gissing and H. G. Wells, Their Friendship and Correspondence, Royal A. Gettmann (ed.), University of Illinois Press, Urbana 1961.
The Letters of George Gissing to Eduard Bertz, 1887–1903, Arthur C. Young (ed.), Rutgers University Press, New Brunswick, N.J. 1961.
The Letters of George Gissing to Gabrielle Fleury, Pierre Coustillas (ed.), New York Public Library, 1964.
The Letters of George Gissing to Edward Clodd, Pierre Coustillas (ed.), Enitharmon Press, London 1973.
London and the Life of Literature in Late Victorian England: The Diary of George Gissing, Novelist, Pierre Coustillas (ed.), Harvester Press, 1978.

Books

CLODD, Edward. *Memories*, Chapman & Hall, London 1916.
COLLIE, Michael. *George Gissing: A Bibliography*, University of Toronto Press, and Dawson, 1975.
—— *George Gissing: A Biography*, Archon Books and Dawson, 1977.
COUSTILLAS, Pierre (ed.) *Collective Articles on George Gissing*, Frank Cass, 1968.
—— (ed.) *My First Rehearsal and My Clerical Rival*, Enitharmon Press, London 1970.
—— (ed.) *George Gissing Essays and Fiction*, The Johns Hopkins Press, Baltimore and London 1970.
—— (ed.) *Gissing's Writings on Dickens*, Enitharmon Press, London 1970.

—— (ed.) *George Gissing at Alderley Edge*, Enitharmon Press, London 1970.
—— (ed.) *Henry Hick's Recollections of George Gissing*, Enitharmon Press, London 1973.
—— and SPIERS, John (eds.) *The Rediscovery of George Gissing*, National Book League, 1971.
—— and PARTRIDGE, Colin (eds.) *Gissing: The Critical Heritage*, Routledge & Kegan Paul, London 1972.
DONNELLY, Mabel Collins. *George Gissing: Grave Comedian*, Harvard University Press, 1954.
GETTMAN, R. A. *A Victorian Publisher. A Study of the Bentley Papers*, Cambridge University Press, 1960.
GORDAN, John D. *George Gissing: 1857–1903* (Catalogue for an exhibition of materials from the Berg Collection of the New York Public Library), New York Public Library, 1954.
HARRISON, Austin. *Frederic Harrison: Thoughts and Memories*, Heinemann, London 1926.
KORG, Jacob (ed.) *George Gissing's Commonplace Book*, New York Public Library, 1962.
—— *George Gissing: A Critical Biography*, Washington University Press, Seattle 1963; Methuen, London 1965.
ROBERTS, Morley. *The Private Life of Henry Maitland*, Eveleigh, Nash and Grayson, London 1923.
SWINNERTON, Frank. *George Gissing, A Critical Study*, M. Secker, London 1912.
WELLS, H. G. *Experiment in Autobiography*, Macmillan, New York 1934.
YATES, May. *George Gissing, An Appreciation*, (Publications of the University of Manchester, English Series No. XII), The University Press, England 1922.

Articles

ADAMS, George M. 'How and Why I Collect George Gissing', *The Colophon*, Part XVIII (1934), no pagination.
ADAMS, Ruth M. 'George Gissing and Clara Collet', *Nineteenth Century Fiction*, XI (June, 1956), pp. 72–7.
BERGONZI, Bernard. 'The Novelist as Hero', *Twentieth Century*, CLXIV (November, 1958), pp. 444–55.
BOWES, Arthur. 'George Gissing's School Days', *TP's Weekly*, (22 January 1904), p. 100.
COLLES, W. M. 'George Gissing', *Academy*, LXVI (9 January, 1904), p. 40.

COLLIE, Michael. 'The Lost Realist', *English Studies Today*, Istanbul (1973), pp. 359–85.

—— 'Gissing's Revision of *New Grub Street*', *The Year Book of English Studies*, IV (1974), pp. 212–24.

—— 'How George Gissing Disappeared', *English Studies in Canada*, I (Winter 1975), No. 4, pp. 434–49.

COUSTILLAS, Pierre. 'George Gissing à Manchester', *Etudes Anglaises*, XVI, pp. 255–61.

—— 'George Gissing et Eduard Bertz: Une amitié littéraire', *Revue de littérature comparée*, XXVII (July), pp. 394–405.

—— 'George Gissing et H. G. Wells', *Etudes Anglaises*, XV, pp. 156–66.

—— 'Gissing and Butler Clarke', *Gissing Newsletter* II (April 1966), pp. 6–7.

—— 'Gissing: Some More Biographical Details', *Notes and Queries* XIII (1967), pp. 68–9.

—— 'Gissing's Feminine Portraiture', *English Literature in Transition*, VI, pp. 130–41.

—— and SPIERS, John. 'A George Gissing Bibliography', *The Book Collecting and Library Monthly*, (September, October, November, 1969).

FARRAR, F. W. 'The Nether World', *Contemporary Review*, LVI (September 1889), pp. 370–80.

FRANCIS, C. J. 'Gissing and Schopenhauer', *Nineteenth Century Fiction*, XV, p. 63.

GETTMANN, Royal A. 'Bentley and Gissing', *Nineteenth Century Fiction*, XI (March, 1957), pp. 306–14.

GISSING, Alfred C. 'George Gissing – Some Aspects of His Life and Work', *National Review*, XCIII (August, 1929), pp. 932–41.

—— *London Times Literary Supplement*, (12 April 1933), p. 261, (27 April 1933), p. 295.

—— 'Gissing's Unfinished Romance', *National Review*, CVII (January, 1937), pp. 82–91.

GISSING, Ellen 'George Gissing: A Character Sketch', *Nineteenth Century and After*, CII (September 1927), pp. 417–24.

—— 'Some Personal Recollections of George Gissing', *Blackwood's Magazine*, CCXXV (May 1929), pp. 653–60.

GOODE, John, 'George Gissing's *The Nether World*', in *Tradition and Tolerance in Nineteenth Century Fiction* by D. Howard, John Lucas and John Goode, Routledge & Kegan Paul, London 1967, pp. 207–41.

GROSS, John, 'Introduction' to *New Grub Street*, Bodley Head, London 1967, pp. v–viii.

HAIGHT, Gordon S. 'Gissing: Some Biographical Details', *Notes and Queries*, pp. 235–6.
HARRISON, Austin. 'George Gissing', *Nineteenth Century and After*, LX (September 1906), pp. 453–63.
KIRK, Russell. 'Who Knows George Gissing?' *Western Humanities Review*, IV, (Summer 1950), pp. 213–22.
KORG, Jacob. 'George Gissing's Outcast Intellectuals', *American Scholar*, XIX (Spring 1950), pp. 194–202.
—— 'Division of Purpose in George Gissing', *PMLA*, LXX (June 1955), pp. 323–36.
—— 'The Spiritual Theme of George Gissing's *Born in Exile*', in *From Jane Austen to Joseph Conrad*, ed. Robert C. Rathburn and Martin Steinmann (eds.), University of Minnesota Press 1958.
—— 'George Moore (and) George Gissing', *Victorian Fiction*, 27, p. 388.
LEAVIS, Q. D. 'Gissing and the English Novel', *Scrutiny*, VII (June 1938), pp. 73–81.
ORWELL, George. 'Not Enough Money', *Tribune*, London (2 April 1953), p. 12.
PARTRIDGE, Colin. 'The Humane Centre: George Gissing's *The Whirlpool*', *The Gissing Newsletter*, IX, Number 3 (July 1973), pp. 1–10.
PREBLE, Harry E. 'Gissing's Articles for *Vyestnik Europy*', *Victorian Newsletter*, 23 (Spring 1963), pp. 12–15.
PRITCHETT, V. S. 'Gissing: Our Only Russian', *New Statesman*, LXXV (14 June 1968), pp. 795–96.
PURDY, Richard L. 'George Gissing at Max Gate 1895', *Yale University Library Gazette*, XVII, pp. 51–2.
ROBERTS, Morley. 'George Gissing', *Queen's Quarterly*, XXXVII (Autumn 1930), pp. 617–33.
—— 'The Letters of George Gissing', *Virginia Quarterly Review*, (July 1931), pp. 409–26.
SHAFER, Robert. *Bookman*, LXXIV, pp. 674–7; *London Mercury*, XXVI, p. 462 (1932).
SICHEL, Edith. 'Two Philanthropic Novelists: Mr Walter Besant and Mr George Gissing', *Murray's Magazine*, III (April 1888), pp. 506–18.
STEINER, Jacqueline. 'George Gissing to His Sister: Letters of George Gissing', *More Books* (Bulletin of the Boston Public Library), XXII (November, December 1947), pp. 323–36, 376–86.
SWINNERTON, Frank. 'The Real Gissing', *The Bookman*, 43, London, pp. 173–4.

Times Literary Supplement (London), No. 2404 (14 February 1948), p. 92, 'The Permanent Stranger'; No. 2861 (28 December 1956), p. 780.

―― (London), 'Gissing's Academic Career' (20 May 1944), p. 252.

WELLS, H. G. 'The Novels of Mr George Gissing', *Contemporary Review*, LXXII (August 1897), pp. 192–201.

―― 'George Gissing, An Impression', *Monthly Review*, XVI (August 1904), pp. 160–72.

―― 'The Truth about George Gissing', *Literary Supplement to Rhythm* (December 1912), pp. i–iii.

WOLFF, Joseph J. 'Gissing's Revision of *The Unclassed*', *Nineteenth Century Fiction*, VIII (June 1953), pp. 42–52.

WOOLF, Virginia. 'George Gissing', in *The Common Reader, Second Series*, Hogarth Press, London 1932.

YOUNG, Arthur C. 'George Gissing's Friendship with Eduard Bertz', *Nineteenth Century Fiction*, XIII (December 1958), pp. 227–37.

―― 'Gissing's *Veranilda*', *Notes and Queries*, IV, p. 359.

―― 'The Death of Gissing: A Fourth Report', *Essays in Literary History*, XVI, pp. 217–28.

Index

Allen, Walter, 174 n3

Balzac, Honoré de, 9, 14, 20, 49
Becker, G. T., 168
Bennett, Arnold, 19
Bentley, Richard, 7–8, 28, 32, 42, 46–7, 54, 58, 59, 60, 106–7
Bertz, Eduard, 18, 41, 66, 106, 107, 111, 136, 137, 141, 174 n4, 182 n16
Black, A. & C., 129, 135, 141, 185 nl
Blackie & Son, 13
Bourget, Paul, 137, 168, 186 n9
Brontë, Charlotte, 20, 26, 99, 106, 124, 138

Cassell & Co., 12
Chapman & Hall, 7, 8, 13, 28, 32, 46, 61, 62
Chekhov, Anton, 128, 138, 143
Colles, W. M., 175 n13
Collett, Clara, 171, 174 n4, 186 n6
Comte, Auguste, 9
Conrad, Joseph, 12
Constable & Co., 13
Cornhill, 64
Coustillas, Pierre, 12, 17, 32, 62, 89, 135, 174 n5, 175 n9, 175 n14, 177 n33, 178 n3, 179 n7, 181 n5, 182 n18, 188 n8

Darwin, Charles, 60, 158
Daudet, Alphonse, 14
Dickens, Charles, 14, 174 nl, 174 n6, 175 n14, 175 n18
Dostoevski, Fyodor, 9, 14, 137, 138, 175 n8
Doubleday Doran, 15, 20, 32
Dumas, Alexandre, 49

Eliot, George, 2, 10, 20, 26, 124, 138, 169, 174 n3

Fleury, Gabrielle, 1, 16, 18, 45, 111, 119, 120, 161, 171, 174 n4, 179 n8, 187 n23
Fortnightly Review, 175 n16
Freud, Sigmund, 70, 117

Gaskell, Elizabeth, 17, 19, 177 n27
Gettman, R. A., 7, 17, 46–7, 175 n8
Gissing, Algernon, 18, 24, 36, 43, 174 n4
—Ellen, 18, 174 n4
Gissing, George: Exeter, 15, 111; first marriage, 7, 18, 41, 43, 45, 46, 136, 171, 174 n4; France, 1, 4, 135, 137; Greece, 4, 107, 110, 135, 137; Italy, 4, 103–4, 105, 110, 135, 137; London, 1, 2, 20, 43–5, 68, 110, 171; North America, 20; second marriage, 8, 10, 111, 136, 137, 171, 174 n4; Wakefield, 6, 24, 43, 48–9, 114; Works, *Workers in the Dawn*, 7, 10, 15, 16, 20–41, 42, 44, 46, 48, 50, 52, 57, 60, 61, 63, 65, 66, 68, 71, 72, 73, 78, 79, 91, 95, 99, 100, 119, 141, 174 n4; *The Unclassed*, 7, 8, 10, 19, 32, 40, 41, 42, 43, 45, 46, 47, 48–61, 63, 64, 66–7, 68, 71, 76, 79, 119, 166, 171, 174 nl, 176 n21, 180 n23, 180 n35; *Isabel Clarendon*, 7, 8, 15, 32, 42, 43, 44, 48, 61–4, 65, 67, 68, 76, 119, 174 nl, 176 n21; *Demos*, 5, 7, 10, 42, 44, 50, 57, 60, 61, 64, 66, 67, 68–71, 72–8, 79, 80, 81, 91, 94, 95, 97, 102, 110, 114, 135, 137, 171, 176 n21; *Thyrza*, 5, 10, 16, 19, 32, 40, 42, 57, 64, 68–71, 72, 76, 77, 78, 79–94, 97, 98, 102, 114, 118, 119, 128, 135, 137, 144, 166, 171, 176 n21, 185 n27; *A Life's Morning*, 42, 43, 48, 61, 64–5, 68, 76; *The Nether World*, 10, 13, 16, 19, 32, 42, 57, 68–71, 72, 76, 78, 86, 94–102, 105, 110, 111, 128, 135, 136, 144, 162, 171, 176 n21, 187 n8; *The Emancipated*, 10, 11, 16, 32, 41, 70, 71, 72, 91, 102,

Gissing, George – *contd*.
104–9, 110, 115, 119, 129, 132, 134, 136, 137, 145, 146, 149, 166, 176 n21, 181 nl; *New Grub Street*, 10, 16, 19, 30, 31, 62, 64, 71, 72, 91, 102, 106, 108, 109–26, 129, 131, 134, 136–7, 141, 145, 149, 166, 171, 175 n20, 185 n27; *Denzil Quarrier*, 11, 32, 149, 176 n21; *Born in Exile*, 5, 11, 15, 19, 22, 30, 40, 57, 60, 71, 74, 102, 106, 123, 127–45, 146, 149, 154, 166, 170, 171, 174 n4, 176 n21, 185 n2; *The Odd Women*, 5, 11, 19, 30, 32, 59, 60, 145, 146, 147, 148, 149, 150–4, 156, 161, 176 n21, 187 n2; *In the Year of Jubilee*, 8, 11, 19, 146, 147, 148, 154–7, 161, 163, 171–2, 176 n21; *Eve's Ranson*, 12, 147, 148, 187 n11; *The Paying Guest*, 12, 147, 187 n11; *Sleeping Fires*, 12, 175 n9, 176 n21, 187 n11; *The Whirlpool*, 8, 11, 19, 31, 44, 59, 74, 146, 148, 154, 157–61, 163, 164–5, 171, 176 n21, 181 nl; *Human Odds and Ends*, 13; *Charles Dickens*, 13, 14; *The Crown of Life*, 11, 146, 147, 148, 154, 161–3, 166, 171, 176 n21, 188 n6; *Our Friend the Charlaton*, 176 n21; *By the Ionian Sea*, 13; *The Private Papers of Henry Ryecroft*, 13, 62, 175 n16; *The House of Cobwebs*, 13; *Sins of the Fathers*, 13; *A Victim of Circumstances*, 13; *Brownie*, 13; *Notes on Social Democracy*, 181 nl; 'Clement Dorricott', 186 n8; 'Dust and Dew', 186 n8; 'Mrs Grundy's Enemies', 7–8, 42, 46–7, 48, 50, 60, 68, 107, 174 n1; 'The Insurgents', 186 n7; 'Godwin Peak' (see *Born in Exile*); 'The Lady of Knightswell' (see *Isabel Clarendon*); 'Miss Lord of Camberwell' (see *In the Year of Jubilee*); 'The Puritan' (see *The Emancipated*)
Gissing, Margaret, 43
Gladstone, W. E., 59, 180 n35
Goethe, Johann Wolfgang von, 9, 43
Goncourt brothers, the, 9

Hardy, Thomas, 8, 9, 17, 28, 48, 66, 83, 117, 137, 168, 175 n7, 176 n20, 177 n28, 183 n25
Harrison, Frederic, 6, 45, 46, 60, 65, 78
Heine, Heinrich, 9
Hugo, Victor, 14
Huysmans, Joris Karl, 127, 168

Ibsen, Heinrik, vii, 3, 9, 10, 55, 127, 128, 137, 138, 186 n10

James, Henry, 12, 109
Joyce, James, 174 n3

Kettle, Arnold, 174 n3
Korg, Jacob, 13, 17, 46, 61, 64, 72, 88, 89, 90, 151, 158, 174 n4, 176 n22, 179 n7, 186 n7, 182 n18

Laforgue, Jules, 127
Landor, Walter Savage, 43
Lawrence, D. H., 43, 117, 169, 170
Lawrence & Bullen, 12, 15, 16, 32, 65, 66, 86, 119, 154, 175 n6, 180 n25, 186 n6

Maudsley, Henry, 86, 180, n28, 183 n29
Meredith, George, vii, 8, 9, 12, 47–8, 61, 66, 76, 118, 119, 143, 167, 168, 176 n20
Molière, 9
Morley, John, 45, 49
Morris, William, 43
Murger, Henri, 9, 10, 20
Musset, Alfred de, 9

Owen, Robert, 181 n4

Pall Mall Gazette, 45
Pinker, J. B., 175 n13
Poole, Adrian, 17

Remington, 26, 27–8, 31
Ribot, Theodule, 86, 158, 180 n28, 183 n28
Roberts, Morely, 64, 171, 174 n4, 181 n46
Rossetti, D. G., 44
Ruskin, John, 43

Sand, George, 9, 20
Schiller, Johann von, 43
Schopenhauer, Arthur, 4, 44, 50, 56, 70, 175 n8, 180 n22
Scott, Walter, 43
Shorter, Clement, 175 n13
Sichel, Edith, 171
Smith, Elder & Co., 16, 32, 46, 64, 91, 120, 141, 175 n6, 181 n48, 183 n47, 185 n27
Sue, Eugène, 9, 20

Thackery, William, 14
Tindall, Gillian, 17, 175 n20
Turgenev, Ivan, 3, 4, 9, 43–4, 49, 89, 127, 137, 138, 175 n8

Unwin, T. Fisher, 12

Vizetelly case, 78, 168

Watt, A. P., 141
Wells, H. G., 19, 45, 174 n4
West, Rebecca, 19
Wilson, Angus, 19

Wolff, Joseph, 174 n2

Young, A. C., 17, 18

Zola, Émile, 9, 20, 21, 77–8, 97, 168, 174 n3, 174 n6, 182 n14